THE RIGHT TO RESEARCH

MCGILL-QUEEN'S REFUGEE AND FORCED MIGRATION STUDIES

Series editors: Megan Bradley and James Milner

Forced migration is a local, national, regional, and global challenge with profound political and social implications. Understanding the causes and consequences of, and possible responses to, forced migration requires careful analysis from a range of disciplinary perspectives, as well as interdisciplinary dialogue.

The purpose of the McGill-Queen's Refugee and Forced Migration Studies series is to advance in-depth examination of diverse forms, dimensions, and experiences of displacement, including in the context of conflict and violence, repression and persecution, and disasters and environmental change. The series will explore responses to refugees, internal displacement, and other forms of forced migration to illuminate the dynamics surrounding forced migration in global, national, and local contexts, including Canada, the perspectives of displaced individuals and communities, and the connections to broader patterns of human mobility. Featuring research from fields including politics, international relations, law, anthropology, sociology, geography, and history, the series highlights new and critical areas of enquiry within the field, especially conversations across disciplines and from the perspective of researchers in the global South, where the majority of forced migration unfolds. The series benefits from an international advisory board made up of leading scholars in refugee and forced migration studies.

6   The Urbanization of Forced Displacement
    UNHCR, Urban Refugees, and the Dynamics of Policy Change
    Neil James Wilson Crawford

7   Finding Safe Harbour
    Supporting the Integration of Refugee Youth
    Emily Pelley

8   Documenting Displacement
    Questioning Methodological Boundaries in Forced Migration Research
    Edited by Katarzyna Grabska and Christina R. Clark-Kazak

9   Voluntary and Forced Migration in Latin America
    Law and Policy Reforms
    Edited by Natalia Caicedo Camacho and Luisa Feline Freier

10 The Right to Research
    Historical Narratives by Refugee and Global South Researchers
    Edited by Kate Reed and Marcia C. Schenck

The Right to Research

Historical Narratives by Refugee and
Global South Researchers

Edited by

KATE REED and MARCIA C. SCHENCK

McGill-Queen's University Press
Montreal & Kingston • London • Chicago

© McGill-Queen's University Press 2023

ISBN 978-0-2280-1454-6 (cloth)
ISBN 978-0-2280-1455-3 (paper)
ISBN 978-0-2280-1565-9 (ePDF)
ISBN 978-0-2280-1566-6 (ePUB)

Legal deposit first quarter 2023
Bibliothèque nationale du Québec

Printed in Canada on acid-free paper that is 100% ancient forest free
(100% post-consumer recycled), processed chlorine free

Library and Archives Canada Cataloguing in Publication

Title: The right to research: historical narratives by refugee and
  Global South researchers / edited by Kate Reed, Marcia C. Schenck.
Names: Reed, Kate (Graduate of University of Oxford), editor.
  | Schenck, Marcia C., editor.
Series: McGill-Queen's refugee and forced migration studies; 10.
Description: Series statement: McGill-Queen's refugee and forced migration
  studies; 10 | Includes bibliographical references and index.
Identifiers: Canadiana (print) 2022040853X | Canadiana (ebook) 2022040867X
  | ISBN 9780228014546 (cloth) | ISBN 9780228014553 (paper)
  | ISBN 9780228015659 (ePDF) | ISBN 9780228015666 (ePUB)
Subjects: LCSH: History—Research—Developing countries. | LCSH: Narrative
  inquiry (Research method)—Developing countries. | LCSH: Refugees—Research.
Classification: LCC D16.R54 2023 | DDC 907.20172/4—dc23

This book was typeset in 10.5/13 Sabon.

Contents

Figures | vii

Preface: An Invitation | ix
Kate Reed and Marcia C. Schenck

Acknowledgments | xii

Introduction | 3
Kate Reed and Marcia C. Schenck

PART ONE
Crossing Borders: Critical Perspectives on
Refugee and Migrant Experiences | 45

1 Fostering Education Services in Kakuma Refugee Camp | 47
Gerawork Teferra

2 Dangerous Crossings: East African Women Refugees and
Migrants Flee Home for Opportunities in the Gulf States | 76
Muna Omar

3 Burundian Refugee Drummers: Practitioners of a Longstanding,
Yet Ever-Changing, Tradition | 109
Aime Parfait Emerusenge

PART TWO
Cultures in Motion:
Continuity and Change in Displacement | 129

4 The Impacts of Displacement on Twa Culture and Tradition 131
Richesse Ndiritiro

5 On Hip-Hop and Mental Migration | 147
Alain Jules Hirwa

6 The Oral History of Local Photojournalism in Kurdistan | 160
Lazha Taha

PART THREE
Identity and (Un)Belonging:
Constructing and Deconstructing Social Identities | 181

7 "Traditional Healers Save Lives":
The Changing Relationship between Traditional Healing
and Modern Medicine in Rwanda | 183
Phocas Maniraguha

8 Until New Dawn ... New Day: The Development of
Gender Awareness across Generations in Syria | 200
Ismail Alkhateeb

9 The Impact of Migration on Intore Traditional Dance | 226
Sandrine Cyuzuzo Iribagiza

Conclusion | 237
*Ismail Alkhateeb, Sandrine Cyuzuzo Iribagiza, Aime Parfait
Emerusenge, Alain Jules Hirwa, Phocas Maniraguha, Richesse
Ndiritiro, Muna Omar, Marcia C. Schenck, Kate Reed, Lazha
Taha, and Gerawork Teferra*

Contributors | 247

Index | 251

Figures

1.1   Secondary school in Kakuma. Image credit: Gerawork
Teferra. | 51

1.2   A primary school in Kakuma. Image credit: Gerawork
Teferra. | 63

2.1   A bomb exploding in Sana'a, Yemen. Image credit:
Muna Omar. | 83

2.2   Water scarcity in Yemen. Image credit: Muna Omar. | 84

2.3   A photograph of Dastow. Image credit: Muna Omar. | 88

2.4   A photograph of Rabia. Image credit: Muna Omar. | 89

2.5   A photograph of Safia. Image credit: Muna Omar. | 92

2.6   Ayesha and her children in their home. Image credit:
Muna Omar. | 95

2.7   Refugees registering to return to their home countries.
Image credit: Muna Omar. | 99

2.8   A photograph of Saeed. Image credit: Muna Omar. | 101

2.9   Refugees stranded in Yemen. Image credit: Muna Omar. | 105

4.1   A Twa potter in Mahama refugee camp. Image credit:
Richesse Ndiritiro. | 141

6.1   A horse leaps after packages are placed on his back.
Image credit: Younes Mohammad. | 165

6.2   A Peshmerga tank. Image credit: Hawre Khalid. | 168

6.3   Raad Hindia. Image credit: Ali Arkady. | 170

6.4   Two Kurdish women make local Kurdish bread.
Image credit: Sangar Akrayi. | 172

6.5   A worker sitting in the middle of the Bazaar of Sulaimani.
      Image credit: Sartep Othman. | 175
7.1   An example of the herbs used by traditional healers.
      Image credit: Phocas Maniraguha. | 185
7.2   Miti shamba. Image credit: Phocas Maniraguha. | 187
8.1   Heyam Almouli, a retired teacher from Salamieh.
      Image credit: Heyam Almouli. | 203
8.2   Rola Ibrahim, a researcher and counsellor.
      Image credit: Rola Ibrahim. | 204

Preface: An Invitation

Kate Reed and Marcia C. Schenck

Dear Reader,

We are grateful and overjoyed to share this anthology with you. The essays collected here represent the culmination of years of research and writing, often under adverse conditions. It has been our pleasure and honour to work with these authors, first as instructors in a history research methods course, and now as editors and colleagues. The authors who have written for this volume are a global cohort, residing presently or previously in: France, Syria, Iraqi Kurdistan, Rwanda, Kenya, Ethiopia, Yemen, Saudi Arabia, and Burundi. Their relationships to these nation-states are reflective of our globally fraught system of sociopolitical organization, including refugee-hood, official and unofficial migrant status, and varying degrees of citizenship. Their research, similarly, captures interstices, liminality, and marginality, and does so from perspectives rarely represented in historical scholarship. By way of introduction, we, as editors from Germany and the United States who do not share these perspectives or positionalities, want to introduce ourselves and share some of the ideas and commitments that guided us in compiling this anthology.

Throughout the teaching, editing, and collaboration process, our basic premise has been that historical research is a form of conversation. We have returned to this touchstone again and again. Whether conceived of as conversation with sources, historiographical conversation with other authors, conversation with colleagues and peers, or eventual conversation with the wider public, the notion of historical research as an intersubjective and dialogical process grounds this volume. It gives us great pleasure to invite you into the conversation we open here.

Dialogue can seem abstract, even utopian. However, thinking about research as a set of overlapping conversations means careful consideration of the positions – material, epistemological – from which each participant intervenes, as well as those factors that obstruct or preclude the participation of certain people in certain conversations. It means thinking about what Michel-Rolph Trouillot calls the "conditions of production" of historical scholarship and the ways these lead to silences/silencing. Trouillot identifies four moments when silencing might take place: in the creation of sources, in the creation of archives, in the creation of historical narratives, and in the compilation of historical narratives to create "history in the final instance."[1] The essays in this volume represent critical interventions along at least three of these axes of silencing. Whether they amount to a shift in "history in the final instance" will depend on how they are received by you, the reader.

First, because they are based on original oral historical research, these essays involved the creation of new sources that document experiences, perspectives, and phenomena that infrequently, if ever, surface in the documentary record. Second, without access to archives in the traditional sense, contributors to this volume built their own archives of interviews, ephemera, and observations, creating a counterpoint to the "archival logics" that govern state and agency archives.[2] And third, as "non-traditional" historians by virtue of training, geography, citizenship, refugee or migrant status, or some combination thereof, the historians whose work appears here bring rarely heard authorial voices and perspectives to the process of narrative creation.

The conversational paradigm entails a commitment to transparency about the context in which, and process by which, these histories were created. This commitment, in turn, requires deviation from "traditional" historical scholarship, both to throw into relief the ligaments connecting author, sources, and narrative, and to draw readers more explicitly into the conversation. To this end, prefacing each essay, you will find a letter like this one, in which the authors introduce themselves and their work, making visible the intellectual and physical paths travelled to arrive at the narratives they share in their research. We ask that you keep an open mind and heart as you read these letters and the essays that accompany them.

In keeping with our commitment to transparency about the conditions of narrative creation, we conclude with a brief word about us, as the editors of this volume. Marcia, from Germany, is a professor of global history at the University of Potsdam where she teaches the Global History Dialogues course (which sparked the idea for this anthology) and researches the history of refugees across the African continent. She received her doctorate in history from Princeton University in 2017. In her free time, Marcia can be found painting, playing piano, and walking with her dog Ellie. Kate, from the United States, is a graduate student in economic and social history at the University of Oxford where she studies labour, land, and migration in Mexico and Central America. She completed her undergraduate degree in history at Princeton in 2019 and worked as a teaching assistant for Global History Dialogues for the first two years of the course. Not as artistic as Marcia, Kate spends her free hours baking, playing with her dogs Flynn and Annie, and spending time with her siblings.

It is perhaps obvious, but nonetheless important to state, that our status as German and US citizens, with abundant research and financial support from some of the most well-endowed universities in the world, both made this anthology possible and indelibly shaped it and the relationships between us and the contributors. Our citizenship affords us near freedom of movement, which was crucial for the development of this anthology. Both of us were able to teach in person in Kakuma refugee camp in Kenya between 2016 and 2019. We not only established lasting relationships with some of the contributors to this book, but, in discussion with her students, Marcia developed the idea for the Global History Dialogues Project, where the journey toward this edited project began. In the formal introduction that follows this letter, we reflect more systematically about our role. For now, we would like to extend our gratitude to the authors, Aime Parfait, Alain, Gera, Ismail, Lazha, Phocas, Richesse, Sandrine, and Muna, for sharing their research here; and to you, for joining us in this conversation.

Sincerely,
Kate Reed and Marcia C. Schenck

NOTES

1   Michel-Rolph Trouillot, *Silencing the Past: Power and the Production of History* (Boston: Beacon Press, 1995), 24. Emphasis in original.
2   Kirsten Weld, *Paper Cadavers: The Archives of Dictatorship in Guatemala* (Durham: Duke University Press, 2014).

Acknowledgments

There are so many people and institutions we would like to thank for helping bring this volume into the world. The Global History Lab (GHL) at Princeton University, and especially its director, Jeremy Adelman, have been foundational to Global History Dialogues (GHD) and everything that has followed from it. This project would have been impossible without them. The 2019 and 2020 teaching assistants for Global History Dialogues – Ray Thornton, Lorenzo Bondioli, Matthew Dowd, Joe Glynias, Oihana Basilio, Isabelle Delorme, Johanna Wetzel – contributed so much as teachers and mentors, both to the students in the course and to the development and realization of students' research projects. The current and former staff of the GHL, especially Jennifer Loessy and Nicole Bergman, were generous with their time and energy, making possible the formidable logistics of organizing a project across three continents. Also at Princeton, we owe our thanks to Marija Naumoski at the McGraw Center for Teaching and Learning, Trisha Thorme at the Program for Community Engaged Scholarship, and Kristy Holmes at Global Financial Services.

In 2019 and 2020, Global History Dialogues was fortunate to work with amazing partner institutions: the UNHCR in Kenya; Kepler in Rwanda; Sciences Po in France; Fundación del Pino in Spain; Whitaker Peace and Development Initiative in Uganda; Panteion University in Greece; and American University Iraq – Sulaimania in Iraq. Our thanks go to all these places and the people who collaborated with us at each of them.

Turning to the drafting and revising of the volume itself, special thanks are due to Louise Thatcher, Lisa Ilmer, and Cibele Kojima de Paula at the University of Potsdam for their assistance preparing the manuscript. We would also like to thank our editors at McGill-Queen's University Press, Jacqueline Mason and Melissa Jean Gismondi, for their early enthusiasm and vision for the book, and Kaitlin Littlechild, for copyediting the manuscript. Two anonymous reviewers provided inspiring and extremely helpful suggestions. Joanne Pisano kept us organized throughout. The Refugee and Forced Migration Series editors, Megan Bradley and James Milner, have been great supporters of the project and our vision; we are thankful to be part of this excellent collection of scholarship. Rhea Stark's incredible artwork, inspired by contributions from all the authors of the volume, graces the cover.

Finally, we would like to extend our sincere thanks to all the student-researchers who have participated in the Global History Dialogues program since its start in 2019. The curiosity, commitment, and brilliance they bring to every class discussion, research workshop, and conference presentation sustain the project.

In addition to these collective acknowledgments, each of us has people and places we would like to thank personally.

Ismail would like to express his warmest thanks to Isabelle Delorme for the continuous support since day one. Jeremy, Marcia, and Kate provided amazing support and brilliant supervision through this project's development until accomplishment. He is extremely thankful for Ghieth, Eleonore, and his family for their constant encouragement and motivation. Most certainly, this project would not have been possible without the inspiring contributions of Heyam and Rola. Finally, Ismail expresses his deepest and warmest gratitude to every Syrian woman, whose stories are worthy to be told to the whole world for many generations to come.

Aime Parfait would like to thank Joselyne Ishimwe and Kepler for inviting him to join Global History Dialogues. The Princeton University Global History Dialogues team has also been supportive. He is grateful for the insights that they provided during the learning process. In addition, their constructive comments and advice during the research and writing were very helpful. He would like to thank the team of researchers for the support. Their comments, companionship and advice were memorable. The Burundian refugee drummers living in Rwanda also contributed a lot by sparing their time and by enriching the research with information. His contribution to this book is dedicated to his two parents, his brother Emmanuel, and the protective love from his sister Yvette.

Sandrine would like to acknowledge Professor Marcia as the head of Global History Dialogues, who eventually equipped her with the necessary skills to conduct research, as well as giving her feedback where it was needed. Moreover, she had the best tutors who made all the work easier; she would like to thank Ray Thornton and Kate Reed who monitored every step from 2019 till now. Finally, she thanks her family and friends who tremendously loved and helped her throughout the entire time of the research. She dedicates this book to you who are reading it; she believes you will enjoy it.

Alain would like to thank Marcia, Kate, and Ray for helping him bring this research paper to completion. Other sincere thanks go to the late Joshua Tuyishime, a.k.a. Jay Polly, and Gatsinda Jean Paul, a.k.a. J.P., for giving him their precious time and knowledge while he interviewed them.

Phocas would like to appreciate and thank Kepler and Princeton University for allowing him to be a part of this program. Immaculate provided necessary information for the research that he conducted. She is located in the Nyabihu district, Rwanda. He would like to thank his teaching assistant, Ray Thornton, for the hard work and direct support to help him reach this goal. He would like to appreciate all the Global History Dialogues staff for the support that they provided in direct or indirect ways. Lastly, he would like to appreciate all the support from his friends and family members.

Richesse would like to thank Tony Mihigo who has been an inspiration to the development of the topic, Kepler for inviting him to join Global History Dialogues, and Princeton University for helping him complete the course. Marcia Schenck, Kate Reed, and Ray Thornton have contributed so much to the accomplishment of the course and the research. The research paper would not be incredible without their constructive feedback, comments, and advice. Much appreciation to Aime Parfait Emerusenge and Iribagize Cyuzuzo Sandrine for their peer reviews and encouragement. His contribution to this book is dedicated to Burundian Twa refugees who found strength to adapt and integrate themselves in Mahama refugee camp.

Muna is overwhelmed with humbleness and gratitude to acknowledge all those who have helped her to put her research together, well above the level of simplicity and into something concrete. Muna is extremely grateful to Professors Jeremy Adelman and Marcia Schenck for the immense knowledge and continuous support they provided during her research. Muna would like to thank Lorenzo

Bondioli and Kate Reed for their insightful comments and assistance at every stage of the research project. Finally, and as always, she would like to thank her mother for the unconditional love and unwavering support. Muna's contribution to this book is dedicated to her mother for all the hardships and sacrifices her mother has made for her.

Kate would like to thank Marcia and Jeremy for inviting her to join the GHD in its first year. Mohamed Hure and Joy Maraka at the UNHCR provided a kind welcome in Kakuma refugee camp. Alexandra Kersley and Eren Orbey read the introduction and provided insightful comments. Other friends provided much-needed companionship and counsel. Working with the GHD has introduced her to so many incredible researchers and historians-in-training; she is grateful for all of them. Finally, and as always, she would like to thank her family for their unwavering love and support. Her contribution to this book is dedicated to the memory of her brother Henry.

Marcia's heartfelt thanks go to Kate and Jeremy for making the GHD possible in the first place, Jeremy through his unwavering faith in the idea and continued financial support of the implementation, and Kate through being first a teaching fellow, then program coordinator, and now a treasured coauthor and friend. She also would like to thank all the participants of this anthology from the bottom of her heart for their patience in traversing the unfamiliar path to publication – without you and your courage nothing would be possible. And last, but not least, she wants to express her sincere thanks to her family for their continued and loving support and patience.

Lazha would like to thank Kashkul, the Center of Arts and Culture at the American University of Iraq-Sulaimani, for their collaboration with Princeton University, which made it possible for her to join Global History Dialogues and write her first ever research project. She thanks the Global History Dialogues team, especially Kate, who worked closely with the researchers and helped them along all the steps; this project would not have been possible without her. Lazha also would like to pay her special regards to Marcia and Jeremy, who made this program the best possible and made it a friendly environment for researchers in underrepresented regions of the world. Finally, she appreciates the support of her family and the unconditional love that has influenced her work.

Gera is highly grateful to Kate and Marcia for the keen, continuous, and helpful supports, as well as insightful comments provided, without which his paper would not have such form. During writing, Kate's encouragement, critical comments, and support in gathering resources, has been immeasurable. He is also grateful to Marcia and Jeremey for creating the GHD training opportunity and inviting him to attend; it has really had an impact. His special appreciation goes to his interview respondents who have shared their experience and made him understand camp education better, which has heavily enriched his work. Lastly, he thanks everyone who has been connected directly or indirectly and has had an influence on his contribution.

THE RIGHT TO RESEARCH

Introduction

Kate Reed and Marcia C. Schenck

After I finished my paper, I read an article that mentioned exactly
what I wanted to mention in my paper in a more candid and appealing
language. If I read that paper before or during my research, without
a doubt my research question would have been changed to an unanswered question, or would have endeavored to refute some of the
points raised in the article. This paper not only poured cold water on
my paper, it also made me think that I spent time and energy to find
an answer to a known thing. This happened because answers are saved
(colonialized) in universities for scholars only.[1]

Gerawork Teferra, Kakuma Refugee Camp, 2020

Gerawork (Gera) Teferra, one of the contributors to this volume,
shared this reflection about his experience doing historical research
in Kakuma refugee camp. He wrote this as part of an ongoing
conversation about the possibilities and limitations of (academic)
historical research conducted in partnerships between institutions
and academics in the United States and Europe and refugee and
host-community students in the "Global South." His words express
a deep-seated frustration: how could he contribute to a scholarly
conversation from which he was excluded, not only because he
lacked access to libraries and databases, but also because of more
fundamental, implicit assumptions about who conducts research
and narrates history? Gera's words are not, however, without some
sense that things could be otherwise. If he could have read the paper
earlier, if systems of knowledge production and dissemination were
more open, less "colonialized," his work could have formed part of
this wider conversation.[2]

The project that led to this volume started with another observation from Gera, this one about the global history course he was taking, which was taught to refugee learners but had little to say about refugees. And it had nothing to say that was spoken by refugees themselves. Put simply, refugees rarely figured as historical actors, and never as historical narrators – as historians.[3]

It would be easy, perhaps, to accept this as a matter of course. Assumptions like this have long been made about the (in)capacity of marginalized groups to be the authorial voices of history. Refugees living in camps are not historians for "historically explicable reasons," to borrow historian Bonnie Smith's phrase.[4] They do not do the things historians do because they cannot. They cannot consult archives, they cannot access university libraries, they cannot depend on reliable internet access, let alone the funding, research support, training, social networks, and material resources that underpin the research and writing of academic history.[5] It is as though (encamped) refugee and historian have been defined as mutually exclusive identities. A person residing in a refugee camp cannot be a historian because a historian, quite simply, cannot be a person residing in a refugee camp.

What if we were to disrupt this tautology? To redefine what being a historian means? What perils do we run, what possibilities do we open? This volume is an overture, an invitation to conversation about these questions. It consists of nine articles authored by refugee, migrant, and host-community researchers living currently or formerly in France, Syria, Iraqi Kurdistan, Rwanda, Kenya, Ethiopia, Yemen, Saudi Arabia, and Burundi.[6] Their work is based on original oral historical research conducted between 2019 and 2020. The authors' essays are both important contributions to historical scholarship and challenges to the norms and assumptions about that scholarship and who is able to participate in it. Drawing on their unique positionalities and lived experiences, as well as the fact that their research unfolded in conversation with each other as part of an experiment in global history education and research, their essays attend both to the hyperlocal – which is so often flattened in top-down studies of "refugeeness" – and to the larger regional and global structures in which those local experiences and processes are embedded. (When using the term *refugee* in these pages, we include those with manifold lived realities not neatly captured by the normative legal category of refugee, such as forced migrants, "economic" migrants, and internally displaced people, as well as people who have moved between these categories over time.)

Contributors researched and wrote their work under the auspices of a project called Global History Dialogues (GHD), which sought to equip them with the tools needed to carry out historical research wherever they lived.[7] If student-researchers received training, support, and structure, the idea went, they could create research that not only included but also spoke from vantages long excluded from global history. Yet, achieving this goal proved fraught, and while we all found much meaning, even joy, in the process of working together, we also share ambivalences, doubts, and criticisms of this project and what it represents. Thus, this volume is not a roadmap for a new practice of historical scholarship and it offers no sweeping vision for what history could be. It works in the interstices, at the edges, starting from existing practices and moving, haltingly and partially, to something new. It grows from WhatsApp messages, lagging video calls, and endless email exchanges. It starts with the idea that anyone can be a historian – already a contentious proposition – and asks what happens next.[8] Where do we go from here?

Addressing that question is one of our tasks in this introduction. First, we offer a brief history of what we might call the global refugee regime to help ground the volume's empirical contributions. We then contextualize the volume and its nine essays, articulating their significance and the possibilities they suggest for moving toward a world in which we can "expand historical discourse to a conception of every one of us, as historical writers, writing as historical actors," as the historian Susan Crane writes.[9] At the same time, we must critically acknowledge the limitations of this project and of the paradigm of inclusion itself. These two purposes may seem at odds with each other. Indeed, recurrent in our conversations about this project was a profound sense of tension, which stemmed from the disjuncture between allowing for, even celebrating, difference, and seeking to participate in structures, systems, and dialogues that are premised on excluding that which is *too* different.[10] As we reminded each other many times in our class discussions, however, one of the most important aspects of historical scholarship is its embrace of complexity. And so, just as we must allow for contradiction, paradox, and incoherence in the pasts we study, we allow for the same in our own experiences and experiments. Such allowance is not meant to dismiss the limitations of this project – far from it. Rather, it is to fix our attention on the concrete, to move us from abstract ideas of inclusion and dialogue to the fraught and messy business of enacting those ideas and coming to terms with their shortcomings. Attention to complexity and ambivalence suggests possibilities for future endeavors that build from the liminal, limited space opened by this volume and the conversations it has sparked.

A BRIEF GLOBAL HISTORY OF
REFUGE AND REFUGEES

The conventional story of our current refugee regime begins with the largescale displacement of European populations during and after the Second World War. The Geneva Convention, which remains the defining international law on refugee protection, and the two international organizations most closely associated with refugees and migrants (the United Nations High Commissioner for Refugees [UNHCR] and the International Organization for Migration [IOM]) were all established in 1951. While wartime displacement and the Cold War were both crucial shapers of the institutional and legal frameworks created at midcentury, focusing only on the European panorama overlooks practices of refugee control that developed earlier in the century in colonial and imperial contexts. Indeed, the colonial origins of thinking about refugees become especially apparent when looking at the language of humanitarianism concerning refugees and the emergence of the refugee camp as an institution for the protection and safeguarding, but also the governing, of displaced people in European colonies in Africa.

Refugee camps, for example, which are one of the defining features of present-day refugee management, emerged during the Anglo-Boer War (1899–1902). The conflict, sparked by the discovery of gold in the Transvaal, saw the use of scorched-earth tactics causing massive displacement. Rural populations were housed in racially segregated camps, referred to, tellingly, as both "concentration camps" and "refugee camps."[11] More than 28,000 Afrikaners and 14,000 Africans died.[12] Several years later, German forces in present-day Namibia adopted the British refugee/concentration camp as part of a war of extermination against the Herero, during what is widely considered the first genocide of the twentieth century.[13] These camps functioned as spaces of control and labour exploitation, with refugees expected to work in the camps or hire out to private employers.[14]

The refugee/concentration camps used during colonial wars meshed with nascent European humanitarianism. By the 1930s, with the Italian invasion of Ethiopia, Bronwen Everill argues that the refugee, rather than the enslaved person, became the object of European (and especially British) humanitarianism.[15] But this was a "reluctant humanitarianism," as the historian Brett Shadle has it, and the techniques of control, isolation, and coercion that characterized camps in southern Africa were redeployed in this "humanitarian" context.[16] Two contradictory logics, extant to this day, shaped camp management in the 1930s: on the one hand, the need to do more than simply sustain life; and on the other, to avoid creating any hope of long-term settlement.[17]

By the start of the Second World War, European governments already had an extensive repertoire of techniques for managing the refugee populations created by their colonial and extractive exploits. The First World War and interwar years, too, saw the rise of international coordination to manage the refugees that resulted from the breakup of large eastern European empires, such as the Ottoman. The passport became a nearly universal requirement for entry and helped nation-states to define themselves as a bounded body of citizens. Identification requirements were especially onerous for refugees who lacked access to this documentation or had been stripped of the legal nationality required to acquire the proper papers. The League of Nations, responding to this shift in migration control, created the Nansen Passport as a form of identification available to refugees, but it imposed no binding requirements on nation-states to receive refugees at their borders or allow them to return to the issuing country. However, this was the first time that stateless persons had juridical status via international agreement and, thus, constitutes a critical precursor to post-Second World War developments in refugee law.[18]

This longer, broader history of refugee management provides an important context for the response to European refugees following the Second World War. Initially, repatriation was the favoured response to refugees (and remains so to this day), but by the 1950s, resettlement to third countries became more prevalent. However, the newly created UNHCR faced serious obstacles from the outset – namely, that the United States and Western European nations were strenuously opposed to any limitations on their sovereignty. This opposition had important ramifications: first, the UNHCR's budget was tiny, and fundraising efforts were subject to approval by the UN General Assembly. Second, the distinction between "refugees" and "migrants" became ever more important, with the IOM set up to deal with migrants and the UNHCR – which was originally a temporary institution – to deal with refugees. Generally speaking, the widely accepted legal definition of a refugee, based on the 1951 Convention and the 1967 Protocol Relating to the Status of Refugees is:

> any person who is outside their country of origin and unable or unwilling to return there or to avail themselves of its protection, owing to well-founded fear of persecution for reasons of race, religion, nationality, membership of a particular social group (an additional ground not found in the UNHCR Statute), or political opinion. Stateless persons may also be refugees in this sense, where country of origin (citizenship) is understood as "country of former habitual residence."[19]

The sharpening division between types of displaced people is reflective of a broader phenomenon: as protections for refugees became more formalized in international law, the issue of who could claim refugee status became more contested and contentious. This has been especially true since the advent of decolonization struggles in Africa and violent civil wars in Central America (in which the United States was often involved), both of which caused increasing numbers of people to seek protection in Europe and the United States. Since the 1980s, these countries have tried to sideline the UNHCR and other international organizations in an effort to impose stricter entry requirements on people seeking refuge. The legal definition of a refugee, which necessitates individual, case-by-case recognition instead of group identification (as had previously been the case), allows states to determine – often arbitrarily – whether an individual's story conforms to the definition and, thus, whether that person is "deserving" of protection. While the specific process varies significantly among receiving countries, claims to protection are generally based on refugees' accounts of their persecution, supported "through documentary and often bodily evidence."[20] However, as Agnes Woolley notes, in practice, "the process relies heavily on the self-presentation of the individual claimant; their ability to convince an immigration officer or judge. The claimant must narrate themselves into a position of legitimacy."[21] We will return to this problem of narrative production – knowledge production – later in the introduction. Now, we move from this crash course in refugee history to a history of the present volume, and what it seeks to do.

STARTING THE CONVERSATION: BECOMING RESEARCHERS, NAVIGATING POSITIONALITIES

We return to the global history class and the absence of refugee historians. Global History Dialogues was conceived as a response to this absence. Working with refugee and host-community learners in Rwanda, Kenya, South Sudan, Uganda, the Middle East and Northern African (MENA) region, France, and Iraqi Kurdistan, the course trained student-researchers in historical research methods. Global History Dialogues focused on methodologies accessible from the students' various circumstances: liminal or no legal status, dependence on (and, therefore, vulnerability to) aid organizations and NGOs, and lack of precedent for "someone like them" to be working as researchers rather than being the subjects of someone else's research. Mindful of these limitations, we chose to focus on oral history, which had the twofold advantage of being highly accessible and introducing a far wider range of perspectives and voices than would be found in official archives.[22]

The course was pragmatic. We attended to the nuts and bolts of research – developing questions, contacting interviewees, obtaining consent, recording, and storing files. It was also complex, drawing into one (virtual) classroom the kinds of differences and inequalities that often keep people in separate spaces, as strangers. The teaching staff, including the authors of this introduction, were white, middle-class academics and graduate students at prestigious universities in the United States and Europe. The student-researchers included refugee and migrant learners as well as host-community students, spread across Southern and Central Europe, Eastern Africa, Northern Africa, and the Middle East. While gender was balanced among the teaching staff, men student-researchers outnumbered women, an imbalance reflected in this volume, which features three contributions by women and six by men.

The inequalities that structured the classroom compelled us to confront them, rather than treat them in the abstract. We did so with fragmentary success. The one inequality that the course explicitly set out to address – the inequality in who authors, and appears as an actor in, historical narratives – was perhaps the terrain where we made the most progress. Other inequalities in access to library resources, internet, technology, safe and comfortable places in which to work, legal status and citizenship, and mobility were so profound and so far outside the scope of what a nine-month course could accomplish, that our "solutions" were stopgap at best. Universities and non-profits helped fund a time and labour-intensive project, paying both for the labour of the teaching staff and for stipends for student-researchers to subsidize the opportunity costs of participation. Teaching assistants used their institutional library privileges to conduct secondary research on behalf of students. We relied on messaging apps and email when lack of internet connectivity prevented students from attending video-call discussion sessions.

This list of limitations and adaptations might seem mundane, but it throws into relief the unspoken assumptions that underwrite common perceptions of teaching and research, and, crucially, who does them. To paraphrase Gayatri Spivak, it is sometimes the most informal, banal, and "marginal" moments that "[give] us a sense of what is 'normal' ... what 'norms.'"[23] "Normal" researchers would have access to libraries and archives, to institutional review boards, colleagues, trainings, and workshops. They would most likely not need to stay up until two or three or five in the morning because those were the only hours of the day that they could reliably access the internet. They would be accustomed to being the one seeking out interviewees and asking questions, rather than being the "research subject." How would research change if we could not assume that researchers have access to the ideas, texts, and authors with whom we expect them to be in conversation, especially if they speak from positionalities that have rarely been taken seriously as productive of knowledge in their own right?

The "conditions of production" of the pieces in this volume – written from the lived realities of refugee, migrant, and host-community historians working outside the traditional bounds of the academy – mark the narratives shared here, highlighting and upending the assumptions and norms that underpin history writing. By "conditions of production," we mean Michel-Rolph Trouillot's formulation:

> What history is changes with time and place or, better said, history reveals itself only through the production of specific narratives. What matters most are the process and conditions of production of such narratives. Only a focus on that process can uncover the ways in which the two sides of historicity intertwine in a particular context. Only through that overlap can we discover the differential exercise of power that makes some narratives possible and silences others.[24]

These pieces show that other narratives are possible; that silenced narratives need not remain so. They destabilize homogenizing concepts and identities. "Refugee" and "migrant," when considered not from the gaze of states attempting to control populations, but rather from within those identities, become so infinitely complex as to be marginally useful as categories of understanding or analysis other than in the broadest terms.[25] Indeed, throughout this introduction and book, the terms *refugee, migrant,* and *host-community member* should be taken only as "broad legal or descriptive rubric[s] that [include] within [them] a world of different socioeconomic statuses, personal histories, and psychological or spiritual situations," following anthropologist Liisa Malkki's critique.[26]

The contributions in this volume also unseat historiographical geographies. With historical scholarship traditionally defined by "the real-world geography of textual sources" to which archive-focused historians travel, at great cost, the basic question of (im)mobility underwrites these contributions.[27] Flight across international borders is, under international law, a basic condition for being a refugee; protracted displacement, with highly restricted mobility, often follows flight.[28] These two geographic (dis)locations are increasingly complicated by "deterritorialized social networks of forcibly displaced people" forged by way of internet communication, electronic remittances, and other forms of geographically unrestricted connection (akin to the project from which this anthology emerges).[29] This tension between displacement and emplacement weaves through the volume, in the vein of what Ulrike Freitag and Achim von Oppen call the "translocal." This is an "intermediary concept which helps to better understand and conceptualize connections beyond the local which are, however, neither necessarily global in scale nor necessarily connected to global moments."[30]

The notion of the "translocal" is useful, too, because it highlights the need to create new archives and to record oral histories that can speak to processes, experiences, and subjectivities that no amount of sleuthing in colonial (or postcolonial state, or NGO) archives, however skilled, could uncover.[31] The two issues – of complicating historians' relationship to place and decentering (colonial) state archives – are intertwined for historians and histories with varied relationships to statelessness. Co-creating archives and oral histories from this place of liminality brings a different perspective than that of outsider-researchers whose very presence in "fieldwork sites" is often premised on citizenship, access to a passport, university funding, and so on. On an interpersonal level, too, "there is a huge difference [between a] researchee [i.e., the person being researched] and researcher's perspective," as contributor Richesse Ndiritiro notes. Taking on the identity of researcher – for several contributors, after many years of being the objects of outsiders' projects – was empowering, inspiring them to learn more, to pursue new questions, and to reach out to residents of their localities with whom they otherwise never would have come into contact. It was also bittersweet. As feminist scholar Sara Ahmed writes, research can be "a process of estrangement, which creates an orientation in which some things come into view that had previously been obscured."[32] With the identity of researcher came new ways of relating to familiar communities: people approached student-researchers with expectations that their research could benefit participants in some way, contributing to what Gera calls cycles of "hope and despair" as student-researchers were unable to change the circumstances of their interviewees.[33] New questions and interpretations became visible through research, but this process did not seem to ameliorate the injustice and suffering that researchers set out to address. So – why research?

THE RIGHT TO RESEARCH: CONVERSATIONS AND COMMUNITIES

The title of this volume is borrowed from anthropologist Arjun Appadurai's eponymous essay, in which he argues that the right to research – to "make disciplined inquiries into those things we need to know, but do not know yet" – should be understood as a "right of a special kind," a fundamental ability necessary for meaningful democratic citizenship in a globalizing world.[34] We wish to articulate a right to research both more robust and less specific than Appadurai's conception. He addresses the "bottom portion of the upper half of the typical population in poorer countries," and, in particular, those people with citizenship in those countries.[35] In his formulation, the right to research and democratic citizenship are intimately connected, a connection not new in Appadurai's work but rather a variation on the much older idea that "taking part in democratic society requires one to be informed."[36]

What of those people who do not have citizenship in the country where they reside, whether because they have refugee status or because they live undocumented? That is, what of people whose

participation in democratic society is restricted or altogether foreclosed by their legal status, or by lack of democratic institutions tout
court? There is no reason to restrict the right to research to those
whose membership in a national political community is (relatively)
secure. Indeed, the uncertainty, unpredictability, and precarity of
life partially or wholly outside regimes of citizenship suggests that
research, as a broadly defined capacity to systematically interrogate
one's environment, might reasonably be understood as even more
important in these contexts.

A second addition we would make to Appadurai's conception
of the "right to research" is an emphasis on the communicative,
interpersonal, and conversational dynamics of research. Research
in this case is not simply an activity one pursues for oneself in the
course of making more informed decisions. Also, and more importantly, research is a process of conversation that unfolds (unevenly
and unequally) on multiple scales and in multiple directions. These
include conversations between the researcher and the community
they study; conversations between researchers in a learning community such as Global History Dialogues; conversations between
student-researchers and instructors – in this case, conversations that
bridge Global North and Global South within a classroom space;
and conversations between researchers and others working in their
field. On our account, then, the right to research is *both* the ability
to systematically inquire into the unknown and the ability to share
one's findings and be taken seriously as a producer and bearer of
knowledge – something that has historically been denied to many
refugees and other people on the move.[37]

For some student-researchers, research required building relationships with strangers they otherwise never would have met. This was a
challenge but not one without its rewards: working to remain open-
minded, to listen to stories and perspectives very different from their
own, cultivated student-researchers' self-confidence and empathy.
Reflecting on the research process, several noted that formulating
questions for interviewees and integrating different voices into their
essays was certainly difficult but left them more confident in their
communication, writing, and analytical abilities. The process of conducting research and writing narratives based on their findings was,
student-researchers found, a transformative one, especially for those
who had been subjects in many outside researchers' projects and
now were able to assume the authorial voice.[38]

Doing this research in the context of a global classroom that brought together refugee and host-community researchers with instructors from the Global North provided other opportunities for conversation and collaboration across boundaries. Equally important as the formal teaching offered by Global History Dialogues was the experience of occupying a space shared with once-strangers, brought together for the simple reason that all shared an interest in history, as well as experiences, whether direct or indirect, of displacement, statelessness, and refuge-seeking.

Of course, the differences and inequalities that we brought into the classroom were a source of friction as well as possibility. Possibility, because to become a researcher, to conduct a systematic investigation into something of personal and community significance, is an inherently generative process. To do so in the company of geographically, linguistically, and experientially diverse peers, even more so. Friction, because the project was premised on including new voices in already-existing scholarly conversations – conversations that, as Gera's opening reflection illustrates, were rarely accessible to the volume's contributors. We prioritized conversations across (rather than within) borders and between Global North and South. We stressed interventions in academic spaces, rather than ways of sharing research findings with local communities. Thus, not only did we tacitly accept (indeed, privilege) the terms of Global North academic conversations, which have historically excluded refugee and Global South voices, but we also sought to intervene in conversations that student-researchers could not hear except in snippets.

If we take seriously the notion of research as conversation, it becomes clear that a "right to research" is not one-sided: it cannot be fully exercised outside of a community. Rather, it depends on the possibility of exchanges in which all interlocutors both speak and listen, and where all participants can be heard. This means that the burden of realizing this right rests not only with universities and educators responsible for training student-researchers, but also – perhaps even more importantly – with the wider scholarly community, which must find ways to make its conversations accessible to researchers who defy entrenched norms of positionality, identity, subject matter, and epistemology. By "accessible," we mean not in the limited, conventional notion of "written for a general audience," but materially (by removing paywalls, prioritizing open-access publications, and creating programs for "non-traditional" scholars to freely access libraries and databases) and dialogically (by expecting, and taking seriously, interventions that destabilize and challenge existing norms, practices, and assumptions).

While all of the contributors to this volume believe firmly that a more open and inclusive scholarly community is an eminently worthwhile goal, and one toward which we hope this volume makes a small contribution, we, as the volume's editors, also recognize that participation in scholarly conversations is not the only, or indeed most important, outcome for research projects of the sort featured here. We also recognize that, even in those areas of scholarship more open to this kind of change, the terms of inclusion remain incredibly burdensome for refugee, migrant, and other authors working outside the academy. Particularly as academic conversations remain inaccessible to many people who are their subjects of study, other forums – whether local or regional, with or without university/academic involvement – may help research reach more important and relevant audiences in formats that are more approachable for them.

With this in mind, we turn to what it would take to more thoroughly realize a right to research for more potential researchers, particularly those with refugee status and those outside of academic institutions in the Global South. To do this, we need to consider the ways their voices have historically been marginalized, both within others' research and as authorial voices in their own right.

ON NARRATIVES AND NARRATORS: ORAL HISTORY, REFUGEE STUDIES, AND REFUGEE STORIES

"In a refugee camp, stories are everything. Everyone has one, having just slipped out from the grip of a nightmare ... Everyone is a stranger, in need of introduction," writes Dina Nayeri, who fled Iran with her family as a child and spent years as a refugee in the United Arab Emirates (UAE) and Italy.[39] But, she continues, the stories refugee people have to share may not be the ones they are expected – required – to tell. Narratives of flight and rescue – the expected stories – may not align with the narratives needed to secure asylum, to "calm casual skeptics," to assure an affirmative answer to the question "Am I a *real* refugee?"[40] And the narrow emphasis on narratives of refuge-seeking restricts the other stories, other knowledge, that people who are refugees may prefer to share. In *The Ungrateful Refugee,* Nayeri interweaves her life history, the life stories of other refugees, and an incisive critique of the way prevailing narratives of "refugeeness" limit, censor, and delegitimize other narratives about what it is to be a refugee. "It is your choice how to hear their voices," she writes, knowing, surely, that some will choose to hear her and her interlocutors as the title of her book suggests: ungrateful refugees.

Nayeri illuminates the dialogical aspects of storytelling, the ways reception informs what is said. "For every story that sees the light of day, untold others remain in the shadows, censored, or suppressed." So writes anthropologist Michael Jackson in an extended reflection on Hannah Arendt's conception of storytelling as an intersubjective practice, a way of "transforming private into public meanings" (and vice versa).[41] Much as the right to research requires a community of interlocutors, storytelling requires an audience. And that audience cannot be passive or inert: it must legitimize the story in some way. It must make the story sayable.

What makes a story unsayable; what silences a storyteller? Trauma, certainly. The fundamental inadequacy of words to describe life is heightened for life – and death – in extremis.[42] But even provided a narrator is willing to share their story, other forms of silencing may intervene. The philosopher Kristie Dotson identifies two such "practices of silencing," which she names "testimonial quieting" and "testimonial smothering."[43] Testimonial quieting occurs "when an audience fails to identify a speaker as a knower," often because the speaker belongs to a stigmatized or objectified group.[44] Testimonial smothering, conversely, occurs when "the speaker perceives one's immediate audience as unwilling or unable to gain the appropriate uptake of proffered testimony" – that is, when the speaker, communicating testimony that is "unsafe and risky," feels the audience will not understand them, and so silences themself.[45]

All three of these – trauma, testimonial quieting, and testimonial smothering – affect refugee stories, albeit in different ways. Importantly, storytelling can provide relief from trauma by being a way to make sense of a shattered world and to (re)assert agency in the face of overwhelming circumstances. But that relief will depend upon a story's audience, that is, on the storyteller's ability to speak and to be heard, to have their testimony recognized and accepted. The choice to withhold a story – to maintain silence – is also a form of agency when confronting a system that demands refugee narratives as proof of "refugeeness," and that works to surveil and control refugee lives.[46] Yet, the choice to maintain silence is often not a choice at all, as Yanery, a Cuban refugee resettled in Canada, writes:

> Being a refugee means being in a contradiction: it means being vulnerable and having to show this vulnerability in order to receive protection, while, on the other hand, having to show resilience. Although I am proud of having received protection, I understand the complexities of the vulnerability-resiliency contradiction. There is no pride in being vulnerable, or in having to show it, particularly when everyone keeps stressing how resilient you are. And this is the essential contradiction that most refugees face.[47]

Yanery's reflection alludes to the limits of the narrative possibilities available to refugees sharing their stories publicly. The ways refugees are represented in (European and US) media are constrained to common tropes: villains posing a threat to hosting nations; victims in need of salvation; and, in far fewer cases, potential sources of (principally economic) benefit to host societies.[48] Public narratives of refugees portray them instrumentally or as objects of humanitarian intervention at best, and as racialized stereotypes who pose a threat to national security and well-being at worst. The form such narratives take is also significant. Relatively few articles include refugee voices, a characteristic even more pronounced in media coverage that is hostile to refugees. Photographs, then, are often the main, if not only, way in which refugees become visible in the news media. This brings its own set of problems; namely, that these photographs are easily decontextualized, as they communicate no narrative of their own, and that, by virtue of their narrative instability, they serve to reinforce the limited and limiting tropes that shape media depictions of refugees.[49]

This objectification of refugees creates the conditions for testimonial quieting. Faith Nibbs describes a particularly acute instance of such quieting in her study of a Hmong mother's interaction with the California public health system as she prepared for, and gave birth to, a baby daughter. Refugees, conceptualized as "'the contagious other to the American [US] body politic' ... read as diseased and deviant bodies in need of control," are subjected to a barrage of tests, trainings, and treatments in preparation for resettlement.[50]

This process continues, she argues, in subsequent interactions with medical spaces and professionals. The biomedical system in Global North countries works as "a continuation of governmentality, or refugee objectification," devaluing refugees' knowledge of their bodies and medical practices, refusing to see them as knowers, in Dotson's terms.[51] As the Hmong mother, whom Nibbs calls Choua, gives induced birth and undergoes medical procedures without informed consent, her requests and questions are consistently misinterpreted or unanswered, and hospital staff admonish her for the ways she cares for her newborn child. Pathologized, refugees are seen as bodies in need of intervention, their own narratives about illness and health becoming secondary to the knowledge produced about them by medical professionals – even well-meaning ones.[52]

The objectification of refugees plays a role as well in testimonial smothering – the inability of people who are refugees to share stories that differ from expected narratives because of the risk this poses to them. A great many studies, encompassing academic, journalistic, and literary works, have examined refugee narratives and the ways they are shaped by the need to satisfy eligibility criteria – to, in Agnes Woolley's formulation, offer an "'asylum story': an idealized version of refugeehood on which the civic incorporation of the asylum seeker depends and which circulates in a narrative economy that sets the terms for the enunciation of refugee experience."[53] In most cases, the applicant's narrative of persecution and vulnerability is the primary – though by no means the only – basis on which refugee status, or asylum, is granted. The stakes of conforming to this narrative and satisfying the inconsistent and often arbitrary criteria employed by immigration and asylum officials are, therefore, extraordinarily high. As Woolley notes, "Such models of ideal refugeehood, produced by a peculiarly restrictive set of narrative conditions, have material effects which can often mean the difference between life and death for asylum claimants."[54] Moreover, in many cases, the difficulties of communicating a narrative that meets the expectations of the interviewer are exacerbated by language differences mediated variously well or poorly by interpreters.[55]

Importantly, the narratives that refugees share during interviews with bureaucratic officials are dialogic; the official asks questions that elicit responses. The narrative is thus co-constructed, shaped by the specific questions the interviewer asks and the respondent's understanding of what constitutes a worthy response to those questions. However, as Katherine Jensen remarks in her study of Brazilian asylum interviews, the co-created nature of these narratives does not typically appear in the official records that go on to become the basis for the asylum seeker's case. "The various markers of the official's presence in the interview are effaced in case documents," meaning that "there is no documentation of the official's somatic state, interpersonal engagement, or subjectivity, [so] these components – though acknowledged as impacting the case – are not considered in decision-making."[56]

The elision of the questioner in these asylum narratives is symptomatic of the ways refugees' knowledge and narratives are devalued relative to what Jensen terms "disembodied knowledge" – knowledge from "objective" sources such as expert witnesses, country conditions reports, and asylum officials themselves. Refugees are expected to speak only to what they personally have witnessed or experienced, and are considered able to narrate only the particular, the local. Even then, the evidence they marshal on their behalf is perceived as biased and subjective.[57] Also illustrative of the extreme skepticism that meets refugee narratives is the privileging of bodily evidence over oral testimony, with proof of scars and other injuries often considered more reliable than a spoken or written narrative or required to "corroborate" such narratives.[58]

In the determination of whether someone has experienced the physical and psychological harms they describe, as well as in the establishment of country conditions, the voice of the (non-refugee) "expert" becomes a privileged interlocutor in the adjudication of refugee status or asylum. Doctors and academics who would take on the role of certifying to someone's experience of torture, or to the credibility of someone's case, navigate a fraught ethical landscape. On the one hand, their intervention is likely to increase an applicant's chance of success.[59] On the other, by agreeing to participate in a process that meets refugee and asylum seekers' claims with extreme skepticism and mistrust, they are complicit in the erasure of these individuals' narratives. Describing medical doctors providing certificates attesting to torture in France, Didier Fassin and Estelle D'Halluin write, "The experts replace the victims. By trying to help refugees, physicians and psychologists deprive them of their truth."[60]

The restrictions on "acceptable" refugee narratives apply not only in the legal realm, though it is there that the requirements are most exacting and the stakes highest. Dina Nayeri recounts a suffocating need to continue justifying her presence as a refugee, even many years after resettlement. "Every day of her new life," Nayeri writes, "the refugee is asked to differentiate herself from the opportunist, the economic migrant."[61] Refugees are vulnerable victims; they are seen to "have no agency," and so pose little threat.[62] They can be refashioned, reprogrammed, turned into people that resemble those who have come to their aid. Economic migrants, on the other hand, steal jobs and livelihoods; they intrude; they had a choice to emigrate and so are undeserving of the promise of salvation-through-assimilation afforded to the "true" refugee.[63]

This examination of the asylum and refugee adjudication process illustrates the ways in which refugee narratives are circumscribed by the interview process, official skepticism (a "culture of disbelief"), and the expectations of what an asylee or refugee *should have* experienced, seen, and endured.[64] It also highlights the assumption that refugees can speak only to the particular, the partial, the embodied. "Objective" knowledge, disembodied knowledge, and its claims to superior authority are the purview of the interviewer, the agency, and the state. This discussion is of clear significance to the question of the right to research as exercised by refugee researchers. When one's very identity as a refugee is situated within and determined by an epistemological landscape characterized by the denial of one's capacity to articulate, let alone produce, "objective" knowledge, and when that landscape is shaped in part by the academic researchers producing the scholarly discourse in which a refugee researcher would hope to intervene, it is not difficult to see how the practices of silencing described here would continue to operate within the academic space. It is to this question – to the terms on which refugee historians might be included within historical scholarship – that we now turn.[65]

STRUGGLING TO HEAR AND BE HEARD: MEDIATION, LEGITIMATION, AND VOICE IN HISTORICAL NARRATIVES

This section grapples with an issue at the heart of this project: inclusion. More precisely, it examines what it means for this volume's authors to seek to be included within the scope of what it means to be a "historian"[66] What possibilities open; what are foreclosed? What risks do we run?

Rita Laura Segato, an Argentinean public intellectual, suggests that there is something inherently disobedient about research and writing conducted by those historically and structurally marginalized in the global economy of knowledge production. "Let's name ourselves, choose our own names ... Let's start from there, thinking from our own position, and not delegating thinking about the world we live in to those on the outside," she writes, attesting to the importance of that which comes "from this ground on which we are rooted."[67] Perhaps it is paradoxical to consider research of this sort both a form of disobedience and a right to which all are (or rather, should be) entitled. But holding these two ideas together illuminates a basic truth: that the realization of a right to research requires disobedience. It requires unlearning what has been accepted and legitimized in the past and expanding conceptions of what research can be to include not only different voices speaking in familiar patterns, but also different voices speaking with different patterns, worldviews, and perspectives.

The notion of disobedience captures well the ways in which inclusion (or perhaps more precisely, the terms on which inclusion tends to occur) in academic spaces serves as a form of disciplining difference. Requirements that scholarship engage in particular ways, adopt particular forms of argumentation, cite certain bodies of literature, and be grounded in certain epistemological frameworks are ways of making difference legible and palatable to the individuals and institutions who have greatest say in determining the standards that, in turn, determine what and who are included.[68] What is needed instead, Segato writes, is a "radically plural world," one in which many different "logics" coexist at once. This contrasts with forms of what she terms "monotheism," in which there is "only one truth, only one way of living well, one god, one form of the future, one form of justice." Such systems "are in this way monopolies, governed by an exclusive and exclusionary logic."[69] In other words, in a fundamental way, inclusion is predicated on the possibility of exclusion.

The abundant literature on "decolonizing" research and scholarship raises similar concerns.[70] As Achille Mbembe writes, such decolonization involves "a process of knowledge production that is open to epistemic diversity. It is a process that does not necessarily abandon the notion of universal knowledge for humanity, but which embraces it via *a horizontal strategy of openness to dialogue among different epistemic traditions*."[71] However, attempts to pursue such strategies – to disobey the logics and systems of knowledge production as they currently exist – have often been met with skepticism, if not reproach.[72]

One increasingly common strategy, which shares a good deal with the methods used in Global History Dialogues, is co-researching, wherein the research process, from question inception to dissemination, is undertaken by a researcher in collaboration with an affected community.[73] Such practices of co-researching or co-production must operate "within the cramped space academia currently offers," limited precisely because of the challenge co-researching poses to the status quo.[74] On a practical level, co-researching disturbs the norms of scholarly production: it does not fit neatly into grant applications; it requires time and labour-intensive participation from all parties; it is more concerned with the context of the community in question than with conversations taking place in academia. This, of course, restricts the ability of (especially precarious, contingent, and untenured) faculty and researchers to embark on such projects, thereby further diminishing their already-fragile viability.

On an epistemological level, these projects face challenges to their credibility. As Warwick Anderson notes of a call to "decolonize" one of the leading journals of history scholarship, the *American Historical Review*, the conversation "shrunk rapidly to debating whether collaboration with Indigenous communities will lead to the distortion of historical evidence."[75] Karen Jacobsen and Loren Landau, writing about the ethics of conducting research on forced migration, caution wariness in the "use of local researchers" who may cause "risk of biased responses" (as if this risk evaporates when only outside/foreign researchers are involved).[76] It is difficult to ignore the parallels between this stance and the privileging of expert testimony in asylum cases. In both contexts, the "local" (the "local researcher," the refugee or asylee) is both "enabled *only* to speak for the particular" and less credible than the "researcher" (who is, it must be noted, also local to somewhere).[77] More subtly, projects that are ostensibly endeavors in "co-researching" may involve community researchers who generate materials that are then analyzed, interpreted, and presented by formally trained researchers.[78]

Of course, this kind of skepticism of the inclusion of new historical narrators and subjects of inquiry is not new. Objectivity, as an ideal of history research and writing, has often been used to dismiss history written by and about marginalized groups. As Bonnie

Smith writes of historiographical debates in the 1980s, "The history of women and blacks, it was said, would politicize the field. Or these subdisciplines – being 'sexy, fashionable, and hot' – could undermine the truth value of *real* history by exposing it to influences (such as ideology and rampant market forces) that operated outside professional standards for what was important."[79] And, as her careful account shows, from the beginnings of professional history, so-called "real" history has been "dependent on [the existence of] discredited voices and devalued narratives."[80]

On the other hand, what has counted as legitimate history – and who has counted as a historian – has changed over time. The introduction of new historian positionalities has, in Myrna Perez Sheldon's word, been a "gift." She writes:

> Different bodies bring with them different intuitions; experiences of sexism birthed feminist epistemology; the realities of the postcolonial state opened up the idea of decolonizing. The gift of critical epistemologies is the ability for others to be trained in these intuitions: because of queer theory, straight people can have an expanded understanding of love and sex; because of critical race theory, those who have become white in the West can gain some insight into the legacy of the legal architectures of blackness.[81]

To open the realm of historical narrators, then, has transformative potential. It invites new forms of empathy and horizontality, perhaps marking a step toward Segato's radically plural world. Particularly because refugees and displaced people are so uniquely positioned vis-à-vis some of historians' favourite concepts – the nation-state, citizenship, territoriality, and the labels "refugee" and "displaced person" themselves – their work has the potential to complicate, nuance, and destabilize these ideas, a potential we elaborate further, with specific reference to this volume's authors, in the final section of this chapter. Beyond historiographical contributions, the urgency of several contributors' examinations of human rights abuses demands a response. As contributor Muna Omar writes, her hope in sharing this work is to "generate social change by inspiring people and helping them better relate to the experience of refugees, immigrants, and asylum seekers."

There is much to be gained from a project such as this, one that aims at the inclusion of refugees as historians. Indeed, as Muna's reflection suggests, there is an ethical imperative to share this work widely. But there are also downsides to the approach we have adopted, many flowing precisely from the idea of "inclusion." Inclusion, as we have pursued it in this volume, requires significant resemblance to what has come before. If the essays in this volume do not resemble works of history written by historians traditionally defined, we must explain and justify this deviation. Through both this introduction and the process of editing and revising the contributions that follow it, our focus has been on making these essays legible within a paradigm that has excluded these authors and their communities as historical agents, let alone historical authors. In other words, we accept some of the exclusionary norms of the discipline in order to participate in it. In this attempt to expand ideas of what history is and who can write it, this volume's authors must seek to be heard in a conversation only fragmentarily audible to them, and which has historically attached little value to voices like theirs.

The conversation is fragmentarily audible because of the material circumstances in which the volume's authors worked. People who are refugees are historians, but refugee camps are not university libraries. The working of history as a field of knowledge is premised on the ability to relate to what has been said before, even when new contributions are intended to challenge old ones: "To contribute to new knowledge and to add new significance, the narrator must both *acknowledge* and *contradict* the power embedded in previous understandings," as Trouillot writes.[82] Yet when the conversation is kept "colonialized" (to again borrow Gera's word) in libraries, databases, and repositories that make access almost impossible for non-traditional researchers, and refugee researchers specifically, we see a tension between research's dialogic aspect and its inclusivity.

Intervening in this conversation, too, posed challenges. The entire project – from classroom instruction to the creation of this volume – was conducted in or translated into English.[83] The pragmatism of this decision, English being the only language in which we could all communicate, as well as the predominant language in global publishing, does not excuse the inequalities inherent in it. Moreover, the expectations we had, as instructors, could feel restrictive and out-of-touch to researchers, whose concern was often to reach audiences close to home and have an impact on policymaking and camp administration. As Gera puts it, "The high standard in language usage, word counts, citation styles, etc., have been constraints for our community-based research. I think such problems arise because of a mismatch in the objective of the research. Our professors wanted to see my research meet reviewers' standards and get published ... On the other hand, my main research drive has been to make voices be heard by whoever is interested." The decision to prioritize conversation between refugee authors and the (Global North) scholarly community, rather than local conversations, undoubtedly has trade-offs with respect to both who participates in the conversation and on what terms they do so.

The final question we posed at the start of this section may sound odd, perhaps even wrong: what are the *risks* associated with a more inclusive understanding of historical narration? To be clear, we are not wringing our hands at the "risk" of losing "objectivity" or lowering standards. Rather, our question is: By presenting these essays in this format, as interventions in a conversation led and shaped by professional and relatively well-resourced historians, do we risk unintentionally erasing the very real, very large challenges that attended the research and writing of these essays? Do we risk flattening the differences, not only epistemological (by emulating, insofar as is possible, the standards of professional historical research), but also material, between professional and refugee historians, particularly those residing in camps? What we wish to underscore here is that a movement towards a more radically plural world must attend to both the material and the epistemological structures of the world that we presently inhabit. Any shift in ways of knowing (or in who is widely considered a knower of certain kinds of knowledge) cannot be wholly separated from the material circumstances in and by which that shift occurs. When we frame research as a form of "conversation," we may be led to focus too narrowly on voices – which voices are heard, how they relate to one another, what ideas they suggest or disrupt, who is silenced or interrupted – and not enough on what is required of the speakers to reach the table around which the conversation occurs in the first place.[84] Philosopher Olúfẹmi O. Táíwò illustrates this risk sharply. Inclusion in certain rooms, he writes, "hold[s] fixed most of the facts about the rooms themselves: what power resides in them, who is admitted" even though "these are the last facts we should want to hold fixed."[85] A constant risk we run is that we are not doing enough with this volume to change the room, to deconstruct and reconstruct the house of history, to attend not only to voices, but also to people, to landscapes, to life.

In short, we do not wish to reduce this volume to merely a historiographical or epistemological intervention, however ground-breaking this might be. The stakes are simply too high to overlook the actual people in the real world who conducted this research and who compose the communities described therein. For this reason, among others, we have been careful throughout the volume to pay attention to process, to attend to the "conditions of production" of these essays, and to provide spaces for authors to articulate what they most wish readers to take from their work.[86] This is a small and incomplete way of signaling the "ethics of responsibility" that engaging with this research might entail, "in the sense of cultivating a capacity to respond to and be responsive to the other, without demanding resemblance as the basis for recognition."[87] There is no one way to respond, but we could not conclude an introduction to these essays without noting that at its core, this project is about justice, historical and historiographical, present and future.

To come full circle: What possibilities? What risks? At its most transformative, inclusion of the kind gestured to here could open doors to ways of thinking about and understanding the past that we cannot grasp from within our present. It might serve as "a rigorous exercise in the cultivation of empathy" and, therefore, a step toward the pluralism and horizontality that decoloniality demands.[88] But without sufficient attention to difference, in all its many forms, we risk losing that transformative potential. And without recognition that this volume is as much about non-refugees as it is about refugees, as much about responsibilities as rights, the invitation offered by this volume – to participate in thinking about and working toward a more just world (and a more just representation of that world) – is lost, too.

In the final section, we take up some of the specific contributions the essays in this volume make to the histories of refuge-seeking, refugeeness, and displacement.

REFUGEES AND HISTORY, AND A NOTE ON STRUCTURE AND CONVERSATION

While the phenomenon of forced displacement is not absent from history and historiography, the presence in history of refugees, forcibly displaced people, and other migrants as individuals exercising voice and agency is sparse, especially if we consider Hannah Arendt's

claim that the refugee is the "historical subject of the twentieth century."[89] This is true even though, as Peter Gatrell suggests, displaced
people have a unique relationship to history: "Refugees have called
upon history to explain their displacement and to help negotiate a
way out of their predicament. Refugees were created by violence
and governed by regimes of intervention, but they gave meaning to
their experiences through engaging with the past. History is a refugee resource."[90] Gatrell's attempt to centre refugees in history is an
important step, as is the recent shift in African history, which has
been marked by a new focus on processes of refuge-seeking on, and
beyond, the continent.[91] But the role of refugees in creating this history remains limited, even as historians have turned to approaches
such as oral history that can help move the field away from its
state-centric bias.[92]

   If we are to take seriously the project of creating histories of refugees that go beyond state- or agency-driven histories, we also need
to take seriously the knowledge produced by refugee historians,
even – especially – when it challenges the norms of justification and
legitimation that structure historical scholarship. That is, we need
to be committed to a right to research that is not limited to inquiry
into what one desires to know, but that extends as well to the reception of that research. We need a right to research that understands
the interdependence of author and audience. "Placing refugees at
the centre of historical enquiry" is an important conceptual shift,
but it must be accompanied by a concomitant openness to historical enquiry *by* refugee researchers and authors.[93] Committing to
a different and broader conception of who researchers are and can
be will require expanding our notions of what research looks like,
how we expect it to relate to and resemble what has come before,
and whose voices are accepted not just as interjections in another's
account, but as narrators in their own right. This volume is a gesture
in this direction.

   Together, these contributions historicize (forced) mobility and
immobility in Africa and the Middle East, as well as the cultural
and artistic consequences of these phenomena. By approaching the
issue of (im)mobility from different angles – straight on, obliquely,
in some cases unexpectedly – they enrich and expand ideas of what
histories of refuge and forced migration encompass. International
organizations figure prominently in only two contributions (Omar
and Teferra), and in these essays, such organizations are most

notable for their incompetence and lack of accountability to refugees and migrants – that is, when they are not engaged in blatant abuses of authority. All the essays, too, argue implicitly against analytical frameworks that treat refugees as objects of study in isolation from the societies from whence they came and in which they reside. For this reason, the volume is not restricted to refugee researchers only, but also includes "host-community" members and their projects. Indeed, an important premise of Global History Dialogues is the need to spark conversations within communities that are divided by legal/refugee status and national origin. Economically, socially, culturally, and politically, refugee and migrant people play critical roles in constituting and shaping the communities in which they live, and vice versa. By paying attention to local, regional, and global movements (often facilitated by new forms of technology and communication), the volume's chapters unsettle geographies of refuge, highlighting the importance of diasporic networks, internet communication, and repeated/return migration in shaping people's relationships to and experiences of place. Whether in their exploration of the effects of migration on musical traditions or their analysis of the role of education in refugee camps, authors speak to the tensions between movement and stasis, change and preservation, in fractured landscapes that speak to each other in spite of – because of – their fracturedness. Indeed, while the chapters are joined by their concern for (im)mobility and border crossing, their disparateness suggests a need to attend more closely to the heterogeneity of identities, experiences, and positionalities lumped under the labels "refugee," "forced migrant," and "host community."

Gerawork Teferra's chapter draws on extensive research about the three decades of Kakuma refugee camp's existence. Juxtaposing official policy and international conventions with the lived experience of narrators who have spent more than a decade in the camp, and his own experience as an educational advisor, he evaluates the camp's educational infrastructure and the ways education functions within the camp as a source of hope, even as the organizational confusion and lack of accountability in the camp, coupled with extended displacement and "waithood," limits the utility of education in improving refugees' lives.

Muna Omar's contribution draws on interviews with Eastern African migrants in Yemen, calling attention to human rights abuses perpetrated by smugglers, Yemeni officials, and NGOs. It pays

particular attention to the experiences of women migrants whose
gender magnifies their other vulnerabilities and who feel caught
in an impossible trap: when they leave for Yemen (usually hoping
only to transit through the country), they have no choice but to go;
when they arrive and find it impossible to continue to their intended
destinations, they regret leaving. By interweaving long and beautifully translated sections of her interviewees' narratives with her
own careful analysis, Omar honours the integrity of their stories
while performing the invaluable service of bringing many testimonies together in a sharp analytical frame.

Aime Parfait Emerusenge considers Burundian drummers from the
precolonial period to the present, tracing their role within Burundian
monarchical, colonial, national, and, finally, refugee society. While
Burundian drummers once played a key role as a symbol of the
king's authority, refugee drummers now rely on their musical abilities to earn a modest living. Weaving together oral histories, myths,
and participant observation, Emerusenge offers a striking narrative
of the ways colonization and displacement have affected Burundian
musical practice and its sociocultural significance.

Richesse Ndiritiro's essay traces the impact of displacement on
the culture of the Burundian Twa people, an ethnic minority group.
Ndiritiro examines practices of pottery making and how the Twa
have adapted to create their pottery in Mahama refugee camp.
Linking material culture to social history, he shows the ways stigmas
and stereotypes about the Twa have changed over time through both
internal and external displacements. Finally, he shows how policies
intended to foster equality – such as those implemented by international organizations – can have the unintended consequence of
perpetuating discriminatory treatment in practice.

Alain Jules Hirwa explores how hip-hop in Africa has created
spaces of sanctuary and resistance for young people excluded
from their countries' political processes. Introducing hip-hop as a
form of "mental migration," he shows that the creation of translocal practices and repertoires of contention that speak directly to
local grievances can be a powerful way for hip-hop artists, and the
communities that coalesce around them, to express alternative histories of the past and imaginaries of the future that diverge from
state-sanctioned narratives.

Lazha Taha takes up the issue of narrative creation most directly,
writing about the role of Kurdish photojournalists in Iraq and their

work to create visual archives of Kurdish heritage and experience. How does the perspective of local photojournalists shape the stories that are told and the images that are created, when compared with the work of foreign photojournalists who often provided mentorship and support for local efforts? What is the impact of violence and displacement on memory and archive creation?

Phocas Maniraguha draws on interviews with Rwandan traditional healers, hospital staff, doctors, and patients to argue that for many Rwandans, traditional healing and Western medicine are not in conflict, but rather lie along a spectrum. Patients move back and forth between these options depending on availability (traditional healers being more prevalent), cost, and efficacy (if the treatment offered by one doesn't work, patients have recourse to the other). However, he observes, the relationship between traditional healing and Western medicine is not an equal one, as recent attempts by the government to regulate traditional healers illustrate.

Ismail Alkhateeb, based on extended interviews with two feminist activists in Syria and his own experience advocating for women's rights there, addresses the complex and multifaceted issue of gender, tracking back and forth between urban and rural, past and present, using the lived experience of his narrators as windows into the experience of women in Syria over the last three decades.

Finally, Sandrine Cyzuzo Iribagiza's history of Intore traditional dance shows the ways in which migration, both voluntary and forced, has shaped this art form in Rwanda. Working with interviews and participant observation, she documents the influence of dances from the Democratic Republic of the Congo (DRC) and Uganda, as well as the impact of the displacement of the Tutsis, to show the intimate connections between the movements of people across geography and the movements of their bodies in dance.

This volume differs from more traditional edited collections in both authorship and structure. Essays are grouped into three thematic sections: "Crossing Borders: Critical Perspectives on Refugee and Migrant Experiences," "Cultures in Motion: Continuity and Change in Displacement," and "Identity and (Un)Belonging: Constructing and Deconstructing Social Identities." However, given that the authors in each section may be writing from enormously different contexts – geographic, legal, and otherwise – and given our emphasis on research as a process of conversation and exchange, we have also introduced some other ways for authors to explore and explain the connections and resonances between their work and experiences.

Prefacing each contribution is a personal reflection by the author, addressing the motivations for the author's project, the ways their work has affected them and their relationship to research, and the experience of planning and conducting research as part of a global classroom including both refugee and host-community student-researchers. Insisting, as this volume does, that a historian's social position matters for their work, these autobiographical introductions give authors space to introduce themselves on their own terms, complicating the shorthand expressions "refugee" and "host community member."[94] These letters invite you into the authors' perspectives, sharing what they found most compelling about their research, why they chose to pursue it, and what they hope you will take from it.

The volume's concluding essay is coauthored by all eleven of us. It takes the form of a polyphonic exchange in which we reflect together on the process of researching, writing, and publishing from our different positionalities and lived experiences. We take up the questions of what it means to become a researcher as a refugee or host-community member; what possibilities and challenges accompanied this project; and what it means to work from liminal spaces that bridge – often uneasily – vast structural inequalities. We also reflect on what continued interventions in this space could look like, because while we are attentive to the shortcomings of the project and this volume as an endeavor in "inclusion," we are also committed to working toward a vision of historical scholarship that takes everyone seriously as a historical actor and historical narrator, and that does not unthinkingly reproduce the violences and exclusions of the world whose history we tell.[95]

To return to a question we posed at the beginning of this introduction: Where do we go from here? There is, of course, no straightforward or singular answer. But a few things are clear. The kinds of inclusion represented by this volume are partial and flawed, as is the paradigm of inclusion itself. Realizing a right to research, one that understands us all as actors in, and narrators of, history, requires more than inclusion. It may require stepping back from attempts to intervene in existing conversations, instead asking us to start altogether different dialogues, drawing on what we find valuable in academic research but using it for other purposes, other discussions, other ways of thinking and being. It will certainly require fumbling, reaching beyond our grasp, stumbling, starting over. It will require acknowledging that we must work from where we are, and that this will involve compromises and frictions of the kind elaborated here. We hope that this volume serves as an invitation to think and converse about this work, the ways it can continue and change, and the ways we all can contribute to it, from wherever we are, in whatever ways we are able.

NOTES

1 Throughout the introduction and conclusion of this volume, we generally do not format lengthy quotations from contributors in block quotes so as to reflect the ways in which their perspectives are inextricable from, and deeply integral to, the presentation of this project. Epigraphs like this are the exception.

2 As Steve Stern's incisive 1993 essay makes clear, even professional academics may have difficulty keeping up to date with all of the research in their field (a circumstance that has likely been made more difficult in the past three decades), so Gera's experience might not be read as anomalous in this respect. However, as Stern highlights, for those with the resources to access this research, the splintering of different subfields, particularly for historians of Africa and Latin America, could be enormously generative: "the art of dialogue across fragmented intellectual boundaries, and a wrestling with theory and paradigm as they had been developed in the West, were preconditions of serious historical research." To discover that someone in a slightly different subfield has already written about one's research idea may be disappointing but also potentially quite productive. In the case of the authors of this volume, however, the possibility for generative exchange is profoundly muffled by restrictions on access and entry. See Steve J. Stern, "Africa, Latin America, and the Splintering of Historical Knowledge," in *Confronting Historical Paradigms: Peasants, Labour, and the Capitalist World System in Africa and Latin America*, ed. Frederick Cooper et al. (Madison: University of Wisconsin Press, 1993), 10.

3 For actors and narrators, see Michel-Rolph Trouillot, *Silencing the Past: Power and the Production of History* (Boston: Beacon Press, 1995), 150.

4 Smith speaks specifically to the historiographical neglect of women historians. While clearly very distinct issues, there are important parallels between the assumptions that women and refugees simply were not

historians. Bonnie G. Smith, *The Gender of History: Men, Women, and Historical Practice*, 1st ed. (Cambridge: Harvard University Press, 2000), 3.

5 Elizabeth Colucci et al., *Free Digital Learning Opportunities for Migrants and Refugees: An Analysis of Current Initiatives and Recommendations for Their Further Use* (Sevilla, Spain: JRC Science for Policy Report, 2017), https://publications.jrc.ec.europa.eu/repository/handle/JRC106146; Negin Dahya, *Education in Conflict and Crisis: How Can Technology Make a Difference? A Landscape Review* (Bonn, Germany: German Federal Ministry for Economic Cooperation and Development, 2016), https://inee.org/resources/landscape-review-education-conflict-and-crisis-how-can-technology-make-difference.

6 For right to research, see Arjun Appadurai, "The Right to Research," *Globalisation, Societies and Education* 4, no. 2 (July 2006): 167–77. We diverge slightly from Appadurai's emphasis on the relationship between the right to research and democratic citizenship, arguing that people with all forms of relationship to (non)citizenship should have the right to research. We also stress the interpersonal, dialogic nature of research. These ideas are addressed in detail in the introduction.

7 Marcia C. Schenck conceptualized and piloted the Global History Dialogues Project in 2019, the year in which some of our authors were student-researchers and Kate Reed worked as a teaching assistant on the course. Since 2020, when the other authors took the course and Kate worked as course coordinator and teaching assistant, the Global History Dialogues Project has been offered on a yearly basis through Princeton University's Global History Lab (see https://ghl.princeton.edu/). We have been working with more partner institutions and as of 2022, we have twenty-five partner universities and organizations on four continents. For student publications resulting from this course, see https://globalhist-orydialogues.org/.

8 A temporally and geographically distant cousin of the present project (though we cannot match its "verve, scope, or ambition") might be found in the History Workshop movement, which resonated around the Anglophone world but was most influential in Britain and South Africa. As Bill Schwartz writes in his history of the British History Workshop, "The distinctive quality of History Workshop in its founding moments was its capacity to create connections between professional historians of radical disposition and an array of amateur-labour, feminist, and local-historians, forging in the process a new intellectual mentality." Arguing that working-class researchers (who became researchers for the first time under the auspices of the Workshop) had perspectives and experiences that

made them "peculiarly well-placed to write about many facets of indus-
trial and working class history," the Workshop's basic claim was that
"the people should not only be represented but should represent themselves." For "peculiarly" see Raphael Samuel, "On the Methods of History
Workshop: A Reply," *History Workshop*, no. 9 (1980): 163; for "the
people" see Bill Schwarz, "History on the Move: Reflections on History
Workshop," *Radical History Review*, no. 57 (1993): 208.

9 Susan Crane, "Writing the Individual Back into Collective Memory,"
American Historical Review 102, no. 5 (1997): 1384.

10 One way to work with this tension is the creation of Third Spaces in
academia, which we discuss in more detail with a group of Global History
Dialogues student-researchers: see Mohamed Zakaria Abdalla et al.,
"Opportunities and Challenges of Oral History Research through Refugee
Voices, Narratives, and Memories: History Dialogues," in *Global South
Scholars in the Western Academy: Harnessing Unique Experiences,
Knowledges, and Positionality in the Third Space*, ed. Staci Martin and
Deepra Dandekar (New York: Routledge, 2021).

11 Brett Shadle, "Refugees in African History," in *A Companion to African
History*, ed. William Worger, Charles Ambler, and Achebe Nwando
(Oxford: John Wiley & Sons, Ltd., 2018), 253.

12 Aran S. MacKinnon, *The Making of South Africa: Culture and Politics*
(Pearson, 2012), 172.

13 Jan-Bart Gewald, "'I Was Afraid of Samuel, Therefore I Came to
Sekgoma': Herero Refugees and Patronage Politics in Ngamiland,
Bechuanaland Protectorate, 1890–1914," *The Journal of African History*
43, no. 2 (2002): 222.

14 Casper Erichsen, "German-Herero Conflict of 1904–07," in *Britannica*,
2010, https://www.britannica.com/topic/German-Herero-conflict-of-
1904-1907.

15 Bronwen Everill, "The Italo-Abyssinian Crisis and the Shift from Slave to
Refugee," *Slavery & Abolition* 35, no. 2 (3 April 2014): 349–65.

16 Shadle, "Refugees in African History," 255.

17 On this see Gerawork Teferra, "Kakuma Refugee Camp: Pseudo-
Permanence in Transience," *Africa Today*, forthcoming 2022.

18 Michael Robert Marrus, *The Unwanted: European Refugees in the
Twentieth Century* (Oxford: Oxford University Press, 1985), 160.

19 Guy S. Goodwin-Gill, "The International Law of Refugee Protection," in
The Oxford Handbook of Refugee and Forced Migration Studies (Oxford:
Oxford University Press, 2014), 38.

20 Agnes Woolley, "Narrating the 'Asylum Story': Between Literary and Legal Storytelling," *Interventions* 19, no. 3 (3 April 2017): 380.

21 Ibid., 380.

22 See Paul Thompson, *The Voice of the Past: Oral History*, 3rd ed. (Oxford: Oxford University Press, 2000).

23 Gayatri Chakravorty Spivak, "In Response," in *Can the Subaltern Speak?* ed. Rosalind C. Morris (London: Afterall Books, 2010), 229.

24 Trouillot, *Silencing the Past*, 25.

25 See Teferra and Omar in this volume.

26 Liisa H. Malkki, "Refugees and Exile: From 'Refugee Studies' to the National Order of Things," *Annual Review of Anthropology* 24 (1995): 496.

27 For quote, see Lara Putnam, "The Transnational and the Text-Searchable: Digitized Sources and the Shadows They Cast," *American Historical Review* 121, no. 2 (1 April 2016): 380.

28 The 1951 Convention relating to the Status of Refugees defines a refugee as someone who "owing to well-founded fear of being persecuted for reasons of race, religion, nationality, membership of a particular social group or political opinion, is outside the country of his nationality and is unable or, owing to such fear, is unwilling to avail himself of the protection of that country; or who, not having a nationality and being outside the country of his former habitual residence as a result of such events, is unable or, owing to such fear, is unwilling to return to it." See United Nations Conference of Plenipotentiaries on the Status of Refugees and Stateless Persons, "Convention Relating to the Status of Refugees" (1951), https://www.ohchr.org/EN/ProfessionalInterest/Pages/StatusOfRefugees. aspx. According to the UNHCR, at the end of 2018, 78 per cent of all refugees, or 15.9 million people, were in what it deems "protracted refugee situations," defined as "one in which 25,000 or more refugees from the same nationality have been in exile for five consecutive years or more in a given host country." See UNHCR, "Global Trends in Forced Displacement" (UNHCR 2018), https://www.unhcr.org/globaltrends2018/.

29 Roger Zetter, "More Labels, Fewer Refugees: Remaking the Refugee Label in an Era of Globalization," *Journal of Refugee Studies* 20, no. 2 (June 1, 2007): 179.

30 Ulrike Freitag and Achim von Oppen, "'Translocality': An Approach to Connection and Transfer in Area Studies," in *Translocality: The Study of Globalising Processes from a Southern Perspective,* ed. Ulrike Freitag and Achim von Oppen (Leiden: Brill, 2010), 3.

31 Ibid., 19.

32 Sara Ahmed, *On Being Included: Racism and Diversity in Institutional Life* (Durham: Duke University Press, 2012), 10.

33 The quote is from Teferra's reflection on the research process; for more about this concept, see a chapter he coauthored: Staci B. Martin et al., "Kakuma Refugee Camp: Where Knowledge and Hope Resides," in *Refugee Education: Integration and Acceptance of Refugees in Mainstream Society*, ed. Enakshi Sengupta and Patrick Blessinger, vol. 11, *Innovations in Higher Education Teaching and Learning* (Emerald Publishing Limited, 2018), 139–55.

34 Appadurai, "The Right to Research," 167.

35 Ibid., 168.

36 Ibid., 177.

37 As Michael Jackson writes, "A Greek Cypriot refugee told anthropologist Peter Loizos: 'Those who aren't refugees do not understand the pain of those who are — it cannot be shared. But the refugee *can* talk about his suffering to another refugee, and between the two of them, the suffering is controlled. The one understands the suffering of the other, but the non-refugees don't feel things, they aren't affected in the least' (cited in Loizos 1981, 127). This is why refugees are the best qualified people to work with refugees. Even if others are prepared to listen, there is often such a manifest discrepancy between the world they inhabit and the world the refugee has survived, that the sharing is inhibited" (Michael Jackson, *The Politics of Storytelling: Variations on a Theme by Hannah Arendt*, 2nd ed. (Copenhagen: Museum Tusculanum Press, 2013 [2002]), 107–8). We do not wish to reify a dichotomous "insider-outsider" distinction, which has been critiqued as both essentializing and insufficiently attentive to the complex interplay of different identities that might be at stake in any given interaction. (See Kirin Narayan, "How Native Is a 'Native' Anthropologist?," *American Anthropologist* 95, no. 3 (1993): 671–86; Kyoko Shinozaki, "Transnational Dynamics in Researching Migrants: Self-Reflexivity and Boundary-Drawing in Fieldwork," *Ethnic and Racial Studies* 35, no. 10 (2011): 1810–27.) However, nor do we wish to dismiss the prevailing dynamics in scholarship and publication on refugees. Consider a recent special issue of the flagship *Journal of Refugee Studies*, focused on refugee self-reliance. Of twenty unique authors (some authors published more than one piece), all were formally trained researchers, twelve were in academic positions in the Global North (primarily in the United States and Britain), and eight held policy, research, or advisory roles for NGOs and other refugee agencies, all but one of these in the

Global North, and none in Africa. *Journal of Refugee Studies* 33, no. 1 (March 2020).

38 More generally, Jackson observes that intersubjectivity is the "indeterminate space" where "our original intentions are often confounded and our assumed identities eclipsed, leading us to do things we did not think we had it in us to do, and obliging us to constantly rethink the very notion of who we are." Jackson, *The Politics of Storytelling*, 18.

39 Dina Nayeri, *The Ungrateful Refugee: What Immigrants Never Tell You* (New York: Catapult, 2019), 6.

40 Ibid., 7.

41 Jackson, *The Politics of Storytelling*, 34.

42 Ibid., 39–40.

43 Kristie Dotson, "Tracking Epistemic Violence, Tracking Practices of Silencing," *Hypatia* 26, no. 2 (2011): 237.

44 Ibid., 242.

45 Ibid., 244.

46 Consider the narrative of Moha in Fred Nyongesa Ikanda, "Animating 'Refugeeness' through Vulnerabilities: Worthiness of Long-Term Exile in Resettlement Claims among Somali Refugees in Kenya," *Africa* 88, no. 3 (2018): 579–96. During his eligibility interview, Moha did not recount the particulars of his own story but rather says to the interviewers: "I am a refugee just like those in other Kenyan camps. The problems that refugees go through are the same ones I also encounter and I know you have heard many stories in that regard so I might tire you if I repeat them. What we have in common is that we are all called refugees so we face the same problems as our label suggests" (579). Moha's response to the interviewer's questions shows a rejection of the terms and expectations of the interview, a refusal to produce a narrative of worthiness that turned on Moha's vulnerability.

47 Yanery Navarro Vigil and Catherine Baillie Abidi, "'We' the Refugees: Reflections on Refugee Labels and Identities," *Refuge: Canada's Journal on Refugees / Refuge : Revue Canadienne Sur Les Réfugiés* 34, no. 2 (2018): 56.

48 See especially Heaven Crawley, Simon McMahon, and Katharine Jones, *Victims and Villains: Migrant Voices in the British Media* (Coventry, UK: Center of Trust, Peace and Social Relations & Coventry University, 2016).

49 For two treatments of this topic, see Liljana Šarić, "Visual Presentation of Refugees During the 'Refugee Crisis' of 2015–2016 on the Online Portal of the Croation Public Broadcaster," *International Journal of Communication* 13 (2019): 992 and Roland Bleiker et al., "The Visual

Dehumanisation of Refugees," *Australian Journal of Political Science* 48, no. 4 (1 December 2013): 398–416.

50 Faith Nibbs, "A Hmong Birth and Authoritative Knowledge: A Case Study of Choice, Control, and the Reproductive Consequences of Refugee Status in American Childbirth," *Hmong Studies Journal* 11 (2010): 3.

51 Ibid., 4.

52 The best-known work on Hmong refugees' interactions with the U.S. healthcare system is Anne Fadiman, *The Spirit Catches You and You Fall Down: A Hmong Child, Her American Doctors, and the Collision of Two Cultures,* (New York: Farrar, Straus and Giroux, 2012 [1997]).

53 Woolley, "Narrating the 'Asylum Story,'" 378–9.

54 Ibid., 379. On the inconsistency of asylum decisions, see for instance Rebecca Hamlin, *Let Me Be a Refugee, Let Me Be a Refugee* (Oxford: Oxford University Press, 2014); Deborah Anker, "Determining Asylum Claims in the United States: A Case Study on the Implementation of Legal Norms in an Unstructured Adjudicatory Environment," *Review of Law & Social Change* 19, no. 3 (1991): 435–528; and Katherine Jensen, "The Epistemic Logic of Asylum Screening: (Dis)Embodiment and the Production of Asylum Knowledge in Brazil," *Ethnic and Racial Studies* 41, no. 15 (8 December 2018): 2615–33.

55 See Anker, "Determining Asylum Claims in the United States," and Cristiana Giordano, "Practices of Translation and the Making of Migrant Subjectivities in Contemporary Italy," *American Ethnologist* 35, no. 4 (November 2008): 588–606.

56 Jensen, "The Epistemic Logic of Asylum Screening," 2623.

57 Ibid.

58 For the French case, see Didier Fassin and Estelle D'Halluin, "The Truth from the Body: Medical Certificates as Ultimate Evidence for Asylum Seekers," *American Anthropologist* 107, no. 4 (December 2005): 597–608. As Fassin and D'Halluin write, sometimes it is only in the medical examination and granting of a medical certificate attesting to torture that an asylum seeker feels they have been recognized: "Drawing up a certificate is a way of recognizing that the person has indeed been a victim of the violent acts to which he or she claims to have been subjected. Not only are the people listened to, they also know that they have been heard" (605).

59 While access to medical certification or expert witness usually leads to a higher chance of success, this is not always the case. For an important counterpoint, see Barbara Sorgoni, "The Location of Truth: Bodies and Voices in the Italian Asylum Procedure," *PoLAR: Political and Legal Anthropology Review* 42, no. 1 (2019): 161–76. Sorgoni argues that by

taking asylum-seekers' testimonies literally, ignoring the contexts of their production, judges are able to dismiss medical or expert evidence and reject applications more quickly. She underscores a crucial distinction between taking narratives *seriously*, according the complexities, interpretive challenges, and power dynamics of their production due weight and taking them *literally*, ignoring the well-documented difficulties associated with providing coherent and consistent narratives of traumatic experiences (166–7).

60 Fassin and D'Halluin, "The Truth from the Body," 602.

61 Nayeri, *The Ungrateful Refugee*, 7.

62 Ibid., 8. Peter Gattrell, in his history of refugees in the twentieth century, notes that it is not only in the popular imagination that refugees are construed as lacking agency. Rather, this is part of the particular form of humanitarianism of refugee-serving NGOs, which "[fashion] the modern refugee as a passive and 'traumatized' object of intervention as compared to the active, purposeful and much-travelled relief worker." See Peter Gatrell, *The Making of the Modern Refugee*, *The Making of the Modern Refugee* (Oxford: Oxford University Press, 2013), 8.

63 Indeed, some of the most prominent scholars working at the intersection of economics and refugee studies continue to articulate a sharp divide between economic migrants and refugees. Alexander Betts and Paul Collier write, "People seeking refuge are not fleeing poverty, they are fleeing danger" (Alexander Betts and Paul Collier, *Refuge: Transforming a Broken Refugee System* [London: Penguin Random House UK, 2017]). Arguing for a slightly expanded legal definition of refugee that includes not only forms of persecution but also insecurity in fragile states, they are clear that "economic migrants" have no place in their rubric. However, since the late 1960s, the Organization of African Unity (OAU) has put forth an alternative definition of refugee that moves away from persecution to encompass a broader range of reasons individuals might need to seek refuge in another country. Other scholars, similarly, have argued for more expansive conceptions of refugee. Andrew Shacknove, in an influential 1985 article, writes that refugees are "persons whose basic needs are unprotected by their country of origin, who have no remaining recourse other than to seek international restitution of their needs, and who are so situated that international assistance is possible" (Andrew E. Shacknove, "Who Is a Refugee?," *Ethics* 95, no. 2 [January 1985]: 277). More recently, Matthew Gibney has echoed Shacknove with a slightly narrower definition that links refuge and migration: refugees, in his definition, are "those people in need of a new state of residence, either temporarily or

permanently, because if forced to return home or remain where they are they would – as a result of either the brutality or inadequacy of their state – be persecuted or seriously jeopardise their physical security *or* vital subsistence needs" (Matthew J. Gibney, *The Ethics and Politics of Asylum: Liberal Democracy and the Response to Refugees* [Cambridge: Cambridge University Press, 2004], 7, emphasis in original).

64 For "culture of disbelief," see Olga Jubany, "Constructing Truths in a Culture of Disbelief: Understanding Asylum Screening from Within," *International Sociology* 26, no. 1 (2011): 74–94.

65 Some norms around research about/in/with refugees and migrants are starting to shift in positive ways. One example is the "Your Rights in Research" Project at the Canadian Association for Refugee and Forced Migration Studies (CARFMS), in partnership with the Canadian Council for Refugees, the University of Ottawa, the Social Sciences and Humanities Research Council, and Access Alliance Language Services. This provides translations and explanations of common terms and concepts in consent forms and other research materials, to help people make more informed decisions about their participation in research projects. See CARFMS, "Your Rights in Research," 3 December 2021, https://carfms.org/new-resource-your-rights-in-research/.

66 The meaning of "historian" is ambiguous; this is intentional. For our purposes, we shall take a historian to be one who conducts historical research and seeks for it to be published, primarily, though by no means exclusively, in academic outlets. Note that we leave open questions of profession, institutional affiliation, and training. These are taken up in due course.

67 Rita Segato, "The Virtues of Disobedience," Rosa Luxemburg Stiftung, July 2019, https://www.rosalux.de/en/publication/id/40778/the-virtues-of-disobedience/.

68 Projit Bihari Mukharji et al., "Open Conversations: Diversifying the Discipline or Disciplining Diversity? A Roundtable Discussion on Collecting Demographics Data," *Isis* 111, no. 2 (2020): 44.

69 Segato, "The Virtues of Disobedience."

70 We place "decolonizing" in quotes to signal that we are using the term metaphorically, understanding that some Indigenous and other scholars oppose the metaphorical use of the term. See, for instance, Eve Tuck and K. Wayne Yang, "Decolonization Is Not a Metaphor," *Decolonization: Indigeneity, Education & Society* 1, no. 1 (2012). In using the term metaphorically, we follow the usage of Achille Mbembe and others to situate this chapter within debates about decolonization (Achille Mbembe,

"Decolonizing the University: New Directions," *Arts and Humanities in Higher Education* 15, no. 1 [2016]). Otherwise, we rely on the list of alternatives provided by Nayantara Sheoran Appleton in "Do Not 'Decolonize'… If You Are Not Decolonizing: Progressive Language and Planning Beyond a Hollow Academic Rebranding," *Critical Ethnic Studies Blog* (4 February 2019): http://www.criticalethnicstudiesjournal. org/blog/2019/1/21/do-not-decolonize-if-you-are-not-decolonizing-alternate-language-to-navigate-desires-for-progressive-academia-6y5 g#:~:text=Decolonize'%20.%20.%20.-,If%20You%20Are%20Not%20 Decolonizing%3A%20Progressive%20Language%20and,Beyond%20 a%20Hollow%20Academic%20Rebranding&text=As%20you% 20can%20imagine%2C%20academia,in%20that%20particular% 20historic%20moment.

71 Mbembe, "Decolonizing the University: New Directions," 37. Emphasis in original.

72 For an example of the criticism leveled at scholars who work substantively with other historical traditions and epistemologies, consider a recent Exchange in the *American Historical Review* (AHR), prompted by David Silverman's critique of two scholars of early American history and their engagement with Native communities and knowledge. Silverman argues that decolonizing methodologies and their attendant political commit-ments – to, in this case, the rights of Native peoples – lead to "avoidance of … difficult history" (525). For responses, see the subsequent AHR Exchange, including: Philip J. Deloria, "Cold Business and the Hot Take," *American Historical Review* 125, no. 2 (1 April 2020): 537–41; Christine M. DeLucia, "Continuing the Intervention: Past, Present, and Future Pathways for Native Studies and Early American History," *American Historical Review* 125, no. 2 (1 April 2020): 528–32; Alyssa Mt. Pleasant, "Contexts for Critique: Revisiting Representations of Violence in Our Beloved Kin," *American Historical Review* 125, no. 2 (1 April 2020): 533–36; Jean M. O'Brien, "What Does Native American and Indigenous Studies (NAIS) Do?," *American Historical Review* 125, no. 2 (1 April 2020): 542–5.

73 Sarah Banks et al., "Co-producing Research: A Community Development Approach" in *Connected Communities: Creating a New Knowledge Landscape,* ed. Sarah Banks et al. (Bristol: Policy Press, 2019), 5–7. See also Staci Martin and Vestine Umubyeyi, "What Works in Education in Emergencies: Co-Researching and Co-Authoring," *NORRAG Special Issue (NSI), Data Collection and Evidence Building to Support Education in Emergencies.,* no. 2 (1 April 2019): 122–5; and Neil Bilotta,

"Anti-Oppressive Social Work Research: Prioritising Refugee Voices in Kakuma Refugee Camp," *Ethics and Social Welfare* 14, no. 4 (2020): 397–414. Global History Dialogues diverges in important respects – namely, researchers pursued mostly autonomous projects about questions that interested them, and beyond the participants in the project developing research and project management skills, there were no longer-term plans for community development of any kind. Shared, however, is an emphasis on taking seriously forms of knowledge and ways of knowing that have not been historically recognized as legitimate or valuable within the academy, as well as expanding the range of voices that are included in the production of research.

74 David M. Bell and Kate Pahl, "Co-Production: Towards a Utopian Approach," *International Journal of Social Research Methodology* 21, no. 1 (2 January 2018): 113.

75 Warwick Anderson, "Decolonizing Histories in Theory and Practice: An Introduction," *History and Theory* 59, no. 3 (2020): 369.

76 Karen Jacobsen and Loren B. Landau, "The Dual Imperative in Refugee Research: Some Methodological and Ethical Considerations in Social Science Research on Forced Migration," *Disasters* 27, no. 3 (September 2003): 193.

77 For "enabled *only* ..." see Birla, "Postcolonial Studies: Now That's History," 96. Emphasis in original.

78 Staci Martin's work, cited throughout this introduction, offers a crucial example and model of a more equal alternative to this hierarchical arrangement of knowledge production.

79 Smith, *The Gender of History*, 2. Emphasis ours.

80 Ibid., 10.

81 Myrna Perez Sheldon, in Mukharji et al., "Diversifying the Discipline or Disciplining Diversity?" 314.

82 Trouillot, *Silencing the Past,* 56. Emphasis ours.

83 For a critique of English as Globish in global history, see Jeremy Adelman, "What Is Global History Now?," *Aeon*, 2 March 2017, https://aeon.co/essays/is-global-history-still-possible-or-has-it-had-its-moment.

84 Some institutions have put in place programs to account for this, as Elise Burton observes of the Max Planck Institute, which provides fellowships for PhD candidates from African, Asian, and Latin American institutions to write and publish their first English-language journal articles. While limited to those already within academia, approaches like this one highlight the ways in which already-existing institutions can create space for new voices and epistemologies through material support. More broadly,

we might extend the argument to one for more robust funding for humanities and research education inside, outside, and between academic and
non-academic spaces. See Burton in Mukharji et al., "Diversifying the
Discipline or Disciplining Diversity?" 335.

85 Olúfẹmi O. Táíwò, "Being-in-the-Room Privilege: Elite Capture and
Epistemic Deference," *The Philosopher* 108, no. 4 (2020).

86 Trouillot, *Silencing the Past*.

87 Birla, "Postcolonial Studies: Now That's History," 93.

88 For quote, see Sheldon in Mukharji et al., "Diversifying the Discipline or
Disciplining Diversity?" 314.

89 On the sparseness of refugee history, see Jérôme Elie, "Histories of
Refugee and Forced Migration Studies," in *The Oxford Handbook of
Refugee and Forced Migration Studies*, ed. Elena Fiddian-Qasmiyeh et al.
(Oxford: Oxford University Press, 2014). For quote, see Hannah Arendt,
paraphrased in Fassin and D'Halluin, "The Truth from the Body," 606.

90 Gatrell, *The Making of the Modern Refugee*, vii.

91 Christian A. Williams, "African Refugee History" (and associated Forum),
African Historical Review 63, no. 3 (2020); Marcia Schenck and George
Njung, eds, "Rethinking Refuge: Processes of Refuge Seeking in Africa,"
special issue of *Africa Today* 68, nos 2–3 (forthcoming winter 2022,
spring 2023).

92 Elie, "Histories of Refugee and Forced Migration Studies."

93 For quote, see Gatrell, *The Making of the Modern Refugee*, 284.

94 This is a small way to "resist classification altogether." See Emily
Merchant, in Mukharji et al., "Diversifying the Discipline or Disciplining
Diversity?" 322.

95 For historical actors and narrators, see both Trouillot, *Silencing the Past*,
and Crane, "Writing the Individual Back into Collective Memory." Or, as
Saidiya Hartman writes, "How does one revisit the scene of subjection
without replicating the grammar of violence?" (Saidiya Hartman, "Venus
in Two Acts," *Small Axe: A Caribbean Journal of Criticism* 12, no. 2
(1 June 2008): 1–14.

PART ONE

Crossing Borders:
Critical Perspectives on Refugee
and Migrant Experiences

Crossing an international border is a definitional moment in the process of becoming a refugee – at least as the legal category of refugee is currently constituted. As the essays in this section show, however, border crossing can be protracted and repeated; confused and confusing. Far from a clear-cut movement from danger to safety, complex patterns of prolonged encampment, partial integration, discrimination, and violence show that border crossing might be conceived as an ongoing process, as the line between citizen and refugee, insider and outsider, surfaces, blurs, and hardens in places far from national boundaries.

In the three essays gathered here, the ramifications of borders crossed weave through explorations of the lives and decisions of refugees and migrants. Gerawork Teferra's essay on education in Kakuma refugee camp examines the effects of a segregated educational system – where refugees are educated in overcrowded and understaffed classrooms separate from Kenyan students – on the ways students relate to schooling and their future prospects. Is education merely a salve, a way to keep students occupied in the present and clinging to unrealistic hopes for their future? Can it ever be anything but this, as long as the border – which, for many residents of Kakuma, was crossed years if not decades ago – remains the defining feature of camp life?

Aime Parfait Emerusenge's essay is also concerned with camp life and the ways refugees draw on existing cultural resources in new ways. What spaces exist for the preservation of Burundian drumming in Mahama refugee camp, in Rwanda? How does the commodification of the traditional practice as a way for refugees to make a living relate to its history of royal and ceremonial use? In exploring the accumulating and conflicting meanings of Burundian drumming in different contexts, Emerusenge shows how the act of crossing an international border refracts through cultural and artistic practices, both creating spaces for refugee drummers to contest the valences of their practice and its relationship to the Burundian state, while also possibly posing a threat to those practices as the material conditions of displacement erode possibilities for subsistence.

Finally, Muna Omar's essay traces the movements of refugees and migrants from Eastern Africa to Yemen and Saudi Arabia. She follows them from the decision to migrate (which in some cases, was not one) to the experience of border-crossing and the ways outsider status continues to inflect everyday life many years after the initial border-crossing experience. The border is an almost omnipresent feature of life for non-citizens, from the moment they set foot on Yemeni lands and are vulnerable to human traffickers and corrupt officials, to accessing medical treatment, to trying to find employment and housing.

These three essays are diverse in geographic focus, as well as in the range of experiences and practices they document. They are drawn together by a concern for the way borders are not discrete but rather processual, enacted over and over in different ways and to different effect. However, even as they highlight the tentacular, sprawling reach of the border into facets of daily life, these essays also underscore the malleability of borders and their construction. If borders are enacted, they suggest, they can be enacted differently – or perhaps, not at all.

Fostering Education Services in Kakuma Refugee Camp

Gerawork Teferra

Dear Reader,

Heading to Kakuma refugee camp, in remote northwestern Kenya, in 2011, I carried six second-hand books, a wooden mirror, and a few needles, thinking that it might be difficult to get such items in the camp. I considered books important items because of the (at least temporary) comfort they would bring as I adjusted to a new life. The plan I had with the books was to read one book every two months so that they would help me for a year. I also thought to buy one more year by rereading them. After that, I thought, I would be able to move along with life. At the time, I had no idea that Kakuma had so many businesses, primary and secondary schools, and international online universities. I did not know that the majority of the camp population consisted of minors. Confronting these realities changed my initial perceptions, giving me the strength and the opportunity to find a sense of meaning, and to live and persevere.

Right after arriving, I began teaching in one of the camp primary schools. Soon, those books became only a reminder of my previously limited knowledge about Kakuma. As I continued teaching and helping students in primary, secondary, and postsecondary training centres for ten years, I also started reflecting on both the opportunities afforded by camp education and its many shortcomings. As I have seen how these schools animate refugee students' hopes, I have also observed the ways many students struggle and the ways the camp's educational provision lets them and their families down. It is a challenge to find space and desks in congested and very hot

classrooms. Students must often go to school and come home with
empty stomachs. It is a struggle to get books or attend lectures from
inexperienced or demoralized teachers, or to muster the patience
to listen and respond positively to abusive instructions, which seem
part of school norms. Observing these things has made me see that,
as refugees themselves are marginalized, shunted into liminal camp
spaces for decades, so, too, is education marginalized within the
camp. From my initially positive assessment of education in the
camp, I came to realize that what I thought would be my own life-
line in Kakuma would instead be a source of great worry.

The Global History Dialogues project allowed me to think more
systematically about this concern. I learned storytelling and research
practices that helped me to conduct interviews and review secondary sources to explain educational practices in Kakuma camp. The
results of this work are shared in the following essay, which points to
a tension between camp education as an opportunity to keep hope
alive and as a way of perpetuating the marginalization and diminished life chances of refugee students. Above all, this research project
serves as a narrative shared by a voice from within.

I am not sure whether it was a fully conscious choice to write
about camp education. My ten years of experience in the camp
were always behind the scenes when I was writing. This experience has also shaped how I conducted the research for the project
and how interviewees responded to me. I researched with fellow
refugees from different communities. Most of them are doing
higher-level education and I knew most of them already. These participants are from diverse communities and backgrounds, but the
common identity we share (refugeeness) and a shared concern for
the research question facilitated the research process. I consider our
shared status as an opportunity because the cultural and communication barriers are relatively fewer, the conversation was freer, and
interviewees couldn't exaggerate or underplay facts as we often do
to stranger researchers. Since there was no time pressure, flexibility
in terms of duration and schedule was another advantage.

However, the flip side of these opportunities was a series of
challenges. For graduate students and formal researchers, there is a
clear way of getting permits and guidelines. Not for me. This infor-
mality, which affects other aspects of camp life, limits access to
data and supportive resources. Our refugee identity, as a constraint,
put me and the interviewees in a vulnerable position and led me to

self-censorship to protect myself and the people interviewed. Self-censorship operated not only in the final analysis, but throughout the research process, as a result of concerns that have affected my choice of interview questions, interviewees' narration, vocabulary used, depth of analysis, scope of argument, and research mood. For instance, while I was conducting an interview, the session was carefully observed. It is not possible to know the reasons behind it, as the camp is a playground for various actors from various pockets of authorities, but it certainly affected the interview process, putting both me and the interviewee in a state of suspicion.

Partnering with higher education institutions and professors has its opportunities and limitations, besides the clear power imbalances. Our professors' knowledge, research experience, exposure, and access to secondary resources have been opportunities to add value to our research. Now I have completed my fifth or sixth draft with the support of my professors. When I read my first draft, I laughed at some of my crude generalizations and some of my arrogance. However, my objectives and those of my professors do not necessarily align.

While our professors focus on the forest – working to share our work with global audiences and pushing us to make connections across time and space – I mainly tried to focus on trees since I am inside the forest. While they raise the Global North and South as categories of analysis, I raise nationals, Muzungus, and refugees based on my experience. While they focus on the consistency of my argument, focusing on specific themes, my effort was to bring out complex, multifaceted, chaotic experiences as they are without reducing their complexity. While they want to see our camp reality (my narration) structured into paragraphs with clear topic sentences (to make it easy for the reader), my wish was to show how reality in the camp (including my chaotic thoughts and thought patterns) is unstructured and complex. As they see down from the top, directing me to see problems in certain directions, my desperate effort, seeing upward, was to point in every possible direction and poke the invisible world that I imagined to be hostile. Bringing these two ways of seeing together in my research has been a challenge.

It has also been a way to build connections. Global History Dialogues connected us with refugee colleagues from different camps and with staff at Princeton. Similarly, researching and writing from our lived experiences connects people who are forced to live at the edge of the world. It creates space to bring voices from different places together and show a bigger picture. These voices and the narratives they create may make organizations and academia understand displaced persons not as objects of study or people destined for mere relief-based life, but as dignified persons who are systematically isolated, desperately longing for inclusion.

Sincerely,
Gerawork Teferra

INTRODUCTION

In the mornings and afternoons, thousands of children walk down the dusty roads of Kakuma refugee camp and Kalobeyei settlement area, travelling to and from school. Many laugh and smile, chatting with friends. Parents watch proudly as they set off for school, and students and parents alike harbor hopes that education will be a ticket out of the camp. But the reality within classrooms is often different: refugee students in camp schools obtain far lower marks than their Kenyan counterparts, and only a few refugees are given the chance to attend Kenyan schools outside the camp. Camp schools tend to be lower quality, with teachers lacking training and compensation. Drawing on official documents; oral histories with students, teachers, and parents; and experience working as a teacher and advisor in Kakuma, in this essay I explore the paradox at the heart of camp education: its extreme valorization by students, parents, and international organizations alike, and the often-underwhelming educational provision that actually occurs.

In 1989, the United Nations (UN), in its Convention on the Rights of the Child, adopted two important declarations that changed the course of refugee education. These declarations required free and compulsory primary education for all, and secondary and higher education that was available and accessible to all. The declarations brought more, and more significant, opportunities to refugees in the Kakuma camp, located in Turkana County in the remote northwestern part of Kenya. Similarly, at the beginning of the millennium, the incorporation of universal primary education by 2015 in the Millennium Development Goals (MDGs) strengthened the global commitment to education in general and became another milestone for refugees. These global shifts prompted changes in the education

Figure 1.1 | The Somali Bantu secondary school in Kakuma, September 2019.

policy and strategy of the United Nations High Commissioner for Refugees (UNHCR), which moved from educating a few high-performing refugee students to expanding access to education to all refugees. The need to educate all refugees has, in turn, drawn attention to the protracted nature of many refugee situations: refugees spend, on average, seventeen years in Kakuma.[1] Educating a few students who were expected to return to their countries of origin to "rebuild" is no longer tenable; new strategies, namely incorporating refugees into the education systems in their countries of residence, highlight the long-term (rather than "emergency") nature of camp education, as well as the need for economic and social, rather than just educational, inclusion.

International policy shifts have translated to some concrete action. There are now more than thirteen pre-primary, twenty-one primary, and seven secondary schools; more than seven vocational centres; and more than four postsecondary and higher education service providers in Kakuma camp and Kalobeyei settlement area.[2] Despite such encouraging developments, however, many students and recent graduates in the camp are still far from seeing the ultimate fruits of this partially integrated education system. Few students successfully

complete their primary and secondary level education, and accessing economic opportunities after completion poses a significant
challenge. For most students, schools are places for social interaction; they are instrumentalized as spaces meant to smooth over the
frustrations and injustices of camp life and keep students occupied,
purposes that have overshadowed the main objective of education as
a way to help students meet their long-term aspirations. This essay
considers refugee education from a historical perspective, showing
that despite the emphasis placed on education by the UN broadly
and UNHCR more specifically, camp education remains at the margins and its quality is insufficient to bring a meaningful change to the
majority of refugee students' lives.

I rely on secondary sources, international conventions, and their
derivative strategies to trace the history of refugee education and
understand the purposes of education as conceived by these international bodies. To unravel the actual camp teaching-learning
experience, I use oral history interviews from eight purposefully
selected students, teachers, and parents following heterogeneous
purposive sampling techniques. The selected individuals were from
diverse communities who have lived in the camp for a decade or
more. Either they or their children studied in camp schools. My
observations and experiences in the camp as a teacher and learning
facilitator for nine years at primary, secondary, and tertiary levels
also served as a tool to analyze the relationship between policy and
practice. Because of limited access to official data and information
from relevant organizations, some initiatives might be underrepresented or omitted, which could be considered as a limitation of
the analysis. Nevertheless, by juxtaposing publicly available information about strategies for refugee education with camp residents'
experiences of education in Kakuma, I highlight the gap that persists
between a vision of education as a means of social mobility, and the
lived reality of education, which is a way to keep students occupied
but which rarely connects to meaningful identity formation, post-
school opportunities, or life chances.

The chapter begins with a brief overview of refugee education
since the 1960s, as well as the policy framework currently in place
in Kakuma. The second section brings the insights of interviewees,
my own teaching experiences, and additional data together to show
how actual camp education practices mean schools are mainly social

spaces rather than learning centres. Finally, I sum up the situation and offer some suggestions for how education provision can be improved in the camp by placing it at the centre, rather than the margins, of humanitarian provision and camp life.

A HISTORICAL PERSPECTIVE
ON REFUGEE EDUCATION

Sarah Dryden-Peterson, in "Refugee Education: The Crossroads of Globalization," provides a wonderful summary of the historical background of refugee education.[3] Supported by archival sources, she illustrates how refugee education has passed through three phases: from fragmented, localized learning centres and elite refugee sponsorship education to centralized global refugee education, and finally to attempts at a local integration system. Here, I offer an overview of Dryden-Peterson's chronological framework and ground it in the context of Kakuma refugee camp.

The first phase, according to Dryden-Peterson, includes the period from 1945 to 1985. Though the United Nations Educational, Scientific and Cultural Organization UNESCO) was the primary mandate holder for refugee education at the beginning of this period, the mandate was transferred to UNHCR in 1967.[4] The UNHCR took over responsibility for refugee education in an ad hoc manner because of its strong presence in refugee camps, or what Dryden-Peterson called its "structural necessity."[5] During this stage, refugee primary education was normally done locally, without integrating into any formal system, either at the national or global level. Self-organized local communities ran learning centres with little support from the UNHCR.[6] The UNHCR provided post-primary scholarships for a few select students to join reputable host schools. The assumption underpinning this model was that these students would return home (to their countries of origin) and participate in rebuilding their country.[7] The focus on returning highly educated nationals to their countries of origin dovetails with the UNHCR's general emphasis on repatriation as its preferred "durable solution" to displacement. At the global level, this kind of elite scholarship started with 1,000 students in 1966. There was no significant increase in the number of scholarship recipients for three decades. In 1982, there were only 1,200 students. By 1987, there were 3,950.[8] To put these figures in context, the number of registered refugees increased from nearly 3.5 million in 1966 to 10.7 million in 1982.[9] Dryden-Peterson calls these few lucky students who received scholarships "elite cadres."[10]

As the number of refugees increased dramatically in the 1980s and early 1990s, not only did the old approach of providing scholarships to send students to reputable schools become uneconomical, but the number of children left out of formal education altogether also increased rapidly. This resulted in the emergence of a new approach from 1985 to 2011. A defining moment in this period was the Convention on the Rights of the Child, established in 1989.[11] The convention included two important provisions: "free and compulsory primary education for all" and secondary and higher-level education made available and accessible to all. These two provisions were milestones for bringing educational opportunities to Kakuma, which was founded just three years later, in 1992.[12] Following the convention, at the beginning of the millennium, the UN incorporated universal primary education by 2015 into the MDGs.[13] Such developments have put pressure on the UNHCR to expand its role from mainly sponsoring refugee education through scholarships to administering the refugee education directly to meet the MDGs, specifically concerning universal primary education. As a result, the UNHCR and partner organizations began a more systematized and codified provision of refugee education. Refugee education moved from a decentralized or localized approach to a more centralized system run globally by the UNHCR.[14]

As a result of this milestone, the UNHCR, supported by UNESCO, has played a bigger role in bringing global "doctrines," and the associated "codified refugee education governance system," to refugee camps.[15] The focus of refugee education during this period shifted from providing individual postsecondary scholarships to a few refugees, or "elite cadres," to expanding primary education to all refugees. In 1986, for example, 95 per cent of UNHCR resource support was dedicated to expanding primary level education.[16] This global focus and commitment brought educational opportunities to Kakuma, which converted new local community centres into more formal schools in the mid-1990s. The timing coincided perfectly with the establishment of Kakuma camp in 1991. Within a few years of its establishment (1994–99), three kindergartens, eighteen primary schools, and one secondary school were built, professional teachers were hired, and formal education officially commenced in 1994.[17]

However, to state that the UNHCR became more directly responsible for education is somewhat misleading as the provision of education service was largely left to implementing partner organizations, mainly the Lutheran World Federation (LWF), under the guidance of the UNHCR.[18] Dryden-Peterson, using specific examples, points out the many "inconsistencies" in implementing global policies at the local level, a situation that has an impact on the quality of education provided.[19] I turn to these problems in detail in the second section of the chapter. During this period there was no formal integration with the host nation's education system, though Kavi, a Sudanese community counsellor in Kakuma, notes that the Kenyan curriculum was used from the very beginning.[20] This is true not only within refugee camps, as Kavi attests: some remote places in Sudan, including war zones like Nubia, have used the Kenyan curriculum in their community learning centres for decades.[21] In general, the objectives of camp education, as well as its particular form, remained unclear in this period. For this reason, both Dryden-Peterson and Bellino describe the outcomes of refugee education as an "ultimate disappointment" or "shame."[22] After two and a half decades, it became clear that the expansion of schooling was not enough. The education on offer was low quality and there were few prospects for school leavers in protracted refugee situations. These realizations triggered a strategic change from global governance to the integration of refugee education with the host education system – the third phase of refugee education.

The third phase started in 2012 when the UNHCR launched a new global education strategy (GES) that promised the "provision and implementation of inclusive, protective, and high-quality education opportunities for children and youth as a key priority."[23] GES was aligned with UNESCO's global education strategy, which recognized quality education as a public good as well as a fundamental right to realize other rights, and underscored its impact on "human fulfillment, peace, sustainable development, economic growth, decent work, gender equality, and global citizenship."[24] The Sustainable Development Goals (SDGs), which were a continuation of the MDGs, also endorsed "inclusive, equitable quality education for all"

as their fourth goal.[25] Following these global consensuses, UNHCR
Kakuma prepared a specific four-year education strategy that cau-
tiously promised the same in 2017. The strategy was developed
based on the 5As framework: availability, accessibility, acceptabil-
ity, affordability, and appropriateness.[26] Significantly, the document
lacks details about what these criteria mean in practice.

In this recent third phase of refugee education, the main long-
term target has been integrating refugee education into the national
system, leaving the former centralized refugee education system at a
supranational level.[27] UNHCR's role in refugee education, as stated
in the preamble of the GES, would also deepen from a "peripheral
stand-alone service to become a core component of UNHCR's protection and durable solutions mandate."[28] The three important reasons
that led to this change of strategy, according to Dryden-Peterson,
were the protracted nature of refugee situations, the impossibility of
"separate schooling" within host nations, and financial constraints
on the funding of separate refugee schools for indefinite periods.
So, to reduce costs and create post-schooling opportunities for protracted refugee students (or to reduce their ultimate disappointment
upon graduating with few prospects), integration was presented as a
better, more sustainable option.

Heading toward this third phase, the intent of integrating camp
schools with the host education system, the basic approach followed in Kakuma was to strengthen partnerships and coordination
with the host community, develop the capacity of camp schools,
and implement innovative uses of technology.[29] For example, I
have observed Kenyan education bureaus vetting new schools and
supervising camp secondary schools. Organizations like LWF and
Windle International Kenya (WIK) have also undertaken changes,
including hiring staff in charge of supervising quality and standards. Recently, refugee primary school headmasters have been
replaced by trained Kenyan nationals to facilitate integration and
improve the quality of education. Of course, this also results in
the displacement of the refugee teachers and principals who had
formerly held those roles and who have far fewer prospects for
employment than their Kenyan counterparts. Technology-based
community learning centres, like Instant Network Schools (INS)
and online tertiary-level education, have also been introduced,
in recognition of the near-total lack of postsecondary schooling
opportunities for encamped refugees.

Since I joined camp life in 2011, the period when the third phase started, I have been teaching and facilitating courses at primary, secondary, and postsecondary levels. In the following section, I share some of my and my colleagues' reflections about camp teaching and learning experiences. I focus on the disjuncture between the symbolism of schools and education and the reality experienced by students, teachers, and families in the camp.

SCHOOLS AS SYMBOLS OF WHAT?

In this section, I highlight Kakuma camp students' learning experiences and their performance in comparison with their aspirations and those of their families. Drawing on interviews, nine years of teaching experience, and informal conversations with students and fellow staff, I argue that despite the expansion of primary, secondary, and tertiary education in the camp, quantity has been prioritized over quality. Schools have become places for students to pass the time but do not offer meaningful post-school pathways. This claim dovetails with Bellino's argument that schools function primarily as a way of "avoiding idleness."[30] There is a fundamental disconnect between the imagined temporal horizon of the school – envisioned as a path of social and geographic mobility for students and families – and the fact that camp schools remain anchored firmly in the present, functioning more as a way to pass the time than as preparation for a desired future.

Since I began teaching in 2011, I have had mixed and confusing thoughts about students' behaviour. When I walk to school early in the morning, I see many passionate elementary and secondary school students putting on their uniforms and rushing to school chatting and laughing. The excitement – indeed, exuberance – is everywhere. What's more, such catchy excitement can lighten a tense camp surrounding. Having seen this behaviour on the way to school, one might easily assume that the students are passionate about learning and happy with their experiences in school. Such a scene itself can attract many young people who would otherwise stay at home, but at the same time, it might mislead many parents to dream much bigger than the actual reality for their children, as well as for themselves.

Indeed, contrary to students' excitement to leave home and arrive in their schools, in classrooms the scene appears very different. The sense of anticipation present on the walk to school dissipates. Many students do not focus on their studies, do not do assignments, regularly sneak out of school, and are always ready to bring excuses to be relieved from their learning duties. Teachers and students have divergent interpretations of this phenomenon. Teachers call such behaviour "ingratitude for the right to learn in exile."[31] Students, on the other hand, point to the poor quality of the service, such as inadequate facilities, learning materials, and equipment; teachers' lack of competence and commitment; and dissatisfaction with teachers' and schools' approach to learning. Having such comforting excuses for low performance, the majority continue performing below the standard pass mark, though this is considered "normal," and they continue to advance through school. Except for a few, most students do not express a sense of care about their performance. On the contrary, passing to the next level is considered a right: a refugee right. If one asks, "How is your grade?" The answer is often the same for many: "It is good, Malimu."[32] They say the same regardless of their grade, even if they are achieving only the lowest marks, which are the most common. If one pushes further and asks, "How can you say such a grade is good?" the common answer is, "Oho Malimu, we are refugees, there are so and so challenges." Most of the challenges they mention revolve around shortages of books and labs, teachers' behaviours, the learning environment, and unfulfilled basic needs.

I often ask students what their vision is and what type of job they would think they would get with the grades they earn. The two common answers are: "I want to be a big man" or "a politician." Since most students are victims of war and ethnic conflicts, there is a strong interest to engage in politics. Most students regularly follow issues related to their home countries' current affairs. However, their school performance is much below the level needed either to lead them to their "big man" dreams or to make them fully understand the prevailing realities and affairs. There is a huge gap between their actual performance and their dreams that eventually leads to feelings of disappointment and failure. Sitting on many different job and training interview panels in Kakuma, I have witnessed so many students' painful hesitation and shame when asked to show their school leaving certificates because of their poor grades.

Students' complaints about educational provision are justified. Jimmy, who has been a teacher, head teacher, and school supervisor for nearly two decades in the camp, has serious worries about the quality of education. He said schools are highly congested; the number of students per class has been increasing; and some teachers' qualifications are below required standards. He also recalled the laying off of eighty teachers in the 2017–18 academic year because they did not have the minimum required qualifications. On the one hand, this seriously diminished the number of educational professionals in the camp but on the other hand, the step towards hiring trained teachers was encouraging.[33] Obtaining enough qualified teachers, as well as spaces for them to teach, has been a continuous problem. For example, in 2015 (three years after the GES launched), the average ratio of classrooms to primary school students in Kakuma was one to 156; the ratio of teachers to children was one to ninety-seven; and the student to desk ratio was one to nine.[34] Though there have been efforts to build more classrooms and train more teachers, these efforts have failed to keep up with the growing number of refugee students in need of education.

The low quality of educational provision and perpetual overcrowding in schools and classrooms have significant impacts on students' performance. In 2014, I tried to calculate the average grades of nearly 1,200 students in one of the secondary schools where I was teaching. The result was disturbing but confirmed my worry. The average grade was D-.[35] Compared with the performance of Kenyan students attending national schools, the result becomes even more worrisome. In Kenyan provincial schools, 43 per cent of students score C+ and above on Kenyan Secondary Certificate Examinations (KSCE), a figure that rises to 90 per cent in national schools.[36]

Such huge disparities obviously put refugee high school graduates at a disadvantage in securing either the limited economic opportunities available to them or opportunities for further study. When the age of refugee students is taken into consideration, as the majority of high school students are above twenty-five and some have already established their own families, such performance is more concerning. In one of the postsecondary training centres where I am currently working, the mean student age is thirty-two. Acknowledging the fact that very few have succeeded in terms of securing higher learning opportunities, obtaining employment, or enhancing their self-worth, the majority schools have lost their meaning as spaces to prepare for a hoped-for future and have become places used mainly for social interaction. Even those who managed to reach postsecondary-level education share mixed feelings about their learning experiences. They focus on the relational aspects of school and the ways it helps them endure the present, rather than on what role education could play in their futures. Saida, who fled to Kakuma with a guardian when she was four, did not have a chance to go to school until she was seventeen years old. Speaking about her experience, she said, "The reason I wanted to go to school was to learn the languages which are spoken in Kenya like English and Kiswahili. Those languages are very important for me because I used to see my age mates communicating with other communities, you know Kakuma is very multicultural."[37] Similarly, Monica, a fifty-two-year-old college student, asserted that her college education experience in the camp has mainly helped her to avoid self-harm and to stay alive. Acquiring knowledge and developing skills that lead to employment and self-reliance seem secondary or impracticable to her, as there are so few opportunities to earn a livelihood that depend on what she learns in her college coursework.[38]

It is easy to point to student performance or the difference between students' attitudes on the way to school versus in the classroom as the problem. But students' low interest and participation in learning activities, poor performance, and disrespectful, even contemptuous behaviour toward school and teachers, indicate a much deeper crisis. The GES hasn't meaningfully addressed issues of quality as stipulated in the strategy document designed a decade ago. There remains a visible difference in the quality of education in refugee and host-community schools, despite integration within the national school system being a priority under the current paradigm of refugee education. For example, in 2018, at the lower secondary levels, the number of subjects offered in refugee schools was cut from twelve to seven. Important basic subjects like business, geography, physics, and agriculture are no longer offered in most camp secondary schools. To cope with the growing number of students and lack of adequate spaces and staff, learning hours were reduced and a two-shift system was introduced whereby students go to school either in the morning or in the afternoon hours only. Moreover, camp secondary students do not have the chance to learn basic computer skills and, therefore, have to look for other opportunities to learn computer skills after they complete their secondary level education. The irony here is that while many potential further learning and self-reliance strategies and job opportunities are business-related and IT-based, taking place online, high school leavers are computer illiterate and business study has been removed from their curriculum. This obviously contradicts some of the principles stipulated in the strategic document: that education should be relevant, accessible, and appropriate.[39]

In comparison, host-country secondary schools are not only full-time schools, but many of them are also boarding schools. A wider range of subject options, including computer skills, are available. I recently had a conversation with Jillo, who was born in the camp and calls himself a "refugee by default." He got a chance to study in schools outside the camp and knew well the quality differences. He received a good grade (B+) in his KSCE exam and has attempted to earn the World University Service of Canada (WUSC) scholarship multiple times but failed because he did not have the proper documentation to certify his refugee status. He was bitter about the situation, observing that over the years, most of the students who succeeded in this scholarship were not camp students but rather elite refugees who got a chance to attend reputable host schools, then came and took opportunities that were meant for refugees who studied in the camp.[40] Now, even though he holds a refugee status document, because he passed the maximum age limit, he cannot qualify for that WUSC scholarship. (WUSC has been providing between twenty-five to thirty-five scholarships, which include permanent resettlement to Canada, for refugee students from Kakuma for more than a decade. Except for a very small number of camp school refugees, the majority of refugee beneficiaries studied in regular Kenyan schools.)

The situation of camp primary level education is different. Anna, who was once a primary student in the camp and now has sent her one child and her late sister's children to primary school, explained the system in the following way.

> If you are starting maybe class one up to class five there is no
> quality education because there are more than 250 pupils in class
> three, four, five, you don't even know who is concentrating, who
> is serious. They are just there. The teacher just comes, teaches
> for forty minutes, walks out, gives exams ... but in upper class
> because the school needs good grade in KCPE [Kenyan Certificate
> for Primary Education] from class six they start reading.[41]

She explained some differences in upper school existed only to protect the image of the school or as a result of competition with similar camp schools. However, even this change does not necessarily lead

to better education, as students are expected to study only for the
KCPE. In fact, because books are hard to come by, past exam papers
are common reading material. In contrast, in Kenyan schools, the
government came up with an ambitious plan to provide a laptop to
each primary school student to meet its vision for the 2030 information and computing technology (ICT) education policy.[42]

It seems the global consensus around achieving quality education
for refugees has been reduced to a policy of "something is better than
nothing," which has made students feel alienated and lose trust in
schools and teachers. Having seen host communities' refusal to send
students to camp schools, and unmotivated teachers who frequently
miss classes or arrive late, refugee students question whether such education can be transformed into employment opportunities or enhance
their self-worth.[43] This feeling reduces their enthusiasm for learning
in classrooms and encourages them to use schools as little more than
social places. Though the UN convention clearly states that similar treatment should be accorded to refugees and nationals concerning primary
education and favourable treatment at secondary and higher levels (a
principle that is also endorsed in the recent Kenyan Constitution), the
reality on the ground does not live up to these promises.[44]

Even as students struggle to find meaning in this second-class
education, schooling continues to be a potent symbol in the wider
community, and for parents in particular. Many parents dream that
one day, the time and sacrifices devoted to their children's education
will pay off and compensate them for the life they have spent in the
camp. Jimmy, a Ugandan refugee who came to Kakuma in 1995 said:

> Everybody who has a child and [is] old always lives to see their
> child prosper ... that alone is an incentive for very many old ones
> here. One thing so hard in my mind since I am here is that while
> opportunities are here especially educational opportunities in the
> camp, now that I have two kids I really have to push very hard
> on them, next year my son will be a candidate, after four years
> he will be graduating from high school, and of course the sister
> will be somewhere too. These are the assets for me in the sense
> that they will ensure the continuity of the family ... by the time
> when [I] cease to be [a] refugee my time has gone ... so my effort
> should be for my kids – working hard to the family members
> who are still young to make it – support them then I have a
> glimpse of them paying in kind when my time is up.[45]

Figure 1.2 | Students gather outside a primary school in Kakuma, September 2019.

Most refugee parents believe and hope for the same things as Jimmy. They think their children will benefit from free education, achieve some form of social and geographic mobility (symbolized by the figure of a "big man" or "politician"), and safeguard them when they get old. A person like Jimmy who is also currently a degree student may push hard to make his children focus despite the disadvantageous circumstances. But most parents' dreams come only from seeing their children's regular morning ritual of putting on the school uniform, going to and coming from school, which gives them the impression and prestige of being a parent of "promising" students. In other words, the ritual suggests future possibilities; a sense of becoming.

However, for the majority, school will not provide the skills, space, or guidance needed to realize those possibilities. Rather, it is limited to creating an opportunity to be connected and interact with others – not unimportant, but oriented to the goal of preserving stability in the camp, rather than students' personal transformation.

What is revealed to me when students say, "Oho Malimu, we are refugees" is that they are saying "We are not like others and are offered substandard education so we are not worthy." Their identity as refugees is reinforced by an educational system that discriminates against them based on their legal status. Their refugeeness matters more to the educational system than their achievements or their potential, and so they, too, come to see refugeeness as their most important identity, the one on which most else in their lives depends. In some cases, schools can even be counterproductive, as participating in a single "social place" that is not well-ordered and where students see that they are not valued drives students to new harmful behaviours and actions in schools and outside. To reverse this, the day-to-day teaching-learning process should reflect their worthiness and make them say "we are students," at least in schools, instead of "we are refugees."

WHAT REALLY MATTERS?

In the first section, I described how camp education, in general, has passed through three stages: decentralized (localized learning), centralized (run globally by the UNHCR), and the current third stage – the ongoing unfinished integration with the host countries' education systems. In the second section, I described how the Kakuma camp education services have been reduced to social spaces, referring to interviewees' responses, my reflections, and previously conducted research. In my explanations of the two sections, I have indicated how learning challenges have continued accruing in all three stages.

In this section, I argue that some of the reasons for poor quality education are related to organizations' functional priorities (which consider education as secondary to other, primary, objectives), and their lack of proper functional arrangements (where different organizations have scattered commitments to different parts of the education system, meaning it is impossible to achieve coherence). The secondary status of education and the dispersion of responsibility across multiple organizations lead to the marginalization of education within the camp. Finally, I offer some concrete steps that could be implemented to improve the quality of education in Kakuma, while recognizing that as a future-oriented endeavor, education will always articulate with students' broader socioeconomic prospects – which are also limited by their refugee status.

When it comes to global education, UNESCO is, technically, the mandate holder. It was UNHCR's strong presence in refugee camps that led to the transfer of the mandate from UNESCO to UNHCR and made that latter a foster organization.[46] To ensure outcome-based institutional accountability – in other words, to ensure that schools and institutions are accountable for students' learning outcomes, rather than just enrollment numbers – there has to be a clear and practicable mandate transfer that helps in building a sufficient knowledge base and administrative capacity in such a way that education is seen as a core function or priority of the fostering organization.

However, UNHCR's priority, as stipulated in its mandate, is the protection and safeguarding of the well-being of refugees, whose number has been overwhelmingly increasing year after year. Safeguarding the well-being of refugees mainly entails ensuring refugees are able to exercise the right of asylum seeking, finding safe refuge, and looking for permanent settlement options.[47] On the ground, this mainly involves coordinating rescue and safety operations and the provision of necessities like food, water, and shelter. Then, education and other social services follow. In a camp like Kakuma, verifying the eligibility of asylum seekers, solving security and protection cases, and looking for permanent solutions (repatriation and resettlement), which are considered core functions, have been the primary activities, occupying the majority of UNHCR staff, relative to staff engagement in overseeing education-related activities. The existing departmental arrangement within UNHCR, the number of staff, and the existing field posts indicate that monitoring education is left at the periphery, something the GES warned against a decade ago. The GES strategy stipulates "provision of refugee education, not as a peripheral stand-alone service but as a core component of UNHCR's protection and durable solutions mandate." Practically speaking, however, quality education remains eclipsed by other priorities and has not been seen as part of a durable solution.[48] It is also clear that the accumulated institutional experience and expertise within UNHCR Kakuma are mainly in those priority areas rather than in education service.

So in Kakuma, though some officers call it the "education camp," education service has remained secondary and left to implementing partners like LWF and WIK. This means that education provision is dependent on the success of their fundraising, rather than being responsible to students' learning outcomes. LWF and WIK are not mandated service providers, but rather work based on memorandums of understanding (MOU) they sign, which allows much of their service provision to be explicitly conditional: targets will be met *if* funding comes through; *if* students enroll; *if* the camp remains open and stable; and so on. Like the UNHCR, their priority and focus on education service in most cases is scattered because of other competing priorities. For example, LWF, in addition to education service, is responsible for camp peace building, security, and child protection. For more than two decades, it had also engaged in food, water, and firewood distribution, as well as environmental protection. These responsibilities stretched organizational capacity and made it difficult to prioritize education, even as an implementing partner. Recognizing the fact that more than 50 per cent of the camp and Kalobeyei population are children and youth, improving the quality of education is only possible if outcome-based accountability is put in place, meaning that implementing partners and the UNHCR alike would be held accountable for students' actual learning.[49] This requires the prioritization of education as a key function of camp service providers.

Such prioritization may require changes to organizational structure and capacity. Organizational capacity in this context refers to existing administrative arrangements and structures related to camp education. Most importantly, it refers to clear alignments of roles, workflows, and staffing across stakeholders in such a way that organizations develop a capacity that makes them accountable based on the outcomes students achieve rather than the inputs organizations provide. Here, it is important to clarify what is meant by inputs and outcomes. Under the UNHCR's education strategy, simply increasing enrollment in schools is considered an outcome. However, when the strategies used to increase enrollment including holding two schools in one building and implementing shift schedules that drastically cut children's instructional hours, increasing enrollment is a fungible target. When speaking of outcomes, then, I refer to the *quality* of education provided, not just enrollments, arguing that what and how students learn deserves greater attention in assessing educational provision in the camp. To show gaps and disarrangements, I highlight existing arrangements of activities across stakeholders, their focuses and practices, and the limited efforts made to improve education in the camp.

As discussed above, UNHCR Kakuma has taken the responsibility of fostering refugee education, not because of its knowledge base and relevancy to the education sector but because of "structural necessity." In other words, the UNHCR has taken on this responsibility because it is *there*, not because it is well-suited to education *per se*. Thus, the UNHCR has effectively outsourced educational provision to its implementing partners while maintaining some nominal oversight capacity. The few UNHCR staff dedicated solely to education in the camp (there are usually one or two) have limited time and capacity to regularly oversee more than forty schools and create a conducive learning environment for close to 100,000 minors. And these estimates do not even include the coordination of tertiary-level education, long one of the most neglected aspects of educational provision in camp settings. The transfer of responsibility from UNESCO to UNHCR, and then from UNHCR to implementing partners, has caused a tolerance for shortages of "educational expertise which resulted in huge inconsistencies" and created loopholes of accountability that led to poor quality education.[50]

Tolerance for compromised quality undermines the global goal of refugee education. In 2011, recognizing the poor quality of refugee education, the UNHCR, in its GES, included a strategic objective to "ensure that 70 per cent of refugee girls and boys achieve quality learning in primary school" by 2016.[51] However, quality education has been an issue even after the implementation of the GES. In the case of Kakuma, quality seems to be deteriorating, rather than improving, as I highlighted in section two. Most of the initiatives undertaken seem mainly targeted at accommodating the ever-increasing number of students, rather than improving the *quality* of education that these students receive. To be sure, every student deserves an education, and returning to the old model of elite scholarships for a few students is untenable. Yet so, too, is this model where hundreds of thousands of students receive an education that does not meaningfully equip them for post-school life. Hundreds of refugee teachers have gotten short-term training; however, this cannot serve as a silver bullet to help more than 160 students congested in a single classroom with limited teaching materials like textbooks. In this context, learning is "narrowed to exam preparation" by "diluting the curriculum or teaching down" so that students easily go to the next grade level.[52] In Bellino's words, accruing a "certificate, rather than the learning it represented, was regarded as the central goal of schooling."[53]

Further evidence diminishing hopes of quality improvement appears in the recent UNHCR Kakuma camp education strategy document, prepared in 2017. Out of the six objectives, five of them focus on increasing the number of students engaged in formal education.[54] These objectives are as follows:

Objective 1: The number of boys and girls accessing secondary education gradually increases.
Objective 2: The number of young men and women benefitting from tertiary education increases.
Objective 3: The number of boys and girls benefitting from programs addressing the root causes of out-of-school children increases.
Objective 4: The number of life skills and vocational training opportunities increases.
Objective 5: The number of children attending pre-primary and primary education gradually increases.
Objective 6: Improved data and information management inform responses.[55]

Notably, not a single objective addresses the quality of education provision or suggests that there may be a link between the poor quality of education and the number of children who participate in it. The omission of quality education in the strategic document tacitly implies either satisfaction with the status quo, or equally disturbingly, an assumption of the impossibility of providing quality education in the camp. Recently, I discussed this phenomenon with one officer who works in the education field. When I was complaining, as usual, about the poor quality of education offered to refugee students, he said, "Camp education is for protection." I asked him for an explanation about what "education for protection" means. He briskly said, "protecting them from predators." The officer's comments reinforce the argument that the purpose of education in the eyes of students and families is very different from the purpose it serves within the camp environment. I argue that this tolerance for poor education, as well as the instrumentalization of education in the service of other priorities, is related in part to the diffuse nature of responsibility for education.

The absence of a clear mandate holder has led to the scattered arrangement of activities that do not always align well with students' needs or the UNHCR's stated objectives. The implementing organizations, mainly LWF and WIK, run camp primary and secondary schools and learning centres. WIK identifies itself as a provider of secondary school services but also runs projects that focus on primary schools, which is LWF territory. Arguably LWF, as one of the longest-running service providers in the camp, is better-equipped to run schools as it could integrate them with other programs and service provision.

Both agencies have desks with the authority to supervise the quality of service delivery and offer assurance. The tricky part is that the quality assurance officers have been working under the control and influence of these service offering agencies. In some cases, the quality assurance officers, who are supposed to supervise the implementation of the education system and ensure (or enhance) quality, also engage in administrative activities like hiring teachers and school management activities. Such engagement dilutes their ability to offer impartial and disinterested assurance of school and teacher quality.

In addition to these two main agencies (LWF and WIK), many community-based organizations have been engaged in education services that have been affected by structural deficiencies. As a person who has been facilitating business and community development training, I have observed many community-based adult education centres and tutorial classes that provide literacy, numeracy, and language training. Different youth groups, associations, individual alumni, youth leaders, etc. from the refugee community have been part of such initiatives. But with exception of a few, the lifespans of these initiatives have been short. The common problems they face include registration, curriculum development, management, and constraints related to teaching equipment and materials. Though the policy allows and encourages such community-based education, a lack of sustained support makes it difficult for quality programs to take root.

Similarly, there is a structural gap in facilitating postsecondary education. Many postsecondary certificates, diplomas, and degree training opportunities have come to Kakuma camp in the last decade; they were preceded by the Don Bosco vocational training centre, established in the mid-1990s.[56] More than a dozen organizations offer onsite and online training opportunities.[57] These organizations select and offer opportunities to students based on their own criteria. This creates equity problems, with organizations often inclined to give opportunities to relatively better students who have already received many opportunities, rather than other students who haven't had access to such additional opportunities yet. Given the generally low quality of primary and secondary schools, this practice can further disadvantage "low-performing" students. By coordinating between providers and standardizing registrations, timelines, offerings, and so on, more students could benefit from a structured and coherent postsecondary experience.

Underlying many of the problems outlined above is the notion of education in emergencies. Refugee education is often associated with temporary sociopolitical crises, acute economic crises, conflict and violence, natural and environmental disasters, technological hazards, epidemics, or other related crises.[58] The main aim of education in such contexts is bridging learning discontinuities, with the expectation that the crisis is quickly resolved. Under the UNESCO-UNHCR framework agreement, "All collaborations between UNESCO and UNHCR in the Education Sector will be guided by the Inter-Agency Network for Education in Emergencies (INEE) *Minimum Standards* for Education in Emergencies, Chronic Crises and Early Reconstruction, which constitute the normative framework for all Education Sector work in emergencies" (emphasis mine).[59] In other words, the emphasis in emergency contexts is (reasonably) to meet a basic minimum.

However, the reality in protracted refugee camps is different since most camps survive after an emergency. For example, Banga in India and Palestinian refugee "camps" have survived for more than half a century, and camps like Kakuma and Dadaab in Kenya have existed for three decades. The formula of "education in emergencies" has not been effective for such camps. Almost three generations of students have passed through emergency education schemes with compromised learning and teaching environments that have benefited only a very few refugees in meaningful ways. Arguments that depict camp refugee education as an emergency intervention obviously contradict reality and only serve as an excuse for either (un)intentional discrimination or second-class education for refugee students.

CONCLUSION

The responsibilities and associated accountabilities related to education service delivery assumed by these players (UNESCO, UNHCR, NGOs, host bureaus, and emerging community-based organizations) have been scattered and fuzzy. This situation has created enough space to diffuse institutional accountability for education. The organizations' structural gap has resulted in "structural disconti-nuities between primary, secondary, and tertiary education" where the "purpose of school in Kakuma seemed to be to produce more school," that is, more social places that failed to connect students to post-school opportunities.[60] Though in Kakuma camp "education is everything," at the same time it also means nothing, with really meaningful educational opportunities lacking at every level. In other words, refugee education, which was meant to "affirm self-worth [of refugees] in a society that systematically excluded and undervalued them," has ultimately contributed to, rather than ameliorated, their continued exclusion.[61]

One of the implications of this chapter is that education provi-sion should become a core purpose of refugee support, especially in protracted refugee situations, where it should be seen as integral to the UNHCR's primary commitment to finding "durable solutions." It may be true that complete integration with the host education system is the ultimate solution, as stated in GES. However, other forms of integration (social, cultural, economic, etc.) are key prereq-uisites to fully and successfully integrating camp education with the Kenyan system. Considering the actual capacity of the host country and the prevailing tensions between refugees and host countries across the world, complete integration may take many decades, if it is ever achieved, and more young generations may be forced to pass through the kind of patchwork, discriminatory system that exists in Kakuma today. International organizations, therefore, remain cen-tral to ensuring high-quality educational provision in refugee camps. For this to occur, organizations must make themselves ready to be accountable, not to inputs they invest, but to the outcomes children and their parents cherish.

To come back to the title of the paper, I borrowed the concept of "fostering" for the title of this essay to show how education service and the lives of unaccompanied minors in refugee camps are in some ways similar. It is a common experience in the camp that most unac-companied minors pass through fostering until family reunification occurs or they get fully adopted. In most cases, these foster parents are well-wishers – often religious devotees or community leaders from the refugee community. They foster unaccompanied minors regardless of their own resources, capacity, or special interest, acting instead in response to immediate necessity, moral obligations, and/or other factors like being in the same family or ethnic group. In short, they do it because they are there. Education in the camp currently works like this – through expedients, however well-intentioned. But much like unaccompanied minors, the educational system cannot persist indefinitely in the limbo of foster care. A permanent solution that takes refugee students seriously as students with the potential to learn, grow, and flourish is imperative.

NOTES

1 UNHCR, "Kalobeyei Settlement" (n.d.), https://www.unhcr.org/ke/kalobeyei-settlement.
2 Kakuma refugee camp has four sections (Kakuma 1–4); the nearby Kalobeyei settlement area was intended to mark a paradigm shift from camp to settlement, thereby decreasing the burden on the UNHCR by making refugees more "self-reliant." See ibid.
3 Sarah Dryden-Peterson, "Refugee Education: The Crossroads of Globalization," *Educational Researcher* 45, no. 9 (2016): 473–82.
4 UNESCO, "Framework Agreement Between UNESCO and UNHCR" (Nairobi, Kenya, 1 April 2011).
5 To strengthen support for refugee education, both parties signed memoranda of understanding in July 1967, January 1969, March 1971, and August 1984, in addition to the recent 2011 framework agreement.
6 Dryden-Peterson, "Refugee Education."
7 Ibid.
8 UNHCR Inspection and Evaluation Service, quoted in ibid.
9 UNHCR, Refugee Population Statistics Database, accessed 1 April 2021, https://www.unhcr.org/refugee-statistics/.
10 Dryden-Peterson, "Refugee Education," 477.
11 United Nations, "Convention on the Rights of the Child" (1989), https://www.ohchr.org/EN/ProfessionalInterest/Pages/CRC.aspx.
12 Kakuma refugee camp, located at Turkana West, was established in 1992 as a safe haven for Sudanese "Lost Boys" who were forced to leave camps in Ethiopia as a result of regime change. Since then, the camp has received refugees from more than ten countries. Currently, with its four clustered camps, Kakuma hosts more than 190,000 forcibly displaced persons.
13 United Nations, "Millennium Development Goals," United Nations, 2000, www.un.org/millenniumgoals/.
14 Dryden-Peterson, "Refugee Education."
15 Ibid.

16 Ibid.

17 Peter Unam Bol, security officer, interview by author, 3 August 2019, Kakuma 1; Manaz Peter, retired carpenter, interview by author, 7 July 2019 and 3 August 2019, Kakuma 2; Chuei D. Mareng, "Reflections on Refugee Students' Major Perceptions of Education in Kakuma Refugee Camp, Kenya," *Intercultural Education* 21, no. 5 (October 2010): 474.

18 Peter Unam Bol, interview by author.

19 Dryden-Peterson, "Refugee Education," 478.

20 Kavi, community counsellor, interview by author, 7 July 2019, Kakuma 3.

21 Ibid.

22 Michelle J. Bellino and Sarah Dryden-Peterson, "Inclusion and Exclusion within a Policy of National Integration: Refugee Education in Kenya's Kakuma Refugee Camp," *British Journal of Sociology of Education* 40, no. 2 (2019): 222–38.

23 Dryden-Peterson, "Refugee Education"; UNHCR, *2012–2016 Education Strategy* (2011), https://cms.emergency.unhcr.org/documents/11982/53527/ UNHCR+Refugee+Education+Strategy+2012+-+2016/8561f5dc-0406-43b 9-b476-983bcab709bd; UNHCR, "Education strategy – Kakuma Refugee camp" (2017), https://data2.unhcr.org/en/documents/download/65138.

24 UNESCO, "Education Strategy from 2014 to 2021" (2014), https:// unesdoc.unesco.org/images/0023/002312/231288e.pdf&ved=2ahU- KEwjH-fqV6-rrAhWMsRQKHS_ICscQFjACegQICBAE&usg= AOvVaw2qa-PIOM7PFhjUPsoRfGkV; UNESCO, "Operational Strategy on Youth 2014–2021," (2014), http://www.unesco.org/new/fileadmin/ MULTIMEDIA/FIELD/Nairobi/pdf/UNESCOoperationalstrategy onyouth20142021.pdf&ved=2ahUKEwjH-fqV6-rrAhWMs RQKHS_ICscQFjADegQIBRAB&usg=AOvVaw3R8S9TMwL FjfHx3GyLiVxo.

25 United Nations, "Sustainable Development Goals" (2015), https://sdgs. un.org/goals.

26 UNHCR, "Education Strategy – Kakuma Refugee Camp."

27 Dryden-Peterson, "Refugee Education"; UNHCR, "2012–2016 Education Strategy."

28 UNHCR, "2012–2016 Education Strategy."

29 UNHCR, "Education Strategy – Kakuma Refugee Camp."

30 Michelle J. Bellino, "Youth Aspirations in Kakuma Refugee Camp: Education as a Means for Social, Spatial, and Economic (Im)mobility," *Globalisation, Societies and Education* 16, no. 4 (2018): 541–56.

31 Jimmy, academic advisor, interview by author, 18 July 2019, Kakuma 3;
    Kavi, interview by author. Quote from Bellino and Dryden-Peterson,
    "Inclusion and Exclusion," 229.

32 "Malimu" in Kiswahili means a teacher.

33 Jimmy, interview by author.

34 LWF, "Rapid Assessment of Barriers to Education in Kakuma Refugee
    Camp: With a Focus on Access and Quality in Primary Education"
    (February 2015), https://kenyadjibouti.lutheranworld.org/sites/default/
    files/documents/Barriers%20to%20Education%20in%20Kakuma%20
    Refugee%20Camp%20Assessment_0.pdf.

35 Understanding the significance of this average grade is difficult as students
    sit exams with four or five to a desk, all able to see each other's work.

36 Rachel Glennerster et al., "Access and Quality in the Kenyan Education
    System: A Review of the Progress, Challenges and Potential Solutions"
    (Office of the Prime Minister of Kenya, May 2011), https://www.
    academia.edu/4158386/access_and_quality_kenyan_education_system.

37 Saida, logistics officer, interview by author, 17 July 2019, Kakuma 1.

38 Monica, online degree student, interview by author, 12 July 2019,
    Kakuma.

39 UNHCR, "Education Strategy – Kakuma Refugee Camp."

40 Jillo, business adviser, interviews by author, 18 July 2019 and 13
    November 2020, Kakuma 1.

41 Anna, community sanitation supervisor, interview by author, 7 July 2019,
    Kakuma 1.

42 Geoffrey Mariga et al., "Computer Laptop Project Strategy for Basic
    Education Schools in Kenya," International Journal of Information and
    Communication Technology Research 7, no. 5 (May 2017).

43 Bellino and Dryden-Peterson, "Inclusion and Exclusion."

44 UN, "The Refugee Convention" (1951), https://www.unhcr.org/4ca34be29.
    pdf ; Dryden-Peterson, 2016.

45 Jimmy, interview by author.

46 UNESCO, "Framework Agreement Between UNESCO and UNHCR"
    (Nairobi, Kenya, April 1, 2011).

47 UNHCR, "What We Do" (n.d.), https://www.unhcr.org/what-we-do.html.

48 UNHCR, 2011.

49 UNHCR, "Children" (n.d.), https://www.unhcr.org/ke/children.

50 Dryden-Peterson, "Refugee Education."

51 UNHCR, "2012–2016 Education Strategy."

52 Bellino, "Youth Aspirations"; Bellino and Dryden-Peterson, "Inclusion and
    Exclusion."

53 Bellino, "Youth Aspirations," 545.
54 UNHCR, "Education Strategy – Kakuma Refugee Camp."
55 Ibid.
56 Manaz Peter, interview by author.
57 Some examples of organizations offering tertiary-level courses include
    UNHCR, LWF, WI, AAHI, GIZ, JRS, PWJ, RAI, KYRON, DONBOSCO, NRC,
    Masindi Moreno University, etc.
58 UNICEF, "Education in Emergencies: A Resource Toolkit" (2006), http://
    education4resilience.iiep.unesco.org/en/node/1025.
59 UNESCO, "Framework Agreement Between UNESCO and UNHCR"
    (Nairobi, Kenya, 1 April 2011). Emphasis added.
60 Bellino, "Youth Aspirations," 545.
61 Bellino and Dryden-Peterson, "Inclusion and Exclusion"; quote from
    Bellino, "Youth Aspirations," 551.

Dangerous Crossings: East African Women Refugees and Migrants Flee Home for Opportunities in the Gulf States

Muna Omar

Dear Reader,

It is with immense gratitude and pleasure that I share this research with you. As this research is a part of me, it is an honour to take you, the reader, on this authentic and raw journey to have a glimpse of the stories of survival shared in refugees' and migrants' own words. Before presenting my research and how I came to this project, let me first introduce myself. I am Muna Omar. My first name is Muna, but everyone calls me Shaema. I am from the Oromia region of Ethiopia and was born and raised in Riyadh, Saudi Arabia. My parents met in Riyadh after they fled from internal conflict in the Oromia region in Ethiopia. They crossed the sea from the Horn of Africa to the Arabian Peninsula. When my mother was seven months pregnant, my father was deported and we never heard from him again. My mother struggled to raise me as a single mother, which was particularly difficult in a country like Saudi Arabia where women always needed to have a male guardian. But my mother was strong. Eventually, we moved to Yemen. Shortly after we settled there, war broke out. After almost seven years living in Yemen, we managed to move to Addis Ababa, Ethiopia, for the first time.

Through my personal experiences, I built a passion for stories and history and developed compassion for the struggles people face. I call myself a global citizen. I studied business management, which taught me about communication and relationships.

I obtained certificates and badges in public health and humanitarian leadership programs from John Hopkins and UNICEF, as well as other humanitarian agencies. I worked as a humanitarian worker with NGOs in Yemen. And I became a Global Young Water Professional with Rural Water Supply Network (RWSN), publishing an article in an international geo-drilling magazine and a guest blog post on the RWSN website about water scarcity in Yemen. I became a dialogue facilitator with Erasmus virtual exchange projects to bring people from all walks of life together to talk about global issues such as identity, stereotyping, immigration, foreign policy, and breaking down barriers. Finally, I launched a program called the Women Leadership Program in Sana'a, Yemen, in May 2019 with Hive Women and as part of the Global Heart Project.

The Global History Dialogues program gave me the opportunity to pursue research that drew on these many experiences. I was overjoyed to have the opportunity to be taught by professional academic researchers. It helped me to recognize that the stories I had grown up hearing should be shared with a wider, global audience. Because I am a refugee living with other refugees, these stories are normalized in my community. Everyone has experienced things like this. Preparing for this project required taking a step back to think about what an outsider would need to know and to contextualize the testimonies of fellow refugees. As someone with a passion for history and storytelling, as well as helping refugees and migrants, my goal throughout the project has been to help refugees and migrants have their voices and stories heard in the way they wish.

Global History Dialogues helped me to gain analytical distance from my experiences, and I knew right away that I wanted to push back against the normalization taking place. Injustice, human rights violations, and sexual and physical abuse should never be normalized. Those stories of survival should be told by their own people and not only by statistics or numbers compiled by international bodies. Behind those numbers there are thousands of stories, and those are worth sharing. Why? Because stories speak of our existence, of our personal experiences, our reality. Our pain and agony are important to share to foster change. For these reasons, my work shares previously untold stories through oral history and participatory research methods.

While conducting the interviews for this project, I lived in war-torn Sana'a, Yemen. This led to many challenges, such as a lack of access to archives and limited internet access. Electricity was also limited, so I worked from midnight until the morning to find times when networks were not overloaded. Doing oral history interviews with refugees and migrants posed other challenges, too. Some of my interviewees would feel a bit closed off when I switched on my recorder so I would always talk with them before recording to make us both feel at ease. But they were open to sharing their stories and encouraged each other to share. They always referred me to someone they knew or heard about so that I could interview that person. They would invite me into their houses for a cup of tea to chit-chat about my project and life in general. They trusted me enough to share freely, and that is an important thing for me and something I try to honour in this work.

Every human being experiences life differently. Our lives are affected by our upbringings, backgrounds, education, family experience, and so on. Therefore, we all have different voices. We need to tell multifaceted and moving stories about refugees and migrants that foreground our voices. They are complex stories and documenting them well and carefully will, I hope, generate social change by inspiring people and helping them better relate to the experience of refugees, migrants, and asylum seekers. It's an opportunity to change the world, to have a clear understanding, to be better.

Sincerely,
Muna Omar

> "An immigrant leaves his homeland to find greener grass. A refugee leaves his homeland because the grass is burning under his feet."[1]

INTRODUCTION

Over the last decade, approximately 100 million people were forced to flee their homes, seeking safety either within or outside of their countries' borders.[2] Women and girls make up around 50 per cent, if not more, of the internally displaced or stateless. Those women that are unaccompanied or underage, pregnant, heads of household, or elderly are particularly vulnerable.[3]

Sub-Saharan Africa alone hosts more than 26 per cent of the world's displaced population.[4] Since the 1950s, many nations in Africa have suffered from internal conflicts, ethnic strife, and deep poverty, resulting in the displacement of many people in Africa. From the 1960s onward, the number of displaced Africans has grown steadily, partly as a result of the Eritrean-Ethiopian war, the independence war in which Eritreans rose up against the Ethiopian state, the bloody civil war in Somalia, the Ethiopian civil war marked by the Marxist regime, the Derg, as well as conflicts within other African countries.[5] Many people from Africa, and especially those from the Horn of Africa, found refuge in Yemen, often as a transit hub to reach its richer neighbour, Saudi Arabia.

Migrants who move through the country are vulnerable to abuse and discrimination. For women and girls, displacement can be especially dangerous as they face various forms of discrimination and violence, including rape, torture, kidnap, murder, detention, sexual exploitation, barriers to education and health care services, and early or forced marriage. My research aims to bring to light the experiences of East African women and girls who migrated to Yemen and how their gender has shaped their migratory experiences. What were the conditions under which they migrated? Who made the decision to migrate? How did they experience their arrival in Yemen? To what extent was migration empowering or disabling?

I undertook this study to document the overlooked and silenced experiences of East African women and girl migrants and refugees in Yemen so that people can see and take action to address the human rights abuses perpetuated against them. The essay is divided into five sections. The first outlines my methodology and the impact of these methodological choices on my research. The second provides long-term historical context for Eastern African migration to Yemen, linking this to the decisions that present-day refugees make to flee their countries. Third, I examine the violence many of these refugees encounter on their journeys and the ways women and girls are differentially vulnerable. Fourth, I consider what happens when refugees arrive in Yemen and seek out the support of international organizations and NGOs meant to help them. Finally, I explore the options available to migrants and refugees while they wait in Yemen: What kinds of labour can they perform? How does their status as (women) migrants affect their work experiences? Overall, I argue that the current humanitarian response to these migrants' needs is insufficient, and that it is important to understand their vulnerabilities and experiences in their own words.

METHODOLOGY

While the world's attention has recently focused on the refugee population fleeing war-torn Syria and journeying to Europe, the parallel tragedy unfolding in Yemen has gone largely unnoticed. Media coverage of Syrian refugees migrating to Europe has led to much conversation on the topic, with a particular focus on women and girls. The United Nations High Commissioner for Refugees (UNHCR), the United Nations Population Fund (UNFPA), and the Women's Refugee Commission (WRC) created a joint venture to protect women and girl Syrian refugees from sexual and gender-based violence. Nothing of the sort happened with East African women and girls migrating to Yemen; it seems like there is little to no international focus on their experiences. Yet, alarming accounts indicate that many suffer severe human rights violations that have not been systematically investigated. Interviews with survivors and eyewitnesses of this violence, conducted for this research, reveal an incredibly abusive environment. The stories of the migrants and refugees in this essay should never be in the shadows. Their unique experiences are crucial to understanding the inhumanity of current border and migratory regimes, especially as many of the agencies that are supposed to protect migrants' rights are implicated in their violation. In fact, while planning my research project, I began by contacting international humanitarian organizations working with refugees in Sana'a, for their side of the story. At first, they were compliant and welcomed me when I reached out, but after learning about the research project, they declined to be a part of it. This has limited my ability to represent their perspectives on the issues discussed in this chapter.

Much of the secondary literature on East African migration to Yemen adopts the perspective of humanitarian intervention when it even engages with refugees at all. The experiences of migrants themselves appear as issues that need to be solved by collecting data and sharing snippets of their stories. But as a person who lives among these refugees and hears their stories daily, I felt that their perspectives needed to be heard, not as problems to be solved, but as the lives of whole people with complex narratives of migration and displacement. These are just desperate people who are looking for things most of us take for granted: home, education, food, water, family, work, and safety. Conducting oral histories offered me a way to explore these themes from a very different vantage than that offered by international organizations who understand refugees as a problem.

The refugees' testimonies gave me a firsthand account of their lives and experiences before and after they came to Yemen, their decision to leave for Yemen, survival stories of extreme human rights violations by criminal gangs, near-death experiences, and their current life in Sana'a, a blockaded city in a war-torn country. Although most of the stories shared similar features, each person had a unique life experience – obstacles, heartaches, and hopes – to share. While it was heartwarming to see their eagerness to share their stories, there were some who hesitated to share because they feared for their lives in a country where there is no system to protect them and where even humanitarian agencies would not assist them if they spoke up about anything that would damage the agencies' image. In all, this dependence on these humanitarian agencies resulted in a sense of helplessness about their situations. I would highlight that even as a researcher trying to create spaces to share stories that have been excluded from mainstream historical narratives, the structural vulnerability that many refugees and displaced people experience makes this a very complicated and a difficult task.

Because of the importance of creating spaces for refugees and migrants to speak for themselves, I have chosen to include long excerpts of these interviews. Rather than a single text, this essay weaves together these testimonies with historical background and analysis to create a multivocal tapestry of migrants' experiences of travelling through and living in Yemen.

HISTORICAL SURVEY OF YEMEN-EAST AFRICA CONNECTIONS AND MIGRATIONS

Historically, Yemen has been at the centre of many commercial routes. Although the history of migration between Yemen and the Horn of Africa has not received much study, one ancient route has linked the Arabian Peninsula and the African continent for centuries. Both the slave trade and more humane forms of commercial exchange took place along this route, leaving their marks on Yemeni lands.[6] A less studied part of this history is the period of Aksumite occupation between 526 and 575, resulting in the establishment of the Al-Qalis church, built by the Ethiopian general and King Abraha in Sana'a, and of a similar one in Najran (present-day Saudi Arabia).[7] Similarly neglected is the reign of the Banu Najah, a dynasty of Ethiopian origin that ruled parts of Yemen between 1060 and 1158.[8] Moreover, traces of the Africa-Yemen connection are found in traditional history and folklore: the popular Queen Balqīs is the Queen of Sheba mentioned in the Bible, the Quran, and the Ethiopians' sacred book, Kebra Nagast (Glory of Kings), and her lineage is inscribed in the 1931 Ethiopian constitution, which states that her son Bin Malek, Emperor Menelik, was the first king of the Solomonic Dynasty.[9] The long-standing cultural, religious, and migratory connections between Yemen and the Horn of Africa continue to this day.

Migration between Yemen and the Horn of Africa has continued for centuries, both as a result of the slave trade and as a consequence of other forms of commercial exchange. Exchange did not happen in only one direction; throughout the centuries, Yemenis have migrated to Ethiopia and integrated into the Ethiopian society as tradesmen and shipowners. This long history of cross migration is reflected in Yemen's mixed heritage population, the Muwalladīn, i.e., the children of marriages between Yemeni men and Ethiopian, Eritrean, Djiboutian, and, more rarely, Somali women. This term can be for any mixed half-Yemeni but it is most widely used for Yemenis who have African heritage. The Muwalladīn, to a certain degree, are discriminated against in the Yemeni community. I encountered women and girls who tended to identify as Yemenis only, not sharing that they have African ancestry, even to East African people. Muwalladīn who have a much lighter skin tone and participate in Yemeni culture can more easily integrate in Yemeni society, and not be seen as African. If they have darker skin, they will be known as Muwalladīn and might face more challenges, including problems obtaining employment or wage discrimination when they do find jobs; physical and verbal assault on the street; challenges in marrying lighter-skinned Yemenis; and so on. Discrimination against darker-skinned people is even more severe for Akhdam or Muhamasheen (meaning "servants" or "marginalized," respectively). These are Yemenis who live in extreme poverty, isolated from the rest of society; lighter-skinned Yemenis view it as a taboo to interact with them. They often work as street cleaners and beggars, living in tents and cardboard boxes. These people have experienced centuries of discrimination, racism, exploitation, and poverty – discrimination based on tribe, region, skin colour, and religion is endemic in Yemen.

Figure 2.1 | A bomb exploding in Sana'a, Yemen. Migrants are particularly vulnerable during the conflict because of their exclusion from much social service provision and their frequent lack of safe places to live.

Figure 2.2 | Water is very scarce in Yemen. Again, the burden falls heavily on migrants. Here, refugee women collect water from the side of the street.

In 1980, the Yemen Arab Republic signed the 1951 Refugee Convention as well as the Protocol Relating to the Status of Refugees of 1967.[10] In 1990, when the South and North of Yemen united, the Convention and Protocol remained in place, forming part of Yemen's obligations to the international community and displaced people. To date, Yemen is the only signatory country in the Arabian Peninsula. In line with this policy, before the 1980s, Yemen accepted refugees from the Horn of Africa. The first wave of new arrivals was made up of refugees fleeing the Eritrean War of Independence from the 1960s onward.

To comply with the requirements of the 1951 Convention, the Yemeni government should guarantee refugees their socioeconomic rights, such as the right to work, education, and healthcare, and should guarantee them recourse to courts. Yet Yemen has dramatically failed in protecting the refugees' rights and in fulfilling its duties as laid out in the Convention. Rather, it has repeatedly violated humanitarian law by failing to ensure these rights. To apply for work permits, refugees must present passports with a guarantor who should be a Yemeni citizen. As people who have fled persecution, refugees find these requirements difficult to meet – not to mention that this is a violation of the 1951 Convention. When refugees find jobs, they are paid low wages. Similarly, no education or healthcare is provided and refugees face discrimination when seeking treatment in hospitals. If refugees are provided education and healthcare through humanitarian organizations, these services are low quality and insufficient. On top of this, many refugees are detained and mistreated by both state and private actors.

Yemen continues to suffer from a political and humanitarian crisis from the war that broke out in 2014 between the Houthi rebels and the official government, which led to the military intervention of Saudi Arabia and its allies in 2015. The war has resulted in high numbers of internally displaced people (IDPs), contributing to the worst health crisis in modern history, including millions of recorded cases of water-borne disease.[11] Cholera has hit the country particularly hard, as the airstrikes hit pipelines and leave the country starved for water. Sana'a could be the first city in the world to run out of water, with less than 55 per cent of its inhabitants having access to potable water.[12] If water scarcity; malnutrition; drought; no electricity; and the lack of sanitation, hygiene, and access to clean water were not enough, the war has also resulted in endless piles of garbage accumulating on the streets of the city.

However, the dire situation of the country has not stopped East African migrants and refugees from moving to Yemen. Although many East African men have migrated to Yemen, job opportunities for women are generally more plentiful as they can find employment as domestic workers. Even though Yemen is one of the poorest countries in the world, Yemeni families do not allow women to work in other people's houses as it is a taboo for women to be seen by strange men. For this reason, they tend to employ other nationalities as domestic workers. Ethiopian and Somali women are highly requested as domestic workers. The women and girls who fill these positions may be women sending remittances back home to their families, while others are underage girls who are trying to escape poverty or have been influenced by others to migrate to secure a better life. Many, though not all, hoped to transit through Yemen to Saudi Arabia. Instead, they find themselves stuck in Yemen and unable to continue to Saudi Arabia. Either they do not have the resources to make it to Saudi Arabia or they face the increased militarization of the border but they have come too far to turn back. Many choose to immigrate to Yemen with high hopes for better futures, escaping from sharks' teeth[13] on a route that is uncertain, but that is also the shortest way to their final destination and less dangerous than crossing the Mediterranean. The next section explores the decision to travel to Yemen, and what happens when migrants set out across the sea.

HISTORIES OF SURVIVORS OF THE SEA CROSSING: DANGERS OF THE JOURNEY AT SEA AND ARRIVAL IN YEMEN

Yemen acts as a transit country for migrants from the Horn of Africa, predominantly Ethiopians and Somalis. Based on recent data collected by the International Organization of Migration (IOM), the estimated number of displaced people who arrived in Yemen in April 2019 was 18,320, and the monthly figure increased to 18,904 in May 2019.[14]

This fluctuation in migration between the Horn of Africa and Yemen is not a new phenomenon; it has been taking place for decades. It involves a range of migrants, including so-called economic migrants (i.e., those who are fleeing social upheaval and extreme poverty), refugees, asylum seekers, and unaccompanied minors from Ethiopia, Somalia, and, to a lesser extent, other East African countries. Some are victims of smugglers, who fed them lies, conjuring up fake dreams and promising a wonderful life in Yemen away from their misery. The smuggling networks profit enormously from these migrants. Taken together, these smuggling networks generate revenues on the order of tens of millions of dollars, according to a global study by the United Nations Office on Drugs and Crime (UNODC) on the smuggling of migrants.[15] Safia, an Ethiopian refugee, expressed what this deception can feel like to a young girl: "I was ten years old. I tried to go to Djibouti, but I couldn't and returned back. At the age of thirteen, I was deceived into coming."[16] The decision to flee, as Safia's experience shows, is often made under false pretenses when it is not compelled by violence or conflict. Once made, migrants face the dangers of a journey at sea.

Thus, migrants not only endure pain, persecution, violence, and poverty in their home countries, but they also face a life-threatening journey, not knowing where they are headed, just thinking that wherever that is, it can't possibly be any worse than where they are. The dangers of the journey are enormous; all the interviewees mentioned that they saw people being thrown off the boat while crossing the sea to Yemen. Abdullah and Aeysha said more than a dozen people drowned after having been thrown off the boat, and Safia witnessed (at the age of thirteen) a man being shot eight times while on the boat.[17] Smugglers throw migrants overboard either to lighten the boat or when someone is too weak to continue the journey. The weakest get thrown off earlier, along with those who get into fights.

When boats draw close to the Yemeni coastline, members of criminal gangs direct the smugglers to the shore. The smugglers strike deals in advance with these gangs: the smugglers get money to alert them of the imminent arrival of migrants so that the criminal gangs can wait for them to arrive on the shore. The gangs are mostly Yemenis, but they also include some people of African origin who work for them.

Upon arrival in Yemen, migrants suffer atrocities such as kidnapping and torture for ransom, sexual violence, abduction,[18] forced detention, and extortion. These are frequent and often lethal hazards for migrants. The details of the brutality of criminals (both Yemeni and African gang members) were shocking to hear. I have decided to include lengthy sections of my narrators' stories as they were told to me to preserve the integrity of their narratives. This is because, while the general contours of the migrant experience are often shared – a hope for anything better than current reality, perilous sea crossings, and violence at the hands of smugglers and criminal gangs – attention to the specifics of each journey is important for understanding the particular ways that gender, age, poverty, and other identities and experiences affect migrants' experiences. Moreover, too often "migrants" are treated as an abstract category, an object of study. By sharing individual stories, narrated by interviewees themselves, I hope to challenge the tendency to generalize and dehumanize migrants.

Many of the migrants were teenagers when they decided to flee from violence and persecution and embark on this dangerous journey. Among these teens were Dastow and her sister, who migrated from Ethiopia and endured physical and sexual abuse and torture for ransom by criminal gangs in Yemen. Dastow watched her sister get raped and die. She shared with me her heartbreaking story.

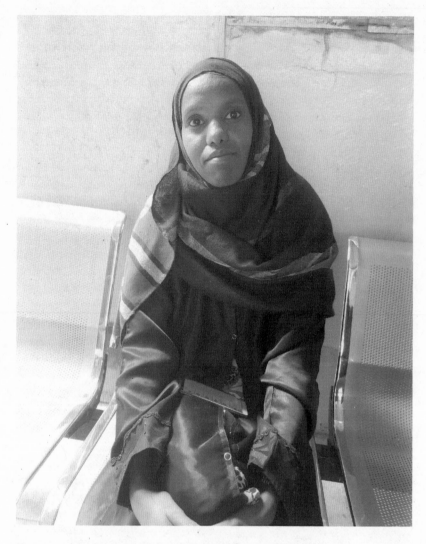

Figure 2.3 | A photograph of Dastow, who migrated from Ethiopia to Yemen
and who shared her story for this chapter.

I didn't have anywhere to go. There was a war in our region
between Oromia and the government – they shot and killed my
father when I was five years old and put my mother in jail where
she died. And so, I had to leave with my younger sister. My aim
was just to survive. I sought safety and a decent life for me and

Figure 2.4 | A photograph of Rabia, one of the narrators who shared her story for this chapter. Rabia migrated across the sea three separate times.

my sister. We went to Djibouti and from Djibouti to Hayyú and took a boat with my sister to the shores of Yemen, where a group of men of 'Abdu'l-Qawī, who are well-known men, forced us into a car with their guns and took us to a tent. They asked for money, but we had none. The four men raped my fourteen-year-old sister.

We escaped. I carried her on my back as we crossed the desert area
and then found a car that took us in the trunk. My sister asked for
water, laying on my arms and lap, but we had no water nor food
for days. Her last words were the Shahada (There is no God but
Allah, and the Prophet Mohammed is the Messenger of Allah) and
took her last breath.[19]

Dastow recounted this story as she cried, remembering that devastating moment of loss and the helplessness she felt to save her
little sister.

Rabia was forced to get married at a young age and escaped
to Assab (now Eritrea). When she decided to escape to Djibouti,
it was during the Mengistu regime and the Derg (Provisional
Military Government of Socialist Ethiopia) in the late 1980s. At
that time, Ethiopia was experiencing a famine that led to millions
of deaths, economic decline, genocide, and internal conflicts of different regions, particularly the Eritrean War of Independence. Her
journey was excruciating – she was recruited by the military of the
Derg regime, witnessed genocide, and was sexually abused when
she decided to flee to and through Yemen. Rabia also crossed the
sea three times, making her story distinctive. The first time, she
recounted:

They wanted to marry me off when I was thirteen years old;
after three months, I escaped to Assab (now Eritrea). I stayed
there where there was the war against the former Prime Minister
Mengistu Haile Mariam, who overthrew and killed the Emperor
Haile Selassie. I was only fourteen years old, and they started to
recruit for the military. I was recruited for two years. We also
used to wear some sort of uniform and serve as waitresses when
there were gatherings of singers or leaders coming to that compound. They made us cheer and sing for the military and take
pictures and videos of us wearing the Ethiopian flag around our
wrist and a red band around our forehead. I watched people
being killed on the streets and their corpses are not allowed to be
picked from the streets. And if they want to kill someone, they
would take him to the streets to be killed in front of the people.
Also, they bury people alive. I attended the big burial ceremony
of a major named Mohammed Yassin, not sure if I recall the
name correctly, though, who was in charge of Assab at the time,

who was killed by Mengistu soldiers. And I remember during the time seeing Cuban soldiers distributing biscuits to poor people on the streets from their trucks.

Then one day, I lied to the woman who was our supervisor, saying that my father was ill and that I had to go to my village but escaped to Djibouti instead. As I was on the bus at the border, I got captured and the man named 'Abdu 'l-Fatāḥ, a leader among them, tried to rape me, but I fought strongly and he kicked my stomach – I bled so hard. I was taken to the hospital. The doctors said my uterus was bleeding and that I would never get pregnant.

I stayed in Djibouti and worked with French and Greek people as a housemaid. I was seeking an opportunity to leave. There was an office where they took people to fight in the war between Palestine and Israel. The men were Pakistani and I went to sign up, but one man convinced me not to sign up.

So, from Djibouti I went to Jazan, Yemeni-Saudi border, where after crossing the sea I walked on hot desert for weeks, I was hungry and thirsty with my friend. I saw a water bottle of gas and drank it. My friend drank her urine. We saw a Saudi soldier with his dogs. We screamed to get him to come take us, but he didn't hear us. But then we found a place and they helped us, and we entered Riyadh.

I got married, and I got pregnant. I was happy to be pregnant, but then my husband left and never came back. I gave birth to my daughter. I worked in the house of a Saudi Princess, Al Jawahara, the sister of Prince Sultan who passed away.[20] I didn't know what they were doing, but at night they would gather women – every night so many – and take them to another prince's house for fun. I didn't know as I worked in the mornings with my four-month-old daughter and at night went home. Then one day, I came and there was no one. I knocked on the door and police showed up and took me to jail and deported me on a boat to Assab. But the boat returned, and I came back to Saudi with my daughter.

The third time was a trap. My daughter was thirteen or fourteen years old; we were legal residents in Saudi Arabia but our sponsor was in Jeddah. There was a Princess' wedding, they said, and they wanted maids so I went and took my daughter so that she could have a good time – little did we know that police cars

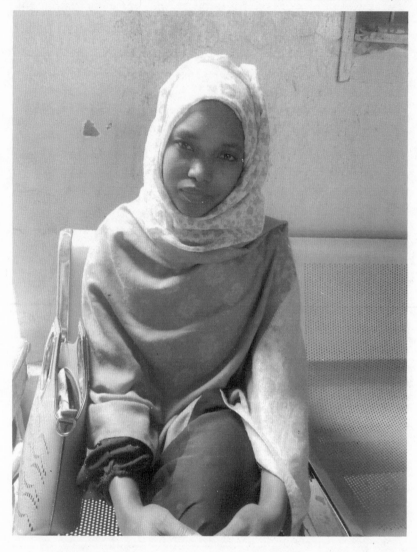

Figure 2.5 | A photograph of Safia, who fled to Yemen at the age of thirteen.

would surround us. They took us to jail, beat us, tore apart our
Iqama (resident permit), which was just two weeks renewed, and
deported us. I had to come back; my daughter became ill. So, the
third time, I came to Yemen. I stayed in Sanaʿa with my daughter
and never went to Saudi Arabia.[21]

This is how Rabia described her remarkable journeys crossing the sea. Her story shows how migrants, even those who manage to obtain some legal status in their receiving countries, remain vulnerable to state violence and abuse, and how that abuse is often exacerbated by their gender.

Safia was another one of those teenagers deceived by the high hopes of a wonderful life awaiting her across the sea, only to have criminal organizations take advantage of her family's situation.

> My father had four wives and they always mistreated me, so I had to escape from that life and interrupt my education. I had no other choice. I was thirteen years old when I came to Yemen. A woman encouraged me to go with her. I walked for one week to Somalia and from Somalia, I took a boat to Yemen. There was a war between the North and the South of Yemen. I was just a kid, and no one would take me for work. Later, I was at the house of some Muwalladīn (people of mixed Yemeni-Ethiopian heritage), and they married me off. I had no choice.[22]

Safia faced a lot of trouble with her husband. She got divorced, and her children were taken from her. She went to Saudi Arabia and returned remarried to another man. He wanted her to get an abortion, but she refused and got divorced again. Now she lives alone with her daughter and has finally contacted her other children. She is sick, as she has problems with her kidneys, and is currently seeking medical assistance.

Aeysha wanted to leave the grinding poverty of her life in Ethiopia, which was causing her mental health problems. Her journey involved a traumatic near-death experience but she survived to tell the tale of her encounter with the criminal gangs.

> We were poor, living in a small village in the Oromia region, and I was married off at a young age and gave birth to four children. Then my two children died suddenly. I got mentally sick and taken to a mental health facility in the city. After I became sane again, I got married[23] and came to Djibouti and from Djibouti to Yemen. I was five months pregnant.
>
> After we crossed the sea, a group of men were waiting at the shores with guns; they forced us inside the car and then took us to a tent. They asked for money – 7,500 Birr for me and 7,500

Birr for my husband so 15,000 Birr. [24] But we didn't have any
money, so they knocked my husband on the head (he later had
surgery) and took him away; they took me with seven other
women to a tent in Hudaydah, near the Saudi Arabia border,
asking us to work as housemaids as a way for us to pay them
the ransom. I said I couldn't work because I was pregnant then
three men started beating me, one holding my hands and two
kicking my stomach and head. I was later thrown on the streets
when a Yemeni man found me and took me to a hospital, I think
to a UNHCR [facility], not sure. A doctor treated me, she was
a Western woman, maybe European. So, I stayed there for one
month and later called my family in Ethiopia who helped me
contact my husband in Sana'a. [25]

These are just a few stories of many that are not widely heard.
The migrant smuggling networks between the Horn of Africa and
the Arabian Peninsula emerged to facilitate the flow of irregular
migrants – those travelling without correct documentation – making
it easier for them to migrate but using their desperation to exploit
them. According to some witnesses, who have survived the transit,
this has been happening since the mid-2000s, but it is not certain
when it actually began.

RESETTLEMENT AND CORRUPTION: ATTEMPTING TO LEAVE YEMEN, INTERFACING WITH INTERNATIONAL ORGANIZATIONS

The dangers of the journey are not the end of migrants' nightmares.
The vulnerable displaced East Africans who manage to reach the
Yemeni coast don't know that the worst is yet to come. From here,
they risk getting kidnapped for ransom, raped, forced to work, and
detained. Some are even forcibly recruited and taken to fight on the
frontlines in the war beside the Houthi rebels.

These migrants left their homes, fleeing for their lives, only to
fall into another trap. I was shocked to find out, by accident, that
I lived in the same building as one of the smugglers. I was vis-
iting his house along with other neighbours, at the invitation of
the man's wife. I remember I got inside the bathroom and saw
a pool of blood. I was shocked when I later found out that the
smuggler's wife had sent a group of four or five men to rape a

Figure 2.6 | Ayesha and her children in their home.

seventeen-year-old migrant girl, and the blood was hers. The man
and his wife were sex-trafficking smugglers.

   I managed to speak to the girl who said she wanted to cross to
Saudi Arabia with a group of men and women from various East
African countries. They made it to Sana'a, where the smuggler
brought them to his house to gather them, take the money, and set
off together to Saudi Arabia. The girl, though afraid of being seen
talking to me, told me that the smuggler took her into the mountains
with other girls to take them to Saudi Arabia but raped them with
his group of men instead. Some were killed. He then brought her
back to his house.

   The smuggler's wife knows what her husband does, but she was
furious at the girl. She later paid other men to rape the girl in her
house, and the smuggler's wife said that she can do whatever she
wants with the girl. The girl was held in the house and not allowed
to leave or even speak to anyone. The girl knew no one and had

no place to go. She was Christian, so I arranged with a priest for her stay in the church since no one would take her in and no one would know who helped her. She was given an abaya (a traditional long black gown with long sleeves worn over clothes when walking on the streets, worn mostly in the Gulf countries) and a scarf and escaped from the balcony. The smuggler's wife was furious and threatened me, saying they would call the police. Since the police in Yemen are easily bribed, and the smuggler is wealthy, she threatened to get revenge.

This young woman's story shows how the economic and legal vulnerability of migrants puts them at even greater risk. Yemen is a country raging with civil war. The resulting lawlessness makes it easier for criminal networks to become entangled with legal authorities. The smugglers bring the migrants across the sea after taking their payment and deliver them to the criminal networks waiting on the shore. The migrants are taken to compounds where they are detained for ransom and tortured, and the unaccompanied women and children are sexually abused. They are then forced to call their families to have money sent to the smugglers. The authorities are bribed to turn a blind eye to these abuses. We also see the ways sexual violence compounds with other forms of abuse, putting women and girls in especially dangerous situations as they attempt to migrate from East Africa to Yemen and Saudi Arabia.

Smugglers are not the only ones to profit off migrants. Criminal gangs collude with smugglers and the authorities. The way I distinguish between smugglers and criminals in this context is that the smugglers are the ones who transport people across the international borders in violation of laws or regulations, and the criminals are the ones who commit immoral activities that violate someone's human rights, such as kidnapping, rape, exploitation, etc. As one of my interviewees stated, "The Yemeni government is living off stealing the money of the African people migrating [by] sea-crossing. Those criminal gangs are well-known, and they have huge compounds where they torture us. The international humanitarian organizations know about it. But no one does anything because they are all cheaters, and they benefit from it. The people who are working in the international organization working with refugees are Muwalladīn – if they were staffed by Western people, it wouldn't be this way."[26]

This comment brings attention to another crucial problem: the widespread corruption among the institutions meant to assist migrants and refugees, namely the international organizations working with refugees. Following are several accounts of abuse by or corruption in the international organizations working with refugees, which emerged as recurrent themes in the interviews. Several interviewees wished to remain anonymous when recounting their interactions with these international organizations. I would state again that I have reached out to personnel from international organizations working with refugees for information or an interview, but they refused to participate.

International humanitarian organizations working with refugees are meant to support the enforcement of humanitarian law to protect the vulnerable people. One of my interviewees, who prefers to remain anonymous, told me, "Fatima and Ahmed [names changed], who work in an international organization [name omitted] working with refugees for many years, take money from refugees in exchange for resettlement. I saw twenty people resettled in Europe this way. I personally know everyone they work with and their sidekicks who work undercover. Fatima and Ahmed stole money from many and never resettled them, they just choose who they want to resettle based on their mood." When asked how the process works, the interviewee continued, "The deal happens outside on the streets. Fatima would drive her car and leave it one block or two blocks away and tell [the refugee] to prepare the money. Then she would go there, there would be no exchange of words, [the refugee would] just hand her the money, and she says she will call, and that's how it goes."[27]

Another one of my interviewees, who also prefers to remain anonymous, said, "I went to an international organization working with refugees to register and they turned down my file. Then Ahmed told me to change my name, and also my story, and to register again for no reason." The interviewee further added that "Those employees wouldn't be able to do it on their own. They have people with them who are in higher positions. They are Western people who do assist them with what they do or how would they be doing this for decades."[28] Dastow, in the same vein, stated, "We can't go to the police asking for justice because they will ask for money for their khat [khat or qat is a narcotic leafy plant, consumed throughout Yemen] and I don't have money. I have no one to turn to."[29]

This accusation, if substantiated, would show that the corruption creeps further up than local employees and has devastating consequences for refugees and migrants seeking protection for their human rights. However, even in the face of widespread corruption, women and girl migrants and refugees dedicate endless energy and resources in the hope of being resettled elsewhere. I once saw a woman crying and screaming in front of the building of an international organization working with refugees. She worked as a housemaid and had made endless sacrifices to put together thousands of dollars. She gave that money to an employee who had promised to resettle her, only to have the door shut in her face. The hard-earned money was gone.

No one seems to be willing to investigate the corruption, which does not stop at money either: sometimes sexual exploitation is involved as well. One interviewee witnessed an employee of one of these international organizations entering and staying at a woman's house; the woman was a registered refugee.

These organizations seem to handle local funds haphazardly, in what appears to my interviewees as involving opaque and arbitrary decisions. For instance, some of my interviewees stated that they received three to six months of cash assistance from one organization, while others did not, despite sharing similar circumstances. Often, employees would visit them to see their houses, registering their names to arrange deliveries of flour, rice, etc. But most never heard back after registering and never found out why they were registered in the first place. To them, it remains unclear what criteria those humanitarian organizations apply in deciding who deserves support and who does not.

Some initiatives have introduced an organized voluntary return of refugees to their homelands. The refugees pay for their passage – around 120,000 Yemeni riyals per person – and can bring no more than twenty kilograms of luggage.[30] Safiya told me, "I registered with [organization omitted] to go back home six months ago, after they told us to go back to my country, but never heard back from them."[31] Safiya's experience is not singular, as many migrants struggle to return home. Yet, organizations like the IOM also successfully repatriate migrants. To quote the organization: "In 2018, IOM helped 1,040 migrants leave Yemen and return home. So far in 2019, the organization has supported the voluntary return of 733 migrants. IOM also works with UNHCR to support the spontaneous return of refugees, helping 2,590 Somali refugees to return from Aden last year."[32]

This is a good initiative to help those who are unable to support themselves or integrate into the host country to have the opportunity to return home but some have been waiting for months to a year to return. Moreover, fees charged for return are expensive

Figure 2.7 | Refugees standing in line, registering to return to their home countries. This process is often expensive and time-consuming, and refugees can only bring a few possessions with them.

for struggling migrants, and the twenty-kilogram baggage allowance does not enable them to bring home possessions that would make their lives easier. Many had hoped to carry more things. For example, I have met some who returned to their home countries crying because they were forced to leave things behind like cooking gas and solar panels that would have helped families struggling with no electricity and cooking over fires. Those who were able to work and can pay, and don't have much to take back, are satisfied and happy to return to their homelands; others who don't have the money are stuck not knowing what to do. The irony of the system is that only those who have some amount of success at obtaining employment in Yemen will be able to return while those who remain unemployed and unable to save hundreds of dollars for their transport are trapped. This brings me to the final section of the essay and the question of labour.

LABOUR: RACISM, VIOLENCE, AND EXCLUSION IN YEMEN

The hope of a decent and dignified life drives people to risk their lives on a dangerous journey, first across the sea and then across the embattled areas of the Yemeni mainland. In my interviews, I focused particularly on working women. While all East Africans endure the life-threatening journey to land a decent job for a better future or to support their families back home, the women are particularly vulnerable, as the preceding discussions of sexual violence have shown. Most women are uneducated; their dream is to seek education yet they work as housemaids instead. The wages do not cover their basic needs, and some cannot find employment because of the ongoing conflict in Yemen. They face discrimination everywhere, even in healthcare, where life-threatening situations occur because of so-called medical mistakes.

I remember seeing a Somali woman moaning in pain on the bench in the hospital. I came close, and she told me she was suffering from pain, but the hospital kept postponing her appointments. She had cancer and it had spread throughout her body because early medical assistance had been denied by the hospital. As I listened to her and saw her pain, I asked a nurse to get her a bed, but the nurse said that none were available and walked away. But from where I stood, I could see empty beds. That night, the woman passed away. No one knew her family in Somalia to contact them, so a group of East Africans gathered some money to bury her.

In another recent case, an Ethiopian woman was found dead in the house where she worked as a housemaid. The police did not investigate, and the international humanitarian organizations overlooked the case, too. Safia remarked on how some employers have

Figure 2.8 | A photograph of Saeed, who works recruiting migrant women as domestic labourers in Yemen.

treated her: "They mistreat me, and they say if you don't want the job, you leave."[33] A migrant's tenuous status in Yemen is always held over her and used to excuse poor treatment, low wages, and other forms of abuse.

Discrimination extends to some local minorities, as well. Saeed Al-Farah is Muwallad (Ethiopian/Eritrean/Yemeni) with Yemeni citizenship and has worked as a mediator for twenty-five years, getting refugees and migrant women to work as domestic workers.

> I took up this work because I couldn't get any job and didn't have a degree or anything, so I started as a mediator. The Yemenis prefer Ethiopians and Eritreans over Somalis or any other. They don't come up to me right away from the sea, they just [find out about me] through other refugees and migrants telling them about me when they seek a job, as I have been doing this for twenty-five years. Even though they don't speak the

Arabic language and no papers are required to work as a housemaid, they work and sleep at their workplace, leaving one day in
a week or a month or sometimes yearly, and learn the language
and get used to it. But the demand is not as high as before the
war, everything is low. I have no income now – I want to go to
Ethiopia as a Yemeni refugee, we are struggling.[34]

Saeed's line of work is predicated on the low wages and vulnerability
of Eastern African women in Yemen, who often have few options
other than the exploitative conditions he describes. The entrenched
preferences of his Yemeni clients illustrate how ingrained this form
of domestic labour is in Yemeni society, to the point where people distinguish between women domestic workers based on their
nationality and ethnicity. In the death of the domestic worker, we
see crystallized many of the identities that make life for Eastern African migrants in Yemen so dangerous: low-paid work in an isolated
context; lack of nearby family to keep watch or even learn of her
death; impunity for those responsible for her death through non-
enforcement by police and the legal system; all underwritten by her
race and migrant status.

CONCLUSION: WHEN THE DREAM
IS WITHIN A FORBIDDEN NATION

As Safia told me, the desire to seek education is one of the driving
factors pushing people to face the risks of the crossing. Yet dreams
are often left behind:

I dream about the future and even now I dream to study and
go back to my education. I need to go back to my country first.
Now if I get an American visa, I will not go. I wish to go back
to my country. There is a proverb that says, "A foreign country humiliates you but your country values you." I wish to go
back to my country. [Crying.] Not only me, but all the refugees,
Syrians, Yemenis, I wish them peace and prosperity in their
countries, and that they return to their countries and live peace-
fully in their own country with their families and people. I don't
wish for anyone to leave their country. This expatriation is hard.
Expatriation is ugly, a monster, awful.[35]

Aeysha similarly stated: "I dream for my children to go to school and have a good education. They are seven and six years old, and they don't go to school now. I wish for me to go to a safe place and also study. No one can study when they are in hardships and circumstances such as we are. When someone has peace of mind, they are able to study and pursue their education."[36] Others dream about a better future for their children – to have a better education, as education is the key for a better life. Rabia stated, "I dream to see my daughter in the best places and that is what happiness is for me."[37] And similarly, Dastow said, "I dream that my children will not live my life. I dream of a better education for them, and that they live with dignity."[38] But Safiya simply prayed for forgiveness to those who contributed to this horrible situation. She tilted her head down and said with so much pain in her voice, "I just want to say may God forgive all human beings."[39]

When I asked the interviewees whether they regretted crossing the sea, they said that had they known the ordeal that was awaiting them, they would not have gone. Yet, at the time, they had no choice but to go to Yemen. They lacked real choices – forced to flee out of desperation but ending up in a situation that might be worse than the one they left. It was a matter of life and death. They could either choose to die in their home country or escape with no papers, often without even having the time to say goodbye to their loved ones.

During their journeys, they faced suffering and abuse, had to learn a new language, familiarize themselves with a different culture, endure injustice, rebuild their shattered lives, and stand up for a better future for their children. If given a chance to work, study, and have a decent living, refugees and migrants, hand in hand with the host country, could contribute to economic development and the well-being of society. But as things stand today, women and girl refugees in Yemen are systematically denied this opportunity.

What makes the situation worse is that this is happening under the eyes of leading refugee advocates and feminist and women's rights organizations who claim to protect human rights on a global level. Even the ease of communication afforded by information technology in the digital era has not been enough to address the abuses and violations that women and girl migrants face in Yemen and increase awareness by international humanitarian organizations.

On 19 September 2016, at the UN Summit, the UN General Assembly and world leaders adopted the New York Declaration for

Refugees and Migrants. There is a series of commitments to protect migrants' human rights, provide safety, protect from violence
in all its forms, and prevent discrimination and xenophobia globally. The New York Declaration for Refugees and Migrants made
strong statements about gender equality and the rights of refugee
and migrant women and girls. Some of these commitments included:

> We recognize and will take steps to address the particular vulner-
> abilities of women and children during the journey from country
> of origin to country of arrival. This includes their potential
> exposure to discrimination and exploitation, as well as to sexual,
> physical and psychological abuse, violence, human trafficking
> and contemporary forms of slavery.
>
> We will ensure that our responses to large movements of refugees
> and migrants mainstream a gender perspective, promote gender
> equality and the empowerment of all women and girls and fully
> respect and protect the human rights of women and girls. We will
> combat sexual and gender-based violence to the greatest extent
> possible. We will provide access to sexual and reproductive health-
> care services. We will tackle the multiple and intersecting forms of
> discrimination against refugee and migrant women and girls.[40]

As it stands, these are just words on paper.

East African women and girls who migrate face gender-based violence. This violence has lasting consequences for these women and
their children, who are born from pregnancies resulting from rape.
Women may have to leave their newborn children at institutions
for adoption or with families they don't know because they cannot
care for them. The adoptive family may change location, and the
mother may never hear from the child. The child may also refuse to
acknowledge the mother when they grow up. In institutions where
children are given up for adoption, they may not know their biological mother because of a lack of legal papers. I have witnessed
these situations and heard the story of a child who was given up for
adoption and came back as an adult to search for his mother. He
was adopted by a European family and lived abroad but returned as
an adult to search for his mother. In his hand, he held a paper with
his biological mother's name and her homeland. He spent months
searching for her in the Oromia region but no one knew her, so he

Figure 2.9 | Refugees from the horn of Africa (mostly from the Oromia region of Ethiopia) stranded in Yemen, homeless with no help living and sleeping on the streets of Aden.

returned back home, heartbroken. Experiences of displacement thus stretch across generations, severing family and community relationships in time and space.

For multiple generations, East African communities have scattered across the globe in search of better opportunities and the stability they lack back home. Their stories have been of disconnection, uprootedness, injustice, and constant wandering in search of a home. This issue is personal; my mother fled the civil war at a young age, migrating to Saudi Arabia. She encountered sexual and gender-based violence. The many East Africans who cross borders and oceans in search of a home share similar experiences. The purpose of this research is not just academic: I intend to raise awareness about an issue that feels so distant from the concerns of the international community.

This study has answered many of the questions I set out to address – about the experiences of women and girl migrants, the reasons they flee, the abuses they encounter, and the ways they are systematically deprived of their rights. The dominant discourse on women and girl refugees, asylum seekers, and migrants is that they are exploited and abused. While the reports of humanitarian organizations focus on human rights violations, the exploitation of East African women and girl refugees and migrants is mostly absent. For example, to my knowledge, no organization oversees the rights of, or helps organize, domestic workers in the Middle East. The women lack access to the medical and psychological help that could improve and quicken their recovery from traumatic experiences. Women should receive more information about their rights as asylum seekers, refugees, and migrants..

All refugees and migrants face multiple challenges associated with forced displacement, but refugee women and girls face additional barriers because of their gender and social status. Women and girls are vulnerable groups. While they are not inherently vulnerable, the refugee experience places them in situations that create vulnerability. The stories of loss, hope, and survival of refugee and migrant women and girls show their strength and courage. The stories and testimonies shared here show how they have risked everything for the chance at safety. There is no wall tall enough or ocean wide enough that can stop them from trying to survive.

NOTES

1 Barbara Law and Mary Eckes, *More Than Just Surviving Handbook: ESL for Every Classroom Teacher* (Portage & Main Press, 2000).

2 UNHCR, "One Per Cent of Humanity Displaced: UNHCR Global Trends Report," 18 June 2020, https://www.unhcr.org/news/press/2020/6/5ee9db2e4/1-cent-humanity-displaced-unhcr-global-trends-report.html.

3 UNHCR, "Women," accessed 8 April 2021, https://www.unhcr.org/women.html.

4 UNHCR, "Africa," accessed 23 November 2019, https://www.unhcr.org/africa.html.

5 "Ethiopia: The Mengistu Regime and Its Impact," accessed 31 March 2021, https://memory.loc.gov/frd/etsave/et_01_08.html; Marie-Laurence Flahaux and Hein De Haas, "African Migration: Trends, Patterns, Drivers," *Comparative Migration Studies* 4, no. 1 (2016).

6 G. W. Bowersock, *The Throne of Adulis: Red Sea Wars on the Eve of Islam* (Oxford: Oxford University Press, 2013), 208.

7 Mattias Schulz Spiegel, "Buried Christian Empire Casts New Light on Early Islam," ABC News, 26 December 2012, https://abcnews.go.com/International/buried-christian-empire-casts-light-early-islam/story?id=18068163.

8 "Najahid Dynasty," accessed 23 November 2019, https://howlingpixel.com/i-en/Najahid_dynasty).

9 "Ethiopian Constitution of 1931," accessed 23 November 2019, http://www.ras-tafari.com/documents/EN_Ethiopian_Constitution_1931.pdf).

10 "Yemen and Refugees: Progressive Attitudes but Policy Void," *Forced Migration Review* (2003): https://www.fmreview.org/african-displacement/hughes.

11 "Yemen: Responding to the World's Worst Humanitarian Crisis," ReliefWeb, accessed 23 November 2019, https://reliefweb.int/report/yemen/yemen-responding-world-s-worst-humanitarian-crisis-v3).

12 UNDP Yemen, "Goal 6: Clean Water and Sanitation," accessed 23 November 2019, https://www.ye.undp.org/content/yemen/en/home/sustainable-development-goals/goal-6-clean-water-and-sanitation.html.

13 Sharks' teeth is a metaphor referring to all of the dangers migrants face along the way, from violence in their home countries to the risks of the journey to the conditions they face in Yemen.

14 "Record Numbers of Refugees and Migrants Arrive in Yemen amidst Intensifying and Complicated War – Yemen," ReliefWeb, accessed 8 April 2021, https://reliefweb.int/report/yemen/record-numbers-refugees-and-migrants-arrive-yemen-amidst-intensifying-and-complicated.

15 UNODC, *Global Study on Smuggling of Migrants* (2018).

16 Safia Abdo Mohammed, interview by author, 9 September 2019, Sana'a, Yemen.

17 Abdullah Mohammed Ali, interview by author, 14 October 2019, Sana'a, Yemen; Aeysha Mohammed Hassan, interview by author, 7 September 2019, Sana'a, Yemen; Safia Abdo Mohammed, interview by author.

18 In this context, the distinction between kidnapping and abduction is as follows: Kidnapping is when migrants are taken away when they are walking on land when they reach Yemen and walking to reach their next destination – for sexual harassment and raping the women. Abduction is when they are forced with fraud to stay detained, and the criminal gangs ask ransom from their families to set them free.

19 Dastow Ibrahim Abdullah Yusuf, interview by author, 9 September 2019, Sana'a, Yemen.

20 The interviewee is not sure of the name.

21 Rabia Saeed Yassin, interview by author, 6 November 2019, Sana'a, Yemen.

22 Safia Abdo Mohammed, interview by author.

23 Aeysha was divorced from her first husband while in the mental health facility in the city.

24 7,500 Birr is 180.24 USD, and 15,000 Birr is 361.69 USD at the time of writing.

25 Aeysha Mohammed Hassan, interview by author.

26 Anonymous, interview by author, October 2019, Sana'a, Yemen.

27 Anonymous, interview by author, October 2019, Sana'a, Yemen.

28 Anonymous, interview by author, October 2019, Sana'a, Yemen.

29 Dastow Ibrahim Abdullah Yusuf, interview by author.

30 120,000 Yemeni Riyals is 479.24 US dollars at the time of writing.

31 Safiya Osman Ali Galmo, interview by author, 28 October 2019, Sana'a, Yemen.

32 "IOM Helps Ethiopian Migrants Return Home from Sana'a, Yemen," International Organization for Migration, 10 May 2019, https://www. iom.int/news/iom-helps-ethiopian-migrants-return-home-sanaa-yemen.

33 Safia Abdo Mohammed, interview by author.

34 Saeed Massed Al-Farah, interview by author, 28 October 2019, Sana'a, Yemen.

35 Safia Abdo Mohammed, interview by author.

36 Aeysha Mohammed Hassan, interview by author.

37 Rabia Saeed Yassin, interview by author.

38 Dastow Ibrahim Abdullah Yusuf, interview by author.

39 Safiya Osman Ali Galmo, interview by author.

40 "New York Declaration for Refugees and Migrants," *International Journal of Refugee Law* 30, no. 4 (2018): 715–43.

Burundian Refugee Drummers: Practitioners of a Long-Standing, Yet Ever-Changing, Tradition

Aime Parfait Emerusenge

Dear Reader,

My name is Aime Parfait Emerusenge, and I am a Burundian refugee living in Rwanda. Before being forced to leave the country, I was pursuing a degree in education at the University of Burundi. I have since graduated from Southern New Hampshire University with a degree in management and a concentration in logistics and operations. Now, I work with a British organization called Jigsaw Consult as a Research Assistant and Youth Researcher, assisting in research about post-primary education for refugees in Rwanda and Pakistan. I am interested in education, business, and technology, and enjoy reading about these topics in my free time.

Another of my passions is history, and this is one of the reasons I became involved with Global History Dialogues and the Global History Lab. As a child, I remember having spent the whole night listening to my grandmother and asking her about the history of my country. It was like an interview. At my high school, I started reading about the two World Wars, the American Revolution, and other conflicts, and I got an opportunity to participate in a presentation entitled "Quand Les Guerres Preparent l'Avenir" (When Wars Prepare the Future). This presentation created great enthusiasm and curiosity about history among pupils of the school. Through these events, I became interested in the relationship between the past and the present, as we learn from past events and make a choice about the present and future. Global History

Dialogues was a chance to pursue my long-standing interest in history – in particular, the history of Burundi.

Burundian drummers have always been a part of my country's culture, playing for important ceremonial events. When I became a refugee, I noticed that refugee drummers used the drums differently than they did in Burundi. This raised many questions for me. I wanted to understand how the role of Burundian drummers and the usage of drums changed. Through the writing of this paper, I discovered how much it meant to me to contribute to the history of Burundian culture. This experience has led me to conduct additional historical research that I hope to share one day.

To investigate Burundian drumming, I interviewed a variety of people involved with the practice. I interviewed groups of refugee drummers living in Rwanda and talked to their representatives and the drummers themselves. This was a chance to ensure that the experiences of refugee drummers were included. I also met with people who are familiar with Burundian culture more generally. Additionally, I reviewed secondary sources such as online articles and online books. However, some books were not available online, and unfortunately, I could not access them in person, as they are in the libraries of my country. There is no doubt that they could have benefited the work. This experience captures some of the challenges of researching Burundi from outside the country with no way to access resources kept there.

Even with these limitations, I hope my paper brings you a new perspective on Burundian drums and drummers, from their role in the Burundian monarchy to the present. This may seem like a small corner of history, but I think it illuminates larger questions about the role of mobility and displacement in shaping cultural practices. Wherever you are from, and whatever your knowledge of Burundi or Burundian drumming, my hope is that this essay resonates with you. Likewise, I hope this essay informs how you read the other pieces in this anthology and vice versa. Perhaps the closest connection is to Richesse's work on the displacement of Twa people from Burundi to Rwanda and how their pottery practice has been affected by life in refugee camps. There are also clear resonances with Sandrine's essay on changes in Intore traditional dance and Phocas's research on traditional healing, both of which discuss the many ways cultural and medicinal practices change and persist in time.

Sincerely,
Aime Parfait Emerusenge

INTRODUCTION

In 2016, I saw a use of Burundian drums that surprised me. I was attending a marriage event, and I noticed that drums had been brought. The drummers took the floor and played for two hours. I wondered if they were conscious of what they were doing. Historically, the use of Burundian drums for private ceremonies and celebrations was strictly forbidden. When Burundi was still a kingdom, Burundian drums were only to be used for the Umuganuro event, a sorghum festival. After independence, Burundian drums were only for national ceremonies like the commemoration of Independence Day, Labour Day, and so on. They were not for personal or private occasions like weddings. Seeing the drums played at this marriage celebration made me wonder: How did it come to be that these drums, with all of their monarchical, and later national, significance, could be played to celebrate a personal event like a wedding?

This question sparked a desire to understand how Burundian drums and drummers have changed over time and space. While drums are generally associated with music, they often have extra-musical functions such as transmitting religious, political, or cultural messages and marking time. In Burundi, drums are credited with magical powers and considered sacred. Both their manufacture and playing involve rituals. During the Burundian monarchy, drummers were considered symbols of the king's power and status and were thought to offer him supernatural protection. In return for this protection, drummers received offerings of cattle. Drums were deeply embedded in Burundian society as an important symbolic representation of power and the social order and drummers formed a distinct and privileged group. What happened when that social order was disrupted, first by colonization and the suppression of Burundian culture, then, after independence, when drummers were forced to flee as refugees?

This paper seeks to address these questions for Burundian drummers, tracing the history of the Burundian drum from precolonial times, through colonization, and up to the present-day experiences of refugee drummers. No longer embedded in their former social and political contexts, these drummers now have another conception and usage of the drum. This essay is based on the experiences of past and present Burundian refugees. Their experience is notably different from their predecessors who had a special social status in

precolonial Burundian society. In addition, they are different from
traditional Burundian drummers who practice drumming in Burundi
today. In the past, Burundian drums were restricted to specific cultural events. However, drumming is a way for refugees to earn a
living and increase socioeconomic status. There has been a shift from
drummers forming a distinct social class with political and economic
privileges to drumming as a trade that expresses pride in Burundian
culture but which is, by virtue of its practitioners being refugees, no
longer a symbol of centralized political authority in Burundi.

Through semi-structured oral history interviews and focus groups
with Burundian refugee drummers living in Rwanda, I documented
how the drums' meaning changed after leaving the national context
and how refugee drummers think about their drums and their role
as drummers today. To identify drummers, I worked with drumming
clubs, which are the main form of organization for refugee drummers in Rwanda. To protect interviewees' identities, I refer to them
by their first names only and do not provide identifying information beyond the location where I interviewed them and the nature
of their involvement with Burundian drumming. While there are
many differences in the use of Burundian drums within and outside
Burundi, one important continuity is that women do not play the
drums and are not part of the drumming clubs. Therefore, I draw on
secondary sources to understand the role of gender in the forms of
power symbolized and reinforced by drumming culture.

This paper shows how the drums' meaning and uses have changed
over time, from the period of the Burundian monarchy, through colonization, into the post-independence national period, and, finally,
in Rwanda, following forced displacement. The essay is structured
chronologically, as the main concern is change over time. Throughout
many changes in the use of drums, one central continuity persists:
the importance of drumming as a cultural practice where questions
of political authority are contested, negotiated, and transformed.

DRUMMING IN PRECOLONIAL BURUNDI

Drumming in precolonial Burundi was intimately related to the
monarchy and its symbolic authority. Understanding the structure
of the Burundian monarchy is thus an important starting point.
Precolonial Burundian society was ruled by a king (Mwami) and
an oligarchy of officials that governed largely autonomous chief-

doms. These officials chosen from the royal princes (Baganwa), and their chiefdoms were, in turn, dominated by a cattle-owning elite.[1] The king relied on various rituals to maintain his power and authority over the dissentious princes. Most important among these was the Feast of the First Fruits, generally called Umuganuro. This word comes from the word *Kuganura*, which means "eating the sorghum paste of the new harvest." The king blessed all the seeds that were cultivated in Burundi, and the princes declared their allegiance to the king (any prince who did not attend was considered to be in rebellion). Drums played an important role in this festival. As Kameya, a former Burundian drummer now living in Kigali, Rwanda, remarked, "It is through Umuganuro that we can really understand the role of drummers and the difference that resides between these two periods [precolonial and postcolonial Burundi]. The main role of drums and drummers is summarized in what happened during the Umuganuro ceremonies."[2]

The Feast of the First Fruits was divided into several steps. The first was the coming of drums. New drums were prepared for the festival and brought ceremoniously to the palace. Then the Abaganuza, who prepared the party, arrived. They were followed by the king's soothsayers. These people were the confidants of the king who predicted happy or bad events for the king and, consequently, had considerable influence on the king's decisions. Next was the eating of the first fruits at Nyamuragura when the king ate a paste made of the first fruits of the sorghum. This was followed by the party at Buryenda, where the temple of Karyenda (the main drum) was located. Next was the ritual hunt, in which the king and the men gathered for the festival took part. After the hunt, the king distributed cattle and the products of the hunt among the people. He could select among the attendees of the ceremonies and give them cows as gifts. This process also marked the close of the ceremonies. After the king finished distributing the goods among attendees, they asked the king if they can go. When the king had given them permission, they could return to their homes.[3]

This summary of Umuganuro shows the centrality of drums and drumming, together with other forms of patronage and obeisance, to the ritual maintenance of the king's authority. The king was also the only person able to authorize the manufacture and use of drums.[4] In what follows, I explore the relationship between drums, drummers, and the king, showing how important the practice was for the precolonial monarchy.

In precolonial Burundi, music was played with many different musical instruments. Drums were, of course, musical instruments, but they were also considered sacred objects, reserved solely for rituals. They were only played under exceptional circumstances and always for ritual purposes. Major events were heralded by the beating of drums, including coronations, sovereigns' funerals, and visits of the sovereign to the various semi-autonomous chiefdoms. The drums kept rhythm with the regular cycle of the seasons, which ensured the prosperity of the herds and fields.[5] Kameya clarified the different types of drums that were used for royal events:

> Drums were even called royal drums. They were of two types: we
> had the palladium Karyenda drum, which was only brought from
> its sanctuary on very rare occasions, particularly during the rites
> associated with the Umuganuro – celebrating the sowing of the
> sorghum. Karyenda was a sacred drum, representing the sover-
> eignty of the Kingdom. It was an emblem of the monarchy, and
> it was only beaten three times, by the king, only on this occasion.
> This annual sorghum festival was [also] the occasion for a mag-
> nificent display of drummers. The drummers used another kind
> of drum while playing: Rukinzo. This drum was the secondant of
> Karyenda ... Apart from [use in] the ceremony of Umuganuro,
> [the Rukinzo] took part in the king's everyday life. It was used
> to show the time to the king and the people at the palace. That
> is, it was beaten in the morning, at midday, and before the night.
> In addition, it escorted the king in all his movements. A group of
> drummers had to go before the king, and they beat Rukinzo. Then,
> all the people around could understand that the king was in the
> vicinity. Rukinzo drums are the drums that we have nowadays.[6]

Kameya's testimony shows the intimate connection between the sound of drums and royal power, including the importance of ritual and hierarchy to this musical representation of royal authority. The drummers, because of their role in supporting royal power, formed a distinct social class within precolonial Burundian society. The drummers were not random people; they came from families that had shown talent in drumming at the beginning of the Burundian mon-archy. Over time, a lineage of royal drummers was developed. Omer, a refugee drummer living in Kigali, provided more details about one of these lineages, the Banyuka:

The example is for the people who were in charge of drums during the Umuganuro Festival. They were the Banyuka. The primary role of the Banyuka was to heal the python's pangs.[7] They were known for this by the whole kingdom. The people who met the pythons could be suffering from rheumatism. In this case, they resorted to the Banyuka, who made sacrifices to the pythons. They lived in Banga in the region of Chief Baranyanka. During the Umuganuro Festival, the Banyuka remained in the place prepared for drums. They had to keep on drumming from the beginning of the Festival to the end.[8]

While drumming was practiced by different lineages, or clans, whose prominence varied somewhat, drummers across these clans formed a distinct social category, the Batimbo (singular Umutimbo). Omer described the Batimbo thus:

Not only the Banyuka were drummers, but also other people from other clans could be in the royal drummers for the normal days. The majority of them came from Gishora, a renowned region for drummers. However, although they came from various clans, they formed a kind of social category: The Batimbo. This name was known in the whole kingdom. It was really a privilege to be among the Batimbo. When you were an Umutimbo, you had many chances to meet the king, and this was a great honour that few Burundians have had. Even if Umuganuro took place, all Burundians were concerned, but they could not all go to the king's palace. The regions were represented. In this way, it was not always easy to see the king during your lifetime. Another thing was that the society could grant you some favours as an Umutimbo.[9]

The formation of the Batimbo as a social category was a sign of the privileges of being a drummer, as well as the ways these were unevenly distributed through Burundian society. As previously mentioned, being a Burundian drummer in precolonial Burundi was mostly a matter of family ties. The culture of Burundi was established in such a way that a son inherited the job of his father. Just as a farmer had to teach his children farming activities, a drummer had to teach his sons how to play drums. Because of the ritual importance of drumming to the status and authority of the king, there were special privileges associated with being a drummer. Drummers were respected among Burundian society, and they could spend a long time at the palace drumming during the Umuganuro festivities.

Drummers were important in supporting the king's authority and the social structure over which he ruled. With the monarchy consist-ing of many distinct chiefdoms, the drums – and the king – were a symbol of unity. This symbolic unity was reinforced by the fact that the king did not belong to any of the three main ethnic groups in Burundi: the Hutu, Tutsi, and Twa. Due, in part, to their proxim-ity to the king, the Batimbo were an important and powerful part of Burundian society. As Samuel, a refugee drummer in Rwanda, said, "The Batimbo were known in the society as the people who played drums. The only privilege they had was to be able to play drums for the king and to do what the king wanted. They were not allowed to play the drums by themselves."[10] Samuel implied that the circumscriptions on the uses of Burundian drums constrained the drummers – and perhaps even that these restrictions were unfair to drummers who may have wished to engage differently with their instruments. Of course, this may reflect Samuel's perspective as a drummer who continues to practice Burundian drumming but not within the traditional ceremonial contexts of Burundi. In the next section, I address some of the traditional prohibitions on the use of Burundian drums beyond the requirement that they are only played with the authorization of the monarch.

CULTURAL TABOOS AND PROHIBITIONS
SURROUNDING THE USE OF BURUNDIAN DRUMS

In addition to needing the king's authorization, drums in precolonial Burundi were subject to various cultural taboos, some of which con-tinue today. The best-known taboo is that women were, and to this day still are, not allowed to play drums. Different perspectives about the reasons for this prohibition exist. Patrice Ntafatiro, a researcher of Burundian culture, states that during the fifteenth century, in the first years of the monarchy in Burundi, women *were* drummers too. Particular clans, including their women, were given the right to beat the drums. However, some claimed that there were cases of incest in instances where family members went into the bush to look for materials to make drums. As a result, the king and the families' elders decided that only men would be allowed to play the drums.[11] Why would men be permitted to continue drumming, but not women? When I asked some of my interviewees about this, Achille, a refugee drummer, responded, "A man has been long considered as superior to a woman in Burundian society. It would have been impossible to keep the tradition of drumming music if we choose women to continue the tradition of music."[12] Kameya supported Achille's perspective: "In case it was in the hands of the women, this kind of music would have even disappeared because women's ideas were not considered in Burundian society."[13] According to Kameya and Achille, the subordinate position of women in Burundian society would have imperiled drumming practices.

However, this is not the only existing account of why women are not allowed to play Burundian drums. According to others, the drum's design mimics the body of a woman. Samuel describes this in great detail:

> The design of a Burundi Royal Drum is said to personify the body of a woman. The female body parts represented on a typical Royal Drum are said to be: the breasts, the navel, the stomach, and the genitals. The breasts are signified by small wooden blocks around which ropes are tied and attached to a cowhide which covers the opening of the drum. The navel of the drum is a small indentation at the bottom of the drum. It is a sign of beauty in Burundian belief to have a navel which is hollow, or curves inward. The belly of the drum is the opening, which is covered by cowhide. When one beats on this skin above the belly, the noise becomes intense. As the belly in the woman carries a child, the drum carries the music to its strong interior. The genitals of the drum are supposed to be the top part covered by the cow skin and are called "Ubwami" (a euphemism in Burundian culture to symbolize the female intimate parts [which] translates as "Kingdom"). It is on this part that we beat with sticks to produce a musical rhythm that is coordinated in a spectacular way. As we imply it, it is obvious that there is a great comparison between women and drums in the Burundian culture.[14]

Perhaps more important for the prohibition of women drummers than the material characteristics of the drums are the ways drumming is imagined to enact a particular set of gendered relationships. One example is the culture surrounding women and secrecy in Burundi. Women are expected to keep secrets – to remain silent about sensitive topics, even when doing so is harmful for them. As Samuel noted, this idea is expressed idiomatically by a phrase urging a woman to keep secrets "in her belly."[15] This embodied expression of discretion and secret-keeping finds its parallel in the woman-shaped Burundian drum, which kept, according to Samuel, "not only the secret of ... tremendous music ... but also the power of the king and the unity of Burundians." Like women, drums were meant to accept the treatment they received by male drummers and still be generous by providing rhythmic music. So, while drums may have been in some ways a symbol of political and social unity, they were also a symbol of gender-based inequality.

There is a final justification offered for the exclusion of women from drum-playing. According to 80 per cent of my interviewees, the first mission of Burundian drums was, and still is, to express the power of each beat and each dance. For this reason, the drummers needed to show that in everything they did. "When people were playing drums around the king, it meant that the kingdom had strong men that could protect the kingdom. This is very important for that time when there were permanent wars between the kingdom of Burundi and other kingdoms like Rwanda and Bushi. It was also a message to the chiefs that could see the power of the king through [the playing of drums]," as Achille said.[16] In this way, the Burundian cultural mentalities attributed strength and power to men. Playing drums was a sign of manhood; it symbolized power and strength.[17]

BURUNDIAN DRUMMERS DURING COLONIZATION (1896–1962)

Burundi was first colonized by Germany at the end of the nineteenth century. During the First World War, Burundi was occupied by Belgian troops, and in 1922 (as Ruanda-Urundi, with Rwanda), made a League of Nations mandate under the supervision of Belgium. The domination and exploitation of European colonizers profoundly impacted the daily life of Burundians, including the denigration of Burundian cultural and moral values. Kiranga, who has been a mediator between Burundians and God for centuries, was degraded; Karyenda, the sacred drum, was no longer available for the king; and the king had to make commitments in the Kiganda Treaty that forced him to recognize German colonial

authority and relinquish his sovereignty as the ruler of Burundi.[18]
The Burundian drum and drummers no longer had a place in
Burundian society; even the national festival of Umuganuro was no
longer allowed. According to the colonizers, this was a way of "civ-
ilizing" the Burundian people. Jules, one of the refugee drummers,
explained: "The colonizers prevented something very special for us
and for our children: that was the Umuganuro and the festivities
around it. It was a very important feast. In addition, our drums
had no longer the value for Burundian people, it was a humilia-
tion and a brainwashing."[19] For Jules, brainwashing meant causing
Burundians to adopt another way of conceiving the world around
them, and compelling them to consider that their own beliefs were
wrong and inappropriate for "civilized" people. Burundian drums,
and the systems of royal authority and patronage that they upheld,
were considered counter to the purpose of "civilization," and the
last Umuganuro was held in 1929.[20]

BURUNDIAN DRUMMERS IN THE NATIONAL PERIOD (1962–PRESENT)

After sixty-six years of domination, the country gained its freedom thanks to a movement led by Prince Louis Rwagasoren, which
resulted in independence on 1 July 1962. The Burundian people
breathed again after a long period of domination, despite the many
wounds inflicted by colonization. When Burundi got its flag, the
drums came back. The king was still there, and it seemed likely that
the national festival (the Umuganuro) could be celebrated again;
drummers hoped their privileges would return. However, it was too
late. Catholicism had taken root in Burundian society, and many
now thought that traditional aspects of Burundian culture were pro-
fane. A new political landscape and post-independence crises also
precluded the kind of unity that Umuganuro had celebrated and
reinforced. The festival did not return on a national scale. However,
the drum did return in the new postcolonial context. As an instrument both popular and revered, it is now used for national celebrations and to honour distinguished guests. The ancient lineages of
drummers have managed to keep their art alive and, in some cases,
have had great success in popularizing it around the world. However, with the new circumstances and new global exposure have
come new fissions. Achille described one of these as follows:

There is a new generation of drummers that is trying to imitate
their elders. There is also another generation that views playing
drums as a talent that they have to exploit. The latter does not
care whether the drums are played on any occasion. Although
the Burundian government had set laws forbidding to play
drums on marriage occasions, drums are played on many similar
occasions outside of Burundi, and this is different from everything that was done in the ancient Burundi.[21]

While the government has tried to restrict the practice of drumming
to ritual occasions still connected to a central authority, some drummers are pushing for the practice to be untethered from these ceremonial occasions. While the Burundian government has passed laws
regulating when drums can be played, these laws do not apply to
the significant number of Burundians who have fled the country as
refugees since the early 1990s. Most of these refugees have gone to
the neighbouring countries of Tanzania, the Democratic Republic of
the Congo, and Rwanda. In the next section, I consider how international displacement has affected Burundian drumming, focusing
on the experiences of refugee drummers or former drummers living
in Rwanda.

BURUNDIAN REFUGEE DRUMMERS

The refugee drummers I interviewed moved to Rwanda because of
the Burundian political crisis that began in 2015. The month of April
2015 ended with demonstrations in the roads of Bujumbura, Burundi's largest city, because of a misunderstanding in the ruling terms
of the then president, Pierre Nkurunziza. Some members of the
intelligence board then attacked the demonstrators. The situation
worsened when there was an attempted coup against the president.
The failed coup resulted in extrajudicial executions on both sides,
causing refugee movements to nearby countries, including Tanzania,
the Democratic Republic of the Congo, Uganda, and Rwanda. This
paper focuses on refugees living in Rwanda, which is where I, as a
Burundian refugee, currently live and work.
    Among the refugees in Rwanda are men who were drummers
in Burundi, though many men remained in Burundi and continue
to play the drums there. The refugee drummers I interviewed live in
various cities in Rwanda and the Mahama refugee camp, located in

eastern Rwanda. When they arrived in Rwanda, they did not give up their passion for the drums, despite the difficulties of their situation. They formed different clubs with weekly rehearsals so they could continue practicing and developing their musical skills. Because the Rwandese people are very familiar with Burundian drums, as many have visited Burundi, the clubs have had a relatively easy time gaining footholds in Rwanda. Moreover, because the rhythm of Rwandese dances is similar to the melodies of the Burundian drummers, it has been easy to put them together and create a mixture of the Rwandese and Burundian songs.

While the drumming clubs are similar in many ways – such as their exclusion of women – they are also very different. Some were created to preserve and teach about Burundian culture. Others were not so invested in cultural preservation and instead sought ways for members to develop their talents as ways to earn money and recognition. Still others have been established, in Mahama, as a way to occupy young people who are stuck waiting in the camp.

The different purposes of the drumming clubs reflect the changing relationship between Burundian drumming and the society where it is practiced. These changes have generated significant controversy both within and outside Burundi. To better understand the different perspectives on refugee drumming, I turned to my interviewees. Achille offered one perspective, saying:

Playing drums is a talent [like] anything else: singing, playing football, etc. In this way, a talent is used anyhow you want. That is why, as a refugee, it is understandable that you can create a club and work together in order to give to the audience the best you have and earn your everyday living.[22]

For Achille, the drum can be used to make a living outside of the traditional ceremonial contexts where permitted in Burundi. But this doesn't mean that drumming loses all its cultural significance simply because it has become more commodified. For Achille and some other authors, playing the drum is also a way of being an "ambassador" for Burundian culture.[23] Drumming outside the national context is thus a way to make a living while preserving a sense of connection to Burundi despite experiences of forced migration and refugeehood.

However, for many drummers and observers, there is a tension in the separation of drumming from its ritual contexts. Kameya reflected on some of the changes he has seen in the use of Burundian drums and the ways they have been separated from the royal or national functions they once played.

> The situation has changed in the usage of Burundian drums. Even in Burundi, Karyenda, the sacred drum, has disappeared during the colonization, and drums are played for official parties. Although the Burundian government forbade the use of drums during the personal festivities for the drummers who remained in the country, the situation has not changed. For Burundian refugees, many clubs are earning money through playing drums and they are not ready to stop. This is because people love them, and they are ready to pay such festivities. There is a lot of interest for people who are endowed with the skills to play Burundian drums. They are no longer representing the Burundian culture. They are now globally known and played by anyone. Here, we have to say that even people who are not Burundians are now in these refugee Burundian drummers' groups.[24]

For Kameya, the changes that have accompanied forced displacement – such as the use of drums at private events and the inclusion of non-Burundians in drumming groups – mean that the practice no longer represents Burundian culture in the way it once did. The fact that non-Burundians are now playing Burundian drums is concerning for him as it dilutes the cultural significance of the drums and their role in Burundian nationhood and political authority.

This perspective is one shared, in part, by the Burundian government. Within Burundi, the government has gone to great lengths to preserve restrictions on drumming. Since 2014, when UNESCO recognized Burundian drumming as part of the "Intangible Cultural Heritage of Humanity," the stakes surrounding when, where, by whom, and for what purposes Burundian drumming can be practiced have increased.[25] In 2017, Burundian Decree No. 100/196 tried to regulate the use of Burundian drums and restrict their use to approved cultural purposes. It also charged anyone wishing to play drums a fee. However, Burundian laws do not apply to refugees living in Rwanda or elsewhere who continue to play their drums for non-ceremonial purposes and to make a living. A flashpoint in this controversy occurred in 2019. The Himbaza Club, a group of refugee drummers living in Rwanda, performed in East Africa Got

Talent (EAGT).[26] Though the drummers identified themselves as Burundian refugees performing Burundian drumming, their outfits and drums bore the colours of the African Union rather than the Burundian flag, as is traditional. While some viewers argued that the performance was an important display of Burundian culture, and refugee culture in particular, others – including a senior advisor to the Burundian president – said the performance was inauthentic, amounting to nothing more than cultural theft by Rwanda.[27] Burundian drums thus became a symbol of older and broader tensions between movements for pan-African unity and the securitization of national sovereignty in the wake of European colonization.

For drumming to have gained such regional and international attention through the performance of artists who have been alienated from Burundi by ethnic and political violence likely displeased Burundi's president, as indicated by his attempts to centralize and control the use of the drums within Burundi. At the same time, by announcing their heritage and identity as Burundian refugees, the drummers continue to believe that their performances represent Burundian culture, even if they wear different colours.

This contemporary conflict over the proper practice of Burundian drumming, while rooted in recent events, echoes back to the long history of the tradition. From the time of the Burundian monarchy, drums have been a site of contestation and an instrument of power. During the early national period, too, they were used to confer legitimacy on the new government through civic ceremonies. Now, with Burundian citizens forced to seek refuge, the drums have emerged again as a place where questions of power and authority are worked out through cultural practice. Though drumming for a living is a pragmatic choice for many refugees, it is also a way of implicitly contesting the Burundian state's attempted monopolization of the practice. For some, the decoupling of drumming from Burundian state authority and the more widespread diffusion of the practice alter something fundamental, causing them to question whether refugee drummers like the Himbaza Collective are performing Burundian drumming or something else. For others, drumming in exile not only preserves Burundian culture, but also inscribes drumming with new meanings, but in ways continuous with prior transformations in the function and practice of drumming. For example, Desire Ngarukiyintwari created a cultural club in Mahama refugee camp to provide young refugees with access to after-school activities, including Burundian drumming. While youth are not involved in the ceremonial rites historically associated with Burundian drumming, learning to play drums in the camp keeps them connected to their cultural heritage and Burundian identity. There is a final important continuity between refugee drumming and drumming practiced in Burundi. Women are still not allowed to participate. While their exclusion was formalized by decree in Burundi, even among the refugee drumming community, women are not permitted to play the drums.[28]

CONCLUSION

Burundian drums have played a significant role in the political and cultural history of Burundi. As this essay has illustrated, this role has changed over time and space. Originally both a representation and affirmation of the king's authority, and one of the most important symbols of Burundian unity, the drums came to fulfill a different, though similar, function after Burundi gained its independence in 1962. Performed for civic ceremonies and other public events, the drums continued to be associated with a central authority. But ethnic and political conflicts and displacements over the last decade have fractured Burundian society and caused many Burundians, including many drummers, to seek refuge elsewhere, changing how drums are used. Now, though the drums continue to be an important national symbol, they are also used by drummers in exile to contest the Burundian government's attempt to control the practice. For many refugees, drumming is both a way to remain connected to their culture and a vital source of income.

Burundians disagree about whether these changes are positive or negative; some even suggest that the practices of refugee drummers are so distant from traditional drumming that their performances are no longer representative of a distinctly Burundian heritage. However, as this paper has shown, the meanings and uses of the drums have never been static. Further research might address how the physical practices and performances of drumming have changed and remained the same over time and whether those changes are linked to political events. There is also a need for more research on how the commodification of drumming affects drummers and viewers. To what extent is this consistent with the historical privileges, both symbolic and material, afforded to Burundian drummers? To what extent do the dynamics of commodification, combined with the separation of drumming from its traditional ritual contexts, represent a distinct relationship to the practice for drummers and audiences? Some authors have posited a sharp tension between "heritage" and "commodification," but the experiences of refugee drummers suggest that this binary is an oversimplification of their relationship to the practice.[29]

To return to the question that initially sparked my research: How could Burundian drums, traditionally understood as symbols of royal power and authority and, to this day, permitted only at official events in Burundi, be played at a private wedding celebration? The answer is at once complex and very simple. The various processes – from colonization to national independence to forced displacement and more – that have affected the meaning and uses of Burundian drums are very complicated, though I have tried to disentangle them in this essay. But simply put, Burundian drumming was never a static cultural practice. It was always connected to wider relationships of power – hence European colonists' determination to end the practice and its renewed importance in the post-independence period. As the political and social context in which the drums were played changed, so too did the ways drums and drummers relate to that context. While it may seem like playing ceremonial drums at a private wedding signifies the stripping away of the drums' political meaning, arguably, it means that the drums have simply acquired a new political valence in the context of forced displacement and refuge. Burundian drums no longer represent the monarch or the authority of the central government – though those aspects of their history remain present. Instead, perhaps more so now than ever before, they have become a visible, audible locus for questions about what it means to be Burundian to be worked out, contested, and transformed.

NOTES

1 African Democracy Encyclopedia Project, "Precolonial Burundi," Electoral Institute for Sustainable Democracy in Africa, 2010, https://www.eisa.org/wep/buroverview1.htm.

2 Kameya, interview by author, 23 August 2019, Kigali, Rwanda. Kameya is a Burundian refugee drummer living in Rwanda. He participated in two focus groups that gathered members of his drumming club performing in Kigali, Rwanda. What he said was both his personal view and he referred

to the history of Burundi, as the history of Burundi was transmitted through the word of mouth in the ancient Burundi, where elders told stories to their children or the youth in general.

3 Joseph Rugomana and Firmin Rodegem, "La fête des prémices au Burundi," *Africana Linguistica* 5, no. 1 (1971): 205–54.

4 Jean Baptiste Nkulikiyinka, "Music and Musical Instruments of Burundi," n.d., http://music.africamuseum.be/instruments/english/burundi/burundi.html.

5 Ibid.

6 Kameya, interview by author.

7 Pythons are one of the dangerous snakes that, according to traditional Burundian belief, could cause pangs when you see them. This was common in the Burundian tradition, and there were people specialized in healing them.

8 Omer, interview by author, 12 July 2019, Kigali, Rwanda.

9 Ibid.

10 Samuel, interview by author, 26 July 2019, Nyamata, Rwanda.

11 Desire Nimubona, "Why the Women of Burundi Are Banned from Playing the Drums," *Culture Trip*, 31 May 2018, https://theculturetrip.com/africa/burundi/articles/why-the-women-of-burundi-are-banned-from-playing-the-drums/.

12 Achille, interview by author, 7 September 2018, Kigali, Rwanda.

13 Kameya, interview by author.

14 Samuel, interview by author.

15 Samuel, interview by author.

16 Achille, interview by author.

17 BBC News Afrique, "A la Découverte du Tambour burundais, un instrument interdit aux femmes," 2017.

18 The Kiganda Treaty was signed between King Mwezi Gisabo and the first colonizers (the Germans). Through this treaty, the king ended any resistance to colonization. In addition, he accepted to pay 424 cows as compensation for what his army destroyed during the resistance.

19 Jules, interview by author, 7 August 2019, Nyamata, Rwanda.

20 Jean-Pierre Chrétien, "Le 'Vol' des Tambours du Burundi," Lamenparle, 2019, https://lamenparle.hypotheses.org/1013.

21 Achille, interview by author.

22 Ibid.

23 Ibid.; Audace Mbonyingingo, Gérard Birantamije, and Constantin Ntiranyibagira, "The Burundian Drum is at a Crossroads between Heritage and Commodification," LSE Blog, 22 June 2020, https://blogs.lse.

ac.uk/africaatlse/2020/06/22/burundian-drumming-crossroads-heritage-commodification-legislation/.

24 Kameya, interview by author.

25 UNESCO, "Ritual Dance of the Royal Drum," last modified 2014, https://ich.unesco.org/en/RL/ritual-dance-of-the-royal-drum-00989.

26 Achille, interview by author; to view the clip of the competition online, see https://www.youtube.com/watch?v=5XrRpVijWaQ.

27 "Burundi Accuses Rwanda of Stealing Drums Culture and Doing It So Badly," *The Chronicles*, 23 August 2019, https://www.chronicles.rw/2019/08/23/burundi-accuses-rwanda-of-stealing-music-performance-group/; Edmund Kagire, "War of Drums: Rwanda Laughs Off Burundi Drum Anger," KT *Press Blog*, 25 August 2019, https://www.ktpress.rw/2019/08/war-of-drums-rwanda-laughs-off-burundi-drum-anger/.

28 Audace Mbonyingingo and Ntiranyibagira Constantin, "Beating Drums or Beating Women? An Analysis of the Drum Universe in Burundi," *Journal of Postcolonial Writing and World Literatures* 1, no. 1 (2020): 15–30.

29 Mbonyingingo et al., "The Burundian Drum."

PART TWO

Cultures in Motion: Continuity and Change in Displacement

A focus on the movement of cultural practices through time and space characterizes the three essays in this section. They address both the process of transmission, considering material culture and the circulation of ideas and knowledge, and the meanings that adhere to the performance of certain practices in new contexts. Questions of ownership and authorship, identity, and the possibility for art to create space for dissent weave through all three essays.

Richesse Ndiritiro's research on Twa people living in Mahama refugee camp connects pottery making to issues of identity, discrimination, and inclusion. While the multicultural context of the camp and the exigencies of camp life have led, in some cases, to the erosion of prejudice against the Twa, some Twa feel the need to abandon their identity and attendant practices (such as pottery) to avoid discrimination and integrate into their new environment. Even though practices of camp administration are superficially egalitarian – for instance, not discriminating against the Twa in the allocation of land – the paradigm in which they operate remains exclusionary. For instance, the Twa believe it is important to leave an area where a relative has died. But assumptions about static land tenure mean that kind of traditional mobility is not possible, at least within the confines of the camp environment.

Lazha Taha's essay concerns another minoritized group: Kurdish people in Iraq. How can current artistic and journalistic practices address the destruction of Kurdish heritage? Taha's interviews with Kurdish photojournalists show how they work to create new narratives and archives of Kurdish experience. She also considers the development of the photojournalism community through workshops, training, agencies, and other institutions and communities of practice. Here, the interface between foreign photojournalists – who often bring with them funding and professional training, as well as connections to major news outlets – and local photojournalists becomes key. Taha's careful exploration of the different ways each group photographs the region, and the purpose behind their images, underscores the importance of local vision and insight in creating the documentary and visual record.

Finally, Alain Jules Hirwa's essay on hip-hop in Africa dovetails with Taha's focus on the reverberation of artistic practices in different contexts. What does hip-hop's irreverence, its origins as protest music in the US context, mean for its adoption and adaptation in Africa? Considering examples from Kenya and Rwanda, primarily, Hirwa argues that hip-hop constitutes a form of "mental migration," allowing artists and listeners access to a refuge where the expression of dissent in contexts of widespread oppression is more feasible. African hip-hop is not derivative, Hirwa argues, but rather a musical genre at once particular to local context and in conversation with a global community.

This tension between local and global is an undercurrent in all these essays. What possibilities do imported practices offer to meet local needs? What processes of negotiation and creation happen at the intersection of local and global? How do displacement and marginalization inflect those processes? There are no easy or universal answers here but the essays in this section offer three ways of approaching the complicated question of what it means to create art, and what art means, in contexts of displacement.

4

The Impacts of Displacement on Twa Culture and Tradition

Richesse Ndiritiro

Dear Reader,
My name is Richesse Ndiritiro, and I am a Burundian refugee living
in Rwanda. It is with great pride that I share my work on the Twa
ethnic group as part of this volume. Looking back just five years, I
had no idea that I would write something like this. I grew up and
studied in the Francophone system until 2015, when I found myself
in Rwanda (which uses the Anglophone system). The process of integrating myself into the Anglophone system was never easy. If anyone
were to see my first application sample at the Kepler University
Program, they would see that my English skills were far from perfect.
Being a part of this anthology and going through the entire writing
and revising process in English demonstrates my progress and commitment, and I am glad to share my work with you here.

Through the Kepler program, I studied healthcare management with a concentration in global perspectives at Southern
New Hampshire University. Along the way, as a Kepler scholar,
I have been a Refugee Student Ambassador, Students Refugee
Representative in the Connected Learning in Crisis Consortium
(CLCC), and a member of the Students Engagement Task Force
for the CLCC, where I advocate for better access to higher education opportunities for refugees. I am passionate about promoting
human rights and well-being by fostering equity and addressing the
social determinants of health. I spend most of my free time writing
poems as a way of expressing my thoughts and values, listening to
music as a way of understanding myself better and blending reality

and imaginary spaces, and working out to improve my health and well-being.

I know that if you, as a reader, had the chance to meet me in person, the first question would not be about my education or hobbies but rather, "Why this topic? Why Twa as a minority group?" (The Twa are an Indigenous ethnic group living in the Great Lakes region of Eastern Africa, forming a minoritized population in Burundi, Rwanda, Uganda, and Congo.)

One afternoon in 2017, as Tony (a Rwandese classmate studying communications) and I walked from the campus to our hostels, we shared our different perspectives on minority groups in both Rwanda and Burundi. Rwanda and Burundi share similar beliefs, cultures, and values and even have the same ethnic groups. Therefore, our discussion was based on understanding perceptions of the Twa minority group in both Burundian and Rwandan contexts. However, though Tony and I thought we could write something based on our discussion, Tony was prohibited from using Indigenous languages within the Rwandan community. When the Global History Dialogues class was introduced in 2019, I saw it as an opportunity to carry out my discussion with Tony.

Indeed, my research topic focuses on the overlooked experiences of Twa living in the Mahama refugee camp and how their story has changed since they settled in refugee camps in 2015. Though deciding on this topic was easy, carrying out the research was challenging but ultimately worth it. Research on ethnic difference and discrimination in Rwanda is extremely sensitive. Given the controversies and prohibitions surrounding the use of Indigenous languages in Rwanda, I had to be exceedingly careful during my interviews about my choice of terms and how I asked some questions. For instance, some questions would be all right to some people and objectionable to others. The flexibility of oral history interviews allowed me to adapt my questions and process to fit the different contexts in which I interviewed people for this project. Nevertheless, both the way I carried myself and the ways interviewees shared their stories and perspectives with me were shaped by these concerns about such a sensitive topic, even if unconsciously.

Finally, I would like to share my gratitude to Marcia and Kate, who have been there for me since the beginning of the Global History Dialogues project.

Sincerely,
Richesse Ndiritiro

INTRODUCTION

"Mobility" is an ambiguous term encompassing both the voluntary movements of nomadic and semi-nomadic subsistence practices and forced displacement due to state or ethnic violence. Considering the Twa of the Great Lakes region, this essay explores the ways different kinds of mobility – both voluntary and forced, within and across the borders of nation-states – affect cultural practices and perceptions of them. I show that the foreclosure of traditional forms of voluntary mobility, such as pastoralism, led to the adoption of new cultural and economic practices like pottery making instead of hunting and gathering. Forced displacement has given rise to spaces like refugee camps, which have somewhat reduced the prejudices confronted by the Twa. However, as I argue, the burden of overcoming discrimination still falls on the Twa, many of whom feel compelled to abandon certain cultural and economic practices to fit in and whose traditional lifestyles are still precluded by the spatial organization and immobilities of camp life.

The Great Lakes Twa are an Indigenous ethnic group living in the Great Lakes region of Eastern Africa. They form a minority population in Burundi, Rwanda, Uganda, and the Democratic Republic of the Congo. Because of their semi-nomadic traditional lifestyle and the forced displacements they have endured because of state and ethnic violence, voluntary and forced mobility have deeply shaped Twa culture. These movements created disparities among the Twa and between the Twa and other ethnic groups, such as the Tutsis and Hutus. This paper asks how displacement has affected Twa culture and traditions over time, as well as how displacement has affected non-Twa perceptions of the Twa. In particular, this paper considers pottery culture among Burundian Twa living in Mahama refugee camp in Rwanda. I conducted interviews with both Twa and members of other ethnic groups over several months in 2019. These interviews were semi-structured, and given the sensitive nature of this topic, I carefully adapted my questions and language based on who I was interviewing. My fieldwork was multi-sited, including some interviewees resident in Mahama refugee camp and others in Kigali.

I will begin with a brief overview of some of the different stories that surround the creation of the Burundian kingdom and how those connect to other ethnic groups (Hutu, Tutsi, and Twa) that live in Burundi today. Then, I will address the shift from a mostly nomadic lifestyle to one based on the production of pottery that Twa adopted in response to the privatization or repurposing of their traditional lands. I distinguish between internal and external displacement to nuance my discussion of mobility and Twa pottery practice. Finally, I summarize how attitudes toward the Twa and their traditional practices have both changed and persisted over time. Perhaps most importantly, I show that ostensibly neutral or equitable policies introduced in international contexts like refugee camps tend to perpetuate, albeit unintentionally, the exclusion and marginalization of the Twa.

BACKGROUND: THE BURUNDIAN MONARCHY AND CONTEMPORARY ETHNIC GROUPS IN BURUNDI AND RWANDA

The people known as the Twa were the first inhabitants of the Burundian kingdom. They occupied the Great Lakes region before the foundation of the Burundian or Rwandan kingdoms in the seventeenth century. The Batwa were descendants of the pygmoid (pygmy) hunter-gatherers. They lived throughout the Great Lakes region of Africa (today the Eastern Democratic Republic of the Congo, Uganda, Rwanda, and Burundi).[1] They were first joined by Bantu farmers (agriculturists) from Central Africa, who were seeking the best land to settle (these people were later called the Hutus), and then by cattle raisers (pastoralists from the north or the northeast seeking land to settle for their cattle; later called the Tutsi).[2] Thus, there came to be three different groups residing in the Great Lakes region. However, only in the present-day territory of Rwanda and Burundi did these groups become the main ethnic groups, the so-called Batwa, Bahutu, and Batutsi. In fact, after the arrival of the Bahutu and Batutsi, these groups came to outnumber the nomadic Batwa.

There are different histories about the foundation of the first Burundian monarchy in the seventeenth century, some of which are based on myths passed down orally. However, there are two main stories about the foundation of the first monarchy: the cycle of Nkoma and the cycle of Kanyaru. In the version of the Nkoma cycle, the first king of Burundi was Ntare Rushatsi, a son of a certain Jabwe who slept with his brother's (Nsoro's) wife. He got the name of Cambarantama, which referred to the sheepskin he wore. In the Kanyaru cycle, Ntare Rushatsi's aunt was the wife of a magician. The magician prophesized that Ntare would be the king of Burundi if he crossed the Kanyaru River and killed a beast that was terrorizing the population. Ntare Rushatsi crossed the river, killed the beast, and made it into an offering. Then, the population declared him king.[3]

There are also different stories about the succession of kings. The Burundian kings would follow the cycle of the names Ntare, Mwezi, Mutaga, and Mwambutsa. However, there have been different findings on how many kings reigned in the Burundian monarchy, whereby there are long cycles of more than sixteen kings and short cycles of around eight kings. The first monarchy was founded in 1680 by Ntare Rushatsi Cambarantama, and the last monarchy ended in 1966. The last king was Charles Ndizeye or Ntare V. In 1966, the year of the last monarch, Michel Micombere founded the first republic as the first president of Burundi. Until the late nineteenth century, Burundi had a society that was based on social classes, families, or clans, not ethnic groups. There were the Mwami (King), Baganwa (Princes), Abatware (Chiefs), and the Abashingantahe, who were supporters and advisors in the hierarchy. For instance, the Baganwa are not an ethnic group but a family or the descendants of the king or king's family. Other families were Abajiji, Abahima, Abanyarwanda, Abenengwe, Abanyakarama, and so on. The categories of Batutsi (now commonly called Tutsi) and Bahutu (Hutu) were assigned to these families based on whether they raised cattle or were farmers, respectively.

However, everything changed during and after colonization. Burundi was colonized by Germany from 1896 to 1916 and by Belgium from 1916 to 1962. In these times, the population was classified as primarily Tutsi or Hutu. These classifications, unlike the earlier versions that were dependent on a family's main livelihood, were based on physical appearance (taller people with long noses were classified as Tutsi, shorter people with flat nose were classified as Hutu, and the shortest were designated Batwa). These classifications, established while Burundi was a Belgian colony, sorted Burundians into different ethnic groups known as Tutsi, Hutu, and Twa. (These are the designations for individuals, while the proper terms for groups of people use the prefix Ba-, as in Batwa.) These ethnic distinctions became the basis for conflict and discrimination in the colonial and postcolonial period.

INTERNAL DISPLACEMENT: VOLUNTARY
AND INVOLUNTARY MOBILITY IN BURUNDI

The Batwa were traditionally hunter-gatherers living a nomadic
lifestyle. Presently, there are between 69,500 and 87,000 Twa in
the Great Lakes region, comprising about 0.2 to 0.7 per cent of
the region's total population.[4] However, the Twa have been disproportionately impacted by changes in land use and control imposed
by postcolonial governments. These changes include government
occupation and control of forest areas to create parks, reserves, and
spaces for military training. In this section, I distinguish between
voluntary and involuntary mobility and describe how both forms
have shaped Twa culture and subsistence practices. Voluntary mobility includes Twa cultural and subsistence practices, such as hunting
and gathering, while involuntary mobility includes forcible internal displacement. The two kinds of mobility are intertwined, with
prejudices against nomadic hunting and gathering – and against the
Twa more generally – informing both everyday practices and government programs that not only failed to support Twa livelihoods,
but actively excluded them from access to the forests and lands they
used to sustain themselves for centuries.

The Twa have experienced a long history of displacement within
Burundi, dating to the movement of pastoralists into the Great
Lakes region. Their hunter-gatherer lifestyle was initially disrupted
by deforestation that accompanied the arrival of agriculturists and
pastoralists. These newcomers took control over the forested land
that was the source of the Twa's livelihoods, and the Twa became
dependent on the farmers and herders.[5] Many Twa became labourers
on the farms of the more recently arrived agriculturalists. However,
when their labour was not needed, landowners would force the Twa
to move off their lands while denying them access to the forest eco-
systems they used for subsistence.[6] The Twa became a small minority
population on their ancestral lands.

While the Twa faced exclusion and displacement even prior to
the consolidation of the Burundian monarchy, the extent and form
of this discrimination have changed over time. During the period
of the Burundian monarchy before European colonization, the Twa
worked as employees of the king, serving as dancers, entertain-
ers, and potters (however, pottery was not their primary source
of income at this time).[7] In addition, the royal family would grant

them land and they would work as the king's messengers and warriors. Some of them gained rank and favour from the king.[8] So, while marginalized from their traditional hunting and gathering practices by the development of agriculture and pastoralism, the social hierarchy was flexible enough to permit mobility for some Twa who managed to gain royal favour. However, things changed radically after the fall of the monarchy. For instance, in Rwanda, as the king (Mwami) was from the Tutsi ethnic group and the first republic was composed of people from the Hutu ethnic group, the Twa that had received the favour of the king were considered Tutsi sympathizers.[9] Indeed, as Clemence Bideri and Hans Petter Hergum note, the Twa have often been pulled into conflicts between the Hutu and Tutsi people as a result of their minority status.[10] This has had devastating effects for the Twa, who are now widely discriminated against.

Salvator, a sixty-year-old Twa man who moved to Mahama refugee camp in 2015, reflected on how this dynamic played out in interpersonal interaction: "Before 1980, people were united and there was no discrimination because we would share and drink beer from the same bottle. However, from 1980 or 1985, the topic of ethnic groups started, whereby people would not call a person by his or her name rather by the name of the ethnic group he or she belongs."[11] Other ethnic groups now consider it taboo to eat with Twa people and even to use the same utensils. Onesphore, a Burundian student living in Rwanda, said, "When I was a child, I used to see Twa coming home to beg for food and clothes. When we gave them food, they never used [a] table; they took the plate of food from the table and put them on the floor and ate from the floor."[12] This story highlights many common stereotypes about the Twa: that they are poor and dirty and that coming into contact with them can contaminate non-Twa. Stereotypes and discrimination are used to justify the marginalization of the Twa and the difficulties they experience in interacting with other communities.

Traditionally, the Twa were dependent on movement through the forested landscapes of Burundi for subsistence, making use of a wide variety of plants and animals to survive. Importantly, in addition to moving around to make use of forest resources, the Twa also have a practice of moving away from any place where a family member has died. This mobile lifestyle came into conflict with agriculture and livestock raising, which involved clearcutting these all-important

forests. The Burundian population depends on land for its livelihood, but in different ways that have come into increasing conflict
as pressure on land has increased over time.

Burundi now has the second-highest population density in Africa,
meaning the average acreage per farmer is less than one hectare.[13]
According to USAID, as of early 2021, 90 per cent of the population
were agriculturists.[14] Unlike the Hutus and Tutsis, few Twa possess
land. Few were granted lands from the king or royal family before
1959, and only 3 per cent received land during the land reforms that
were implemented when Burundi became independent in 1962. After
independence, those few Twa who did receive land from the royal family were considered Tutsi sympathizers and forced to leave their land.[15]
The entrenchment of ethnic categories during colonization continued
to harm the Twa following independence with national reforms –
like land reform – failing to benefit them in any meaningful way. In
addition, the government took the forested land that the Twa used
for wildlife conservation, larger agriculture projects, military training, and farming. Hunting was prohibited in 1970.[16] The Twa never
received compensation or replacement land.[17] Many are now dependent labourers, servants, or landless potters scraping out what living
they can without access to the forests that used to provide for them.[18]

EXTERNAL DISPLACEMENT: FLIGHT TO RWANDA

Persecution has caused many Twa to flee Burundi to neighbouring
Rwanda. Both countries have experienced ethnic violence since 1959,
including massive killings in Burundi and genocide in Rwanda.[19]
Though the Twa were not typically the main targets of these fights,
they have often been the victims of violence as suspected sympathizers of one or the other main groups in the conflict.[20] According to the 2018 Mid-Year Report from the United Nations High
Commissioner for Refugees (UNHCR), 68,306 Burundian refugees
have been hosted in Rwanda since 2015, the year that the Mahama
refugee camp opened, becoming the sixth (and largest) refugee camp
in Rwanda.[21] The main factors that influenced the movement across
the border were war and political crisis. Thierry, a refugee living in
Rwanda and pursuing higher education, recalled, "Considering the
poverty I lived in since my childhood, I have never thought of crossing the border. But the war did it."[22] Violence was the catalyst that
drove many ethnic Twa to leave Burundi.

Because the Twa live throughout the countries of the Great Lakes region and face similar prejudices in all of them, moving to refugee camps such as Mahama does not free the Twa from discrimination. However, the exigencies of camp life and the (at least formal) equality of treatment by the camp administration have lessened the exclusion many Twa faced. This change is demonstrated by the perspective of a non-Twa woman whom I will call Beatrice. Beatrice arrived in Mahama refugee camp in 2015 with her husband and three-year-old son. Her neighbourhood was home to both Twa and non-Twa residents. She shared with me some of the stereotypes she believed about the Twa before she began to live side by side with them in the camp.

> Before living with Twa, what I knew was that they were dirty persons and people that can never get clean. So, talking with Twa was a shame to the family and to the community. In addition, now my son plays with Twa child[ren], which I tolerate because I realized that they are like other people and good ones.
> However, if my family knew that my son lives with Twa children and in Twa neighbourhood, they would worry about my child's health, hygiene, and sanitation.[23]

Beatrice's account shows that her experiences have lessened some of the prejudices she was taught before moving to Mahama. However, she remains worried about what her family would think, knowing that they continue to hold more negative feelings about the Twa and what it means to socialize with them, as her son now does.

The inverse perspective was offered by Emerence, a Twa woman who had also lived in Mahama since 2015. As Emerence said,

> In [the] early 1990s, Twa could not exchange bride[s] with others, which has made our ethnic group and the family circle too small. However, since we are put together with other people in the refugee camp, we have adapted to live with them through sharing neighbourhood and some material. It has opened doors to many things, even exchanging bride[s].[24]

The Twa were a close and isolated community that kept its distance from outsiders; therefore, it took living in close quarters with other communities to disrupt the ideas that the Twa and non-Twa had

about each other. Living together in the Mahama refugee camp collapsed the social distance between the Twa and other ethnic groups
and eroded some of the prejudice against them through simple proximity. The diversity and mixing in refugee camps facilitated their
integration into the new community. In Rwandan refugee camps,
refugees live all together; share the same utensils, food, and hygienic
materials; and attend the same schools. These circumstances have
led to greater social and cultural integration and even the joining
of families through marriage, something that might have remained
unthinkable outside the camp context. At the same time, both wom-
en's accounts show that prejudice toward the Twa has not vanished
entirely and concerns about what it means to socialize with them
persist for many non-Twa. Displacement across international borders to the liminal space of Mahama refugee camp marks both
change and continuity for the Twa. In the next section, I consider
what this has meant for Twa pottery practice, which, since the colonial period, has become one of their key sources of livelihood.

POTTERY PRACTICE AND PREJUDICE IN
THE MAHAMA REFUGEE CAMP

The Twa began relying on pottery as an important source of income
because they were excluded from access to forests and land in
Burundi.[25] Pottery culture has come to distinguish the Twa from the
other ethnic groups, and it is now central to their identity. However,
for many Twa, this pottery practice did not last long. For instance,
some Twa who fled from Burundi to Rwanda in 2015 stopped creating pottery for many reasons, including a scarcity of raw materials
and desire to distance themselves from Twa identity. When offered
the opportunity, many Twa chose to abandon their cultural practices to achieve a greater measure of social acceptance. Based on oral
history interviews with Twa potters in the Mahama refugee camp,
this section illustrates the factors that shaped their decisions about
whether to continue making pottery.

   The Twa continue to face discrimination in the camp, even if it
has somewhat lessened. This means that some Twa feel ashamed of
making pots because they fear their neighbours, who, in the refugee
camp, are of different backgrounds, will recognize them as Twa and
look down on them. Some even abandon pottery because they want
to overcome the stereotypes that other ethnic groups have about the

Figure 4.1 | A Twa potter in Mahama Refugee Camp in 2019. Despite lacking access to many of the proper materials, Twa continue to make their traditional pottery in the camp.

Twa and gain community acceptance. "Making pot[s], in refugee camp, is not that easy. I am living with people from different backgrounds and communities. I feel ashamed though I would like to make pottery," Salvator noted.[26] Salvator's words show that while pottery remained a part of his identity and he wished to continue this work, he felt shame from such a public display of his marginalized ethnic identity. Many Twa share Salvator's perspective. They believe that if they were to stop making pottery, they would feel greater community acceptance. "Living with other people makes us feel accepted in the community. In Burundi, we were living in different sites that the government built for us. Within the community, people were the same; there were no outsiders, only Twa. Therefore, [now that we are in refugee camps,] to avoid discrimination based on our culture, some of us quit pottery. If you make pots, you are a Twa. That name angers us all," Emerence notes.[27] Some Twa have felt compelled to give up pottery in the hopes of fitting in better with the diverse community in the camp. This highlights one of the paradoxes of the impact of external displacement on Twa culture and identity: while the Twa experience less overt discrimination in Mahama than they did in Burundi, they also feel that if they changed aspects of their identity, they could escape the remaining prejudices they do confront. The somewhat greater sociocultural mobility and flexibility of the camp are, thus, contingent upon erasing lingering markers of that which is too different.

There are material reasons for the shift away from pottery, too. Land scarcity in the camp and the different materials available in Mahama versus Burundi have made it hard to continue the pottery tradition. The clay from the refugee camp is different from the clay used in Burundi. Salvator recalled that "finding clay for a person who does not possess any land is very difficult and complicated. We used the clay found in our employer's field back in our country or we could walk kilometers to find them."[28] Even in Burundi, accessing materials could be a challenge; in Mahama, with limited access to land and mobility, it is even harder. Moreover, what materials are available are inferior compared to those in Burundi. Emerence described for me why this was:

> In Burundi, to make the pot we used three types of clay such as nabirambira, namiryige, and nabasore; however, any type of clay can make the pot strong as long as it is mixed with Intsibo.[29] Nevertheless, here in refugee camp there is no Intsibo so we have to use amabuye (pebbles). Pots made of Intsibo are stronger than pots composed of amabuye, which means that pots that we make here in refugee camp are less strong than the ones which we used to make in Burundi.[30]

In addition to the lack of proper clay and sand for manufacturing pots, the geography in Mahama poses a challenge. There is a lack of plain, flat surfaces to make and dry the pots. "Rwanda is a country of hills. Even in the camp there is no plain surface that we can use to make a huge amount of pot[s] as we used to make in Burundi," Emerence added.[31] Natural resources and the physical landscape, in addition to the social and cultural landscape of the camp, make pottery a less-feasible livelihood than it was in Burundi.

The issue of land offers another example of the paradoxes of displacement for the Twa. The equality in the administration of Mahama camp has alleviated some of the material deprivation the Twa faced in Burundi. Land distribution in the camp was required to be done without regard for ethnicity: "There has been no discrimination in site distribution in the refugee camp. All people were considered equal regardless of their ethnic group. The distribution of houses in the camp was based on the family size rather than on the ethnic group. For instance, one room was to be given to two people," Aime, a young Burundian refugee and a volunteer with the American Refugee Committee, noted.[32] Houses were allocated by family size and need, with no regard to ethnicity or other factors.

On the other hand, the paradigm of land use and settlement in the camp continues to exclude Twa cultural practices. As noted before, the Twa move away from places where relatives have passed away. The strict allocation of housing within the camp means that this practice is impossible. As Salvator said, "Where would we move to, in the country where we are not allowed to own land, in the country where we live in the place set by the government and UNHCR?"[33] For the Twa, whose lifestyle has been characterized by voluntary and involuntary mobility, the restrictions on movement in a refugee camp are difficult. Camp rules do not allow them to move as they want. "There has been one house distribution and if a person wants to move from one house to another, he or she has to have a special and understandable case. For instance, if there is a misunderstanding between two people in the community and that misunderstanding disturbs other community members, there are different steps it takes sometimes to community leaders or to the security," Aime noted.[34] The death of a family member does not qualify under this rubric, meaning that the formal equality of distribution continues to exclude Twa spirituality.

A final indicator of the complexity of displacement for Twa identity is the terms by which Twa preferred to be called. Emerence, who noted that the name Twa angers her, shared terms that some people prefer to use to distance themselves from a discriminated identity. These include "abafaransa" in Kinyarwanda and Kirundi and "abaterambere" in Kinyarwanda.[35] While these individuals continue to maintain a distinct ethnic identity, they attempt to do so in a way that escapes some of the prejudice directed towards the Twa. The question of naming captures a tension at the heart of this chapter: the desire to preserve one's unique community and cultural identity while also escaping the hurtful and harmful prejudices that adhere to that identity, even in increasingly tolerant and diverse spaces like the Mahama refugee camp.

CONCLUSION:
THE PARADOXES OF MOBILITY AND DISPLACEMENT

Voluntary and involuntary mobility have had profound effects on Twa culture and subsistence. This essay has shown how the exclusion of Twa from landholding, coupled with discrimination and marginalization in Burundi, caused the Twa to become dependent on pottery production during colonization and the early national period. Pottery became closely associated with the Twa identity and is a source of pride and identification for many Twa who are no longer able to practice their traditional hunter-gatherer lifestyle. However, forced displacement to refugee camps like Mahama complicated Twa pottery practice, both in terms of its cultural associations and access to materials and space. Without large expanses of flat land and the proper clay and sand, pottery in Mahama is not as strong or abundant as it was in Burundi. Moreover, the erosion of some prejudices against the Twa people in the multicultural, diverse space of the refugee camp has had the paradoxical effect of making some Twa give up markers of their identity for more complete integration. In this vein, the incompatibility of camp practices surrounding land tenure with traditional Twa practices illustrates the continuing marginalization of the Twa, even within spaces of ostensible equality, such as the UNHCR-administered camp.

Even though parts of life in the refugee camp, such as land distribution, the possibility of living with other communities, and reduced discrimination, have contributed to greater equality, the Twa remain marginalized, bearing the burden of integrating into the Mahama community. For instance, that some Twa feel the need to give up traditional handicrafts to avoid being associated with Twa or that some prefer the name *abaterambere* to *Twa* suggests that, while ethnic identity may be more fluid in the camp, the stigma associated with being Twa has not disappeared. By taking on a different name and abandoning parts of their traditional culture, Twa sought to become more integrated. The burden of integration, though, rests with them, not with those who have long held prejudices against them. The Twa feel compelled to give up parts of their way of life that identify them as Twa to fit in, suggesting that whatever increased tolerance there is for the Twa in Mahama remains shallow and partial.

NOTES

1   Philip Briggs and Janice Booth, *Rwanda: The Bradt Travel Guide* (Bradt Travel Guides, 2006), 6–7.
2   Ibid.
3   Yaga, "Les origines du premier roi du Burundi: Entre mythes et histoire," Yaga Burundi, 20 January 2020, https://www.yaga-burundi.com/2020/origines-premier-roi-burundi/.
4   Dorothy Jackson and Katrina Payne, Twa Women, Twa Rights in Great Lakes Region of Africa (Minority Rights Group, 2003), https://reliefweb.int/report/burundi/twa-women-twa-rights-great-lakes-region-africa.
5   Jerome Lewis, *The Twa Pygmies: Rwanda's Ignored People* (2006), https://discovery.ucl.ac.uk/id/eprint/43527/. Published in French as "Les Pygmées Batwa du Rwanda: un peuple ignoré du Rwanda," in Séverin Cécile Abega and Patrice Bigombe Logo, eds, *La margininalisation des pygmées d'Afrique Centrale* (Langres, France: Africaine d'Edition/Maisonneuve et Larose, 2006).
6   Clemence Bideri and Hans Petter Hergum, *The Pygmies of the Great Lakes* (Norwegian Church Aid, 2004), 6, http://citeseerx.ist.psu.edu/viewdoc/download;jsessionid=482C0B0F5C8E993D3654D621AE5E0491?doi=10.1.1.602.3176&rep=rep1&type=pdf.
7   Briggs and Booth, *Rwanda*, 30.
8   Lewis, "The Twa Pygmies."
9   Ibid.
10 Bideri and Hergum, "The Pygmies of the Great Lakes."
11 Salvator, interview by author, 12 June 2019, Mahama refugee camp. Throughout the essay, I use interviewees' first names to protect their identities.
12 Onesphore, interview by author, 11 September 2019, Kigali.
13 Bideri and Hergun, "The Pygmies of the Great Lakes," 14–15.

14 USAID, "Burundi – Agriculture and Food Security" (2021), https://www. usaid.gov/burundi/agriculture-and-food-security.

15 Lewis, "The Twa Pygmies."

16 Minority Rights Group International, *World Directory of Minorities and Indigenous Peoples – Burundi: Twa* (2019).

17 Lewis, "The Twa Pygmies."

18 Bideri and Hergun, "The Pygmies of the Great Lakes," 17.

19 Peter Uvin, "Ethnicity and Power in Burundi and Rwanda: Different Paths to Mass Violence," *Comparative Politics* 31, no. 3 (1998): 253–71.

20 Lewis, "The Twa Pygmies."

21 UNHCR, "Rwanda: 2018 Regional Report, Burundi Regional RRP," 4 September 2018, https://data.unhcr.org/en/documents/details/65434.

22 Thierry, interview by author, 11 September 2019, Kigali.

23 Beatrice, interview by author, 15 June 2019, Mahama refugee camp.

24 Emerence, interview by author, 12 June 2019, Mahama refugee camp.

25 Lewis, "The Twa Pygmies."

26 Salvator, interview by author.

27 Emerence, interview by author.

28 Salvator, interview by author.

29 Intsibo is special sand that is used to make pots by mixing it with one of the types of clay.

30 Emerence, interview by author.

31 Ibid.

32 Aime, interview by author, 20 June 2019, Mahama refugee camp.

33 Salvator, interview by author.

34 Aime, interview by author.

35 Emerence, interview by author.

5

On Hip-Hop and Mental Migration

Alain Jules Hirwa

Dear Reader,

My name is Alain Jules Hirwa, and I am an essayist, poet, and short-story writer living in Rwanda. I have published works in *Wasafiri, The Carolina Quarterly, Jalada, Lolwe,* and elsewhere. I am also a graduate of Southern New Hampshire University, where I completed a bachelor's degree in communications. I am currently an MFA candidate at Texas State University through their online programming. From 2018 to 2020, I served as a teaching assistant in communications at Kepler Kigali University Program. My hobbies include writing, photography, and fashion design.

The conditions under which I produced my research were quite good, including having my research funded. While some of my interviews were conducted through phone calls, those that required my narrators and I to meet caused no difficulties since I had enough money for transportation. The hostel where I lived provided Wi-Fi, allowing me to access the internet, and a teaching assistant from Princeton helped me locate articles and other secondary sources.

Like some essays in this anthology, this essay tackles the theme of migration. Like Richesse's essay about pottery and Aime Parfait's essay about Burundian drums, it asks what happens when cultural practices migrate. However, singularly, my essay tackles a metaphysical migration. It offers an interpretation of hip-hop as a form of metaphorical mobility and real resistance. I hope that the essay will allow you to think of mental migration in areas of life other

than music. In what ways is mental migration applicable to you?
In what ways does mental migration apply to the youth in your
country? Those are some of the questions I wish you'd ask yourself
as you finish reading this essay.

Sincerely,
Alain Jules Hirwa

INTRODUCTION

When thinking about migration and refuge, the movement of people – often across international borders – comes to mind. But other
things migrate across borders, too: ideas, technologies, art forms.
They transform, and are transformed by, movement. In some cases,
the movement and transformation of culture creates spaces of refuge
for people who do not, or cannot, migrate themselves. This essay
explores one such instance: the way hip-hop created a space for African youth to find alternative ways of being, both as a community
and in relation to society at large. Through a kind of metaphysical
migration that I term *mental migration*, young people used hip-hop
both as a space of refuge from political oppression and as a form of
resistance to that oppression.

By considering hip-hop as a global cultural phenomenon with
particular local manifestations and resonances, I argue that we can
understand young people's use of hip-hop as a form of metaphysical
migration – they may not leave their homelands, but by adopting
and reconstituting particular cultural and musical practices (like
hip-hop), they can escape some of the confines imposed on them by
their governments and societies, while simultaneously reconfiguring
their relationship to those governments and societies through musical resistance. In this way, young hip-hop artists in Africa become
akin to "refugees" in that hip-hop offers them a (somewhat) pro-
tected cultural space from which they can challenge their exclusion
from political and social life.

The essay begins by tracing the creation of hip-hop as a way for
disaffected Black and Latino youths in the United States to form a
community and critique the racism and neglect they experienced.
It shows that while hip-hop may have first emerged in this context,
it is a truly global musical movement that both draws on diverse
influences and has different local resonances. Through a series of

examples spanning the United States, Senegal, Uganda, Kenya, and Rwanda, I show how hip-hop has created spaces for young people to seek refuge from and contest exclusion in their respective political, economic, and social systems. These examples are elaborated through semi-structured interviews, archival study, and participant observation methodologies. In choosing interlocutors, I focused on their experience in hip-hop, including those who were among its pioneers in Rwanda and those who were new to it. I also watched and analyzed music videos of hip-hop artists whose lyrics had something to do with the idea of mental migration. I conclude by arguing that it is the tension between the international, national, and local that allows hip-hop to serve as a space to challenge dominant national identities and narratives.

BACKGROUND: HIP-HOP AS REFUGE AND RESISTANCE FOR BLACK AND LATINO YOUTH IN THE UNITED STATES

"To me, hip-hop says, 'Come as you are,' we are a family," said DJ Kool Herc (Clive Campbell), who is from Jamaica and is one of the founders of hip-hop in the Bronx.[1] These words show two important features of my research. The first one is movement, as in "Come." There is a sense that DJ Kool Herc is inviting people into a space, one that they can occupy together, comfortably. The second one is the search for a place where one is accepted and valued, as in "family." The first – movement – is relevant because migration is always a transition, a move from one place or medium into another. The second – search for a place where one is accepted and cared for – is linked to the idea that hip-hop offers young people an alternative space of belonging when they were shut out of political life and a way to push for their greater inclusion. To understand the history of these ideas, I start with the development of hip-hop in the United States.

Hip-hop is a cultural art form with four main elements: rapping, deejaying, breaking (dance), and graffiti art. These elements coexist, allowing artists to maximize their individual expression through combinations of these different components.[2] Hip-hop was created by Black Americans and Latinos in the streets of New York in the 1970s as a movement of resistance against societal neglect.[3] As documented by sociologist Raquel Rivera, social conditions and economic prospects for young people living in poor urban communities during the 1960s and 1970s were appalling.[4] Both African Americans and Latinos disproportionately called these poor communities home. One of the worst places to live at that time was the Bronx, which was riddled with poor housing, fierce gang rivalries, and drug use. According to ethnomusicologist Cheryl Keyes, Afrika Bombaataa, a former African American gang member himself and deemed the "Godfather of Hip-Hop," asserted his concept of youth solidarity by rechanneling violent gang rivalries into artistic competitions.[5] In 1973, Bombaataa formed a nonviolent coalition called the Youth Organization, later renamed the Zulu Nation. This organization was a youth organization incorporating breakdancers (mainly Latinos), DJs, and graffiti artists. After the foundation of hip-hop, artists started to use it for resistance. For example, "hip-hop groups and artists like Public Enemy, Brand Nubian, Ice Cube and X-Clan started promoting a political message of resistance in its music to a greater extent than any popular genre at the time. Rappers attacked the crack trade, white supremacy and police brutality in scores of songs, from Public Enemy's 'Night of the Living Baseheads' to Ice Cube's 'I Wanna Kill Sam.'"[6] Hence, right from its creation as a new genre and musical culture, hip-hop served as a tool of resistance for Black Americans and Latinos.

One way that hip-hop functioned as a tool of resistance was through the relationship between hip-hop and enslaved people's history in the United States. J.P. (Jean Paul Gatsinda), a Rwandan music producer who produced his first hip-hop song in 2007, explained this to me:

> You see, they [rappers] put on sagging baggy jeans. That, I know the reason, but don't think many people know it. I heard them say it is because they are memorializing slavery. In America, they used to dress the black slaves in clothes that didn't fit, that had chains, and their numbers. In fact, they sewed clothes without sizing up the slaves. So, you'd find one in clothes that didn't fit. So, in America, they made it a style, a business. They live on it.[7]

JP's claim is supported by the evidence that the trend of wearing saggy pants has a history in slavery, when masters wouldn't allow enslaved men to wear belts as a way to degrade them.[8] In the United States educational system, slavery is mistaught, mischaracterized, sanitized, and sentimentalized and contemporary issues of race and racism are misunderstood. An artist might choose to put on sagging pants, not simply as a fashion statement but as a way to challenge mainstream narratives through a different vernacular.[9] While particular spaces – such as the classroom – remain difficult to access and change, the use of fashion, music, and other cultural practices can be a way to dissent, offering an alternative account of the past and its ramifications for the present.

GLOBALIZING HIP-HOP, LOCALIZING HIP-HOP

When considering the movement of hip-hop around the world, questions arise about the meaning of the word and its practice. Some authors, for instance, insist that African hip-hop is simply derivative of US hip-hop. In this vein, in his book *Hip-Hop Africa*, Eric Charry writes that American rap was the source of African rap.[10] This raises many questions. Is all (African) rap necessarily just derivative of American rap because American rap happened to come first, chronologically? The statement that American rap was the source of African rap also raises another important question. To what extent is hip-hop American? According to the legendary drummer Sheila E., the bongo drums originated in Cuba as a derivative of traditional African drums.[11] Tracing the roots of the bongo drums in Cuba, one goes to the strong historical presence of Africans from the Congo/Angola region in Eastern Cuba. "Most sources on Afro-Cuban cultural history argue that the bongo derives from Central African (Congo/Bantu) drum models, noticeable in the open bottoms. Additionally, a Santería influence from Yoruba culture in the symbolic twin drum is assumed," Jonathan Overby adds.[12] This history of material culture shows that American hip-hop was strongly influenced by African and African-diasporic musical traditions and that drawing a bright line between original and derivative traditions is misleading.

Indeed, the attempt to attribute a national heritage to hip-hop is used by those who would seek to delegitimize it by labeling it as foreign or other and, thus, not a worthwhile musical or protest tradition. "It's vital to know, though, that many Americans dislike hip-hop and might call it foreign or African, displaying a racist fear that the music could have a revolutionary potential that challenges white supremacy," said Ray Thornton, a historian of Kenya and one of my interlocutors. He added, "Would a right wing American (e.g.,

Donald Trump or Ronald Reagan) see a [N.W.A., a California hip-
hop group] radical protest song entitled 'Fuck Tha Police,' a song
that caused the FBI to protest against it, as 'American?' Or would
they think of it as a threat to their idea of America?"¹³ Yes, is the
quick answer to this question. Yes, they would think of it as a threat
to their idea of the United States. In the white supremacists' United
States, Black and brown people are minority groups that should
have no say in how the country is run. Cultural production associated with Black and Latino Americans may be dismissed as foreign
and hence, to xenophobes, as degenerate.

This sterile conflict about whether hip-hop is American can be
resolved by the writer Taiye Selasie's proposal: "Don't ask where I'm
from, ask where I'm a local."¹⁴ Instead of trying to define hip-hop
as American, we should look at it through where it is local and the
work that it does in different local contexts. Location is important –
the ways the genre is used in different places to express concerns and
resistance in local contexts. At the same time, the global nature of
hip-hop, as well as, in certain contexts, its veneer of "foreignness,"
allows us to understand these struggles together as part of a wider
story of resistance against oppression.

The hip-hop movement has now become global, following the
movement of immigrants and members of different diasporas. In
Africa, hip-hop first took off in Senegal. "With the rise of cable TV
and the return of Senegalese living abroad carrying the latest hip
magazines and music, early American rap artists like LL Cool J and
Salt-n-Pepa inspired young people," writes Msia Kibona.¹⁵ She refer-
ences the introduction of hip-hop to Africa, specifically Senegal, which
was achieved largely by the diaspora who brought it in magazines
and cassettes whenever they visited or returned to the continent. On
the continent, hip-hop by American artists kept inspiring more people. The Rwandan hip-hop artist Jay Polly said, "Yeah, of course, in
1998, there were still the feuds between BIG and Tupac, and the East
Coast-West Coast hip-hop rivalry was still going on in America. So,
we followed all of that news. I got interested a lot to follow those people, to know who they were, to know how it was done."¹⁶ His words
emphasize that hip-hop was a form of dialogue deeply grounded in
local contexts. While artists based in the United States used hip-hop
to critique systemic racism and social neglect, as well as to express
rivalries within and between hip-hop communities, hip-hop took on
new valences and functions in the places to which it migrated.

Artists in other places adapted hip-hop to their local contexts and political demands differently. As discussed above, hip-hop is not simply something imported wholesale from the United States but is a form of expression that can speak to local lived realities in new ways. Indeed, the very presumption of hip-hop's foreignness in Africa is part of what has allowed it to create space for resistance. The belief that hip-hop is only an American import, not something grounded in specific local contexts, gives hip-hop artists in Africa more freedom to express resistance. It gives them some protection. For this reason, the concept of "refuge" is important to understand – refugees, legally defined, are people who have sought protection by crossing an international border to seek protection outside of their home countries. Similarly, the intervention of something "foreign" to a particular political context creates a space of refuge for its practitioners, a space from which they can articulate local demands in a vernacular that has some degree of protection from persecution as a globally visible and internationally inflected art form.

THE KENYAN HIP-HOP PARLIAMENT

I will take as my point of departure the Hip-Hop Parliament in Kenya, which best portrays a metaphysical form of migration. Media scholars Charity Marsh and Sheila Petty show that the Kenyan political system of the early twenty-first century has been closed to young people. In 2007, a contested election resulted in political and ethnic violence that left over 1,000 people dead and several hundred thousand displaced. It was in this context that the Hip-Hop Parliament first took shape. Marsh and Petty write, "The Hip-Hop Parliament is a youth initiative comprised of hip-hop MCs and artists, formed to offer the youth a voice and a place from which to participate in the social, political, and cultural processes of Kenya."[17] In other words, this movement of artists was formed in search for a door into a house in which the youth formerly had no place. The closure of the political system to young people led the creators of the Hip-Hop Parliament to search for a different avenue of social, cultural, and political participation for Kenyan youth.

The decision to refer to the movement as a "parliament" – explicitly invoking institutions of governance – illustrates the ways the Hip-Hop Parliament has contested existing structures of power through the creation of an alternative space of political engagement. Several aspects of Kenyan hip-hop made it well-suited to this task of creating new venues for political awareness and action. First, as a youthful phenomenon, the movement spoke to the many newcomers to Nairobi – 80 per cent of migrants to the city in recent years have been under the age of eighteen. Second, as official electoral politics inflamed tensions among tribal and ethnic groups, the Hip-Hop Parliament used the vernacular Sheng (a mix of English, Swahili, and tribal languages) to overcome the differences in ethnic, educational, and class backgrounds that are more evident when speaking in English or Swahili. Third, the Parliament has been a way to draw international attention – to the extent that the Parliament itself submitted a declaration to the United Nations expressing its discontent with the political process and culture in Kenya.[18]

Thus, hip-hop proved an effective space from which young people could engage in the political system, going so far as to imitate (in name) the institutions of the state as a forum for alternative political and cultural ideas. There are two key aspects of the Hip-Hop Parliament that exemplify my argument that I will address in more detail through the rest of the essay. The first is that hip-hop, with its international/global valences, can offer a modicum of protection for dissident ideas, enabling kinds of free speech that might be suppressed in other media. The second is the way vernaculars – both cultural and linguistic – in hip-hop help consolidate group identities and articulate counter-narratives to the idealized, sanitized myths that form the basis for many projects of national identity formation.

HIP-HOP AND FREE SPEECH IN AFRICA

Hip-hop not only makes oppressed histories visible but also offers a way to seek refuge from oppression in the present and express resistance to that oppression. Some examples from African hip-hop include the 2012 collaboration of artists in Senegal, which produced the song "Doggali" ("Finishing up a killing"), in which they say,

You have completed your term
The whip must strike you

The country needs other minds
You must make way for them.

Such songs were used by the Y'en Marre movement to protest
against Abdoulaye Wade's administration. Wade opposed a consti-
tutional two-term limit but eventually lost to Macky Sall, the current
president of Senegal. The lyrics of the song "Doggali" show a high
level of free speech, which is rare to find in the state-controlled mass
media. Sometimes, people who live in places where the broadcasters
are owned and controlled by the state migrate in search of a place
where they can voice opinions contrary to those tolerated by the
state. Sometimes, that is done physically by relocating to exile. Other
times, the use of hip-hop or other practices afford a buffer of freedom because of their "foreignness."

An example from 2013, according to Corey-Boulet, is the rapper
Smockey who helped found Balai Citoyen, or Citizen Broom. This
was a movement of artists and musicians that called on youth to
rise against a bid by the then president of Burkina Faso, Blaise
Compaoré, to change the constitution and extend his rule. The
songs Smockey wrote and recorded during this period provided
a soundtrack to the president's political demise. Within a week,
Compaoré's allies' coup attempt fell apart and a transitional government was restored.[19] On a continent where states often limit
free expression, occasionally through the imprisonment of those
who try to publicly voice their opinions, hip-hop offers an avenue
of expression. That said, it is by no means without risks. Consider,
for example, the incarceration of Stella Nyanzi. Stella Nyanzi was
accused of cyber harassment against the president of Uganda,
Yoweri Museveni, for a poem she wrote insulting the president
and his mother. Nyanzi, as a woman, outspoken feminist, and ally
to ILGBTQ+ people, may have faced persecution because of these
identities and commitments.

Indeed, as Anna Sobral's work on Angola shows, musicians and
rappers are far from immune to imprisonment or other forms of
repression. However, their public platform and the way music
affords them some cover for expressions of dissent, which might
otherwise be censored, have made hip-hop and rap critical forms for
contesting the status quo.[20]

SLANG AND VERNACULAR AS SPACES OF
ALTERNATIVE MEMORY CONSOLIDATION

Another important aspect of hip-hop, in addition to creating space for resistance against oppressive state structures, is how it offers a representation of experiences that lie outside dominant narratives. This is somewhat similar to the way the clothing associated with hip-hop in the United States offered artists a way to contest prevailing narratives of slavery and Black experience. By expressing themes of suffering and exclusion within a popular and dynamic musical framework, hip-hop artists reject straightforward narratives of national unity and progress, creating a public space to express the tensions, injustices, and violence of national projects.

Take the example of Rwandan hip-hop group Tuff Gang's "Amaganya," in which Green P sings, "I know well that the creator didn't do mistakes. He can't. He can't. I'm allowed to live like a hound. When the world go crazy, no one listens to the suffering."[21] This lyric is a monologue of the suffering and the poor, representing traditionally excluded and marginalized people. Projects of state consolidation and national identity formation, as memory scholars have shown, often depend on idealized narratives of the past that gloss over inequality and injustice. Especially in the Rwandan context, where a sanitized national identity has become a major concern of the government since the 1994 genocide, there is often little space afforded to experiences and narratives that run counter to dominant ones. Hip-hop artists use music, slang in particular, to complicate notions of homogeneous national identity. While many people consider slang to degrade or otherwise sully "national" languages, I argue that it is a form of vernacular that symbolizes the ways hip-hop artists complicate and undermine mainstream narratives.

Indeed, as JP observed, the influence of hip-hop has been so pronounced in Rwandan popular culture that slang used by hip-hop artists has made its way into the mainstream. JP said to me,

> Hip-hop musicians brought slangs. We classify the language
> in our culture because Rwandans speak one language. So, if
> when people normally say "Kugenda," and in hip-hop we call it
> "Gutigita," and people are starting to use it at the street, that is a
> big influence that is visible. Or instead of saying, "Urabona," they
> say, "Urayoka." Kugenda is "to walk." Gutigita is "to shake."

Urabona is "you see." Urayoka can loosely be translated as "you get it." It is not only hip-hop artists who say it, it has become things for all Rwandans.[22]

This means that hip-hop has had a huge influence on the Rwandan culture already, modifying the country's only mother tongue. This also shows that hip-hop is accessible to people outside of the musical community through slang terms that they meet everywhere they go. Lastly, it shows that a language can create spaces for self-expression, community, and resistance. Slang offers a way for the influence of hip-hop to transcend "musical" spaces, becoming a practice that Rwandans can engage in through daily speech.

Anna Sobral makes a similar argument, again for the Angolan case. Through an analysis of three Angolan rap songs, she shows that all draw on national symbols and stories, but in a way that is "very much at odds with the official political discourse."[23] Reappropriating national symbols and combining them with parts of Angolan history that the government would prefer to avoid allows these artists to situate themselves firmly within a national history of protest and liberation movements – one the government has tried to claim for itself through the elision of its abuses and inadequacies.

CONCLUSION

The Somali-British poet Warsan Shire asks, "Where do you go when you go quiet?" While this question implies themes of loneliness and quietude, it also indicates the possibility of abstract movement into a metaphysical world. To paraphrase P.G. Smith, there are things beyond the physical world that we can understand at an almost internally perceptive level, and this is where abstract concepts such as music find their home.[24] Hip-hop, as both a musical and cultural form, offers a metaphysical space of refuge for musicians and their fans to find some protection from repression, as well as particular vernaculars that contest dominant narratives and identities.

What I wish to highlight by using the terms "refuge" and "migration" is the unique tension between the national and the international that is at play in many of the movements and practices described here. The Hip-Hop Parliament in Kenya sought recourse with an international body – the United Nations – as avenues for national political participation were foreclosed. Hip-hop is a markedly international phenomenon. But at the same time, the instantiations of hip-hop discussed here have all been decidedly local, engaged with political and cultural questions situated in distinct national contexts. The use of vernaculars like Sheng, the deployment of national symbols, and the focus on contested moments in national politics all reflect this. What I wish to suggest, then, is that the way hip-hop both transcends and embeds in local contexts is part of its power in contesting dominant narratives of national identity formation. By offering a space that is at once firmly within African nation-states, and yet deeply shaped by transnational or hyperlocal processes and categories, hip-hop both explicitly and implicitly complicates the neat stories of nation-state formation and national identity used to quiet dissent and opposition.

NOTES

1 Jeff Chang, *Can't Stop, Won't Stop: A History of the Hip-Hop Generation* (London: Picador, 2005).
2 Ornella Teta, "Fighting Censorship with the Revolutionary Power of Hip-Hop," *The McGill International Review*, 21 April 2019, https://www.mironline.ca/fighting-censorship-with-the-revolutionary-power-of-Hip-Hop/.
3 Eric Charry, *Hip-Hop Africa: New African Music in a Globalizing World* (Bloomington and Indianapolis: Indiana University Press, 2012)
4 Raquel Z. Rivera, *New York Ricans from the Hip-Hop Zone* (New York: Palgrave MacMillan 2003).
5 Cheryl L. Keyes, *Rap Music and Street Consciousness* (Champaign: University of Illinois Press, 2002).
6 Jeffrey O.G. Ogbar, "In Tupac's Life, the Struggles and Triumphs of a Generation," *The Conversation* (Melbourne, 2017), http://theconversation.com/in-tupacs-life-the-struggles-and-triumphs-of-a-generation-79266.
7 JP, interview by author, 21 July 2019, Kigali, Rwanda.
8 Dan Klepal, "Pair Focuses on Pants Problem: Campaign Seeks to End Sagging Trend," *Louisville Courier Journal*, 2008.
9 Melinda D. Anderson, "What Kids Are Really Learning About Slavery," *The Atlantic*, 2018.
10 Charry, *Hip-Hop Africa*.
11 MasterClass, *How to Play Bongos: A Basic Guide to Bongo Drums* (2020), https://www.masterclass.com/articles/how-to-play-bongos.

12 Jonathan Overby, *Instruments of Cuba Series No. 2 – Bongos* (Madison, Wisconsin Public Radio, 2015), https://www.wpr.org/instruments-cuba-series-no-2-bongos.

13 Ray Thornton, personal communication, 2019.

14 Taiye Selasi, "Don't Ask Where I'm From, Ask Where I'm a Local," TED-Global (Vancouver, TEDGlobal, 2014), https://www.ted.com/talks/taiye_selasi_don_t_ask_where_i_m_from_ask_where_i_m_a_local.

15 Msia Kibona Clark, "Senegal: The Politics of Hip-Hop in Dakar," *AllAfrica*, 17 August 2007, https://allafrica.com/stories/200708170863.html.

16 Jay Polly, interview by author, 31 May 2019, Kigali, Rwanda.

17 Charity Marsh and Sheila Petty, "Globalization, Identity, and Youth Resistance: Kenya's Hip-Hop Parliament," *Musicultures* 38, no. 1 (2013).

18 Daniel Howden, "Kenya's Hip Hop Parliament: Where the MCs Challenge MPs," *The Independent*, 18 February 2009.

19 Robbie Corey-Boulet, "The Soundtrack to Burkina Faso's Revolution," *Al Jazeera*, 28 January 2016, http://america.aljazeera.com/articles/2016/1/28/burkina-faso-a-rappers-role-in-revolution.html.

20 Anna Sobral, "Trenches of the Mind: Rap Music in Angola and the (Re)construction of National Identity," in *Literatura e outras artes: construção da memória em Angola e Moçambique*, ed. Ineke Phaf-Rheinberger, Ana Sobral, and Selma Pantoja (Frankfurt: Peter Lang, 2017).

21 Tuff Gang was one of the early Rwandan hip-hop groups. It was made up by Bull Dogg, P-fla, Green P, Jay Polly, and Fireman. It started in 2008. Green P is a Rwandan rapper. His family names are Ellie Rukundo.

22 JP, interview by author.

23 Sobral, "Trenches of the Mind," 128.

24 Patrick Smith, "The Metaphysics of Music," accessed July 2019, https://p-g-smith.com/home/category/Essays.

6

The Oral History of Local Photojournalism in Kurdistan

Lazha Taha

Dear Reader,

I am Lazha, a twenty-four-year-old from Iraqi Kurdistan. I have lived all my life in the city of Sulaimani, and I am also a graduate of media studies at the University of Sulaimani. I currently work as a researcher and translator of Kurdish literature at Kashkul, the Center of Art and Culture at the American University of Iraq, Sulaimani. I am part of a team working on translating a selection of articles written by the early twentieth-century Kurdish journalist, writer, and poet, Piramerd. My hobbies are reading, watching movies, designing jewelry, long walks, and photography.

From the time I entered media studies, my focus has been on photography. It felt liberating for me to express myself through photography, and that is how I found my strength in photography rather than in other mediums. When I was a student at university, I worked as a photographer for a cultural website, DidiMn. I was also a photographer in a student organization that was formed by a group of students with different academic backgrounds, trying to establish a better connection between students and the university. Taking photos of people, events, and occasions was a joyful practice for me and a way to work within those groups and do my part. All this helped me form a deeper connection with photos and photography in a more practical sense. When I participated in Princeton University's Global History Dialogues project, I had the opportunity to do research and dig into a topic I had been interested in for a long time but had never had the knowledge or the tools to research. Preparing for this research gave me the courage to face my fear of not knowing enough about photojournalism or photography. I learned how to plan for a research project, conduct oral history interviews, integrate my ideas with interviewees' ideas in my writing, and edit and revise my work. The course allowed me to interview five of the photojournalists that I have looked up to for years. As a young woman still in search of my academic path, it was very important to me to be a part of this course. Witnessing the intimate creation of the work I love has helped me revisit my creative process and expectations of what I make.

The COVID-19 pandemic imposed restrictions on my work including meeting with the photojournalists I interviewed over Zoom. However, I had the opportunity to build connections with the photojournalists whom I otherwise would not have met and ask them questions that were exciting and meaningful to me. For example, I was planning to interview at least eight photojournalists, but because I had other work obligations and was under the stressful situation of being in quarantine for an uncertain amount of time, I did not have enough time to do so. Eventually, I ended up only interviewing five photojournalists. Beyond the interviews, I made use of books and online resources, both of which were limited. Lockdowns meant I could not use the rich library and archival collections in Sulaimani. The online resources were limited in scope because there is truly no proper research available online about Kurdish photojournalism in either English or Kurdish. I had to use the books from my personal library, which contains volumes I collected over the years as photojournalism books caught my eye.

My research explores the rise of a new form of journalism in the Kurdistan Region of Iraq. I delve into how the first group of Kurdish photojournalists learned their trade and subsequently began to teach another generation of journalists. I examine these photojournalists' missions and how their work is different from the work of those who preceded them. I also touch upon how they play a pivotal role in creating Kurdish memory and identity.

I hope my research shows you the hard work of a group of photojournalists who are eagerly trying to tell the stories of their land with their own life experiences. Their stories are full of wars, uprisings, and fearful flights from their home country. They tell the stories of a country that is becoming more unstable day by day, but it is also a country that holds hope for them, a country that has endless stories to tell and share with the world. I hope this writing can serve as a brief introduction to the beginnings of photojournalism in Kurdistan and can open doors for future researchers to work on this topic in Kurdistan and Iraq.

    I am thrilled that my research is a part of this book alongside other essays mapping histories that have not been told or not yet told in these ways and from these perspectives. Ultimately, I believe that humans, wherever they may be around the world, face a shared set of problems. This book is a good way to read about "the others" of the world. By hearing a diverse set of people from the world talk about their lives and struggles, we are compelled to listen. This will make us contribute to each other's shared knowledge about the world, as well as humble us when we take stereotypes about a region to be true.

Sincerely,
Lazha Taha

INTRODUCTION

Kurds are the largest ethnic group in the world without a country.[1] Since 1916, they have been divided between Iraq, Iran, Turkey, Syria, and the Soviet Union. This essay is about Kurds living in the northern part of Iraq. After the end of British colonial rule, the Iran-Iraq war, the Anfal campaign, the Halabja chemical attack, and many uprisings under Sadam Hussein's rule, they were given an autonomous region called Kurdistan. This series of conflicts has shaped Kurdish history both as that history unfolded and in retrospect: because of these conflicts, Kurds have lost the majority of their archives several times. All that exists now is what could survive outside of Kurdish lands. Our experience as Kurds complicates the historical relationship between the discipline of history and the formation of nation-states.

    Related to the loss of archives and territorial fragmentation is the fact that the history of the Kurds, and Kurdistan, has been mostly written by outsiders, colonial administrators, early travellers, and, most recently, Western journalists and photojournalists. Susan Meiselas, in her photographic history book about the Kurds, *Kurdistan: In the Shadow of History*, writes about photographs of Kurdistan taken by Western scholars and travellers and says: "We have the object, but it exists separated from the narrative of its making."[2] Kurds were represented only through the work of outsiders and their subjective perspectives. We have mostly seen ourselves in others' narration rather than our own, which means the personal opinions and judgments of these Western authors and photographers, which concentrate on only a section of the Kurdish community, are all we have. With archives so sparse, photographs are a key site of memory formation for many Kurds, and we rely on photographs to form memories of, and relationships with, our more distant past. However, these photos were mostly taken by outsiders. In my own life, many of my childhood memories feature photos of Kurds and Kurdistan taken by foreign photographers. Up to now, whenever I think of schools, my mind recalls a photograph by the French photographer Rosy Rouleau, which displays a girl in a Kurdish dress. Written on the blackboard behind her are the words, "Kurd, Kurdi, Kurdistan" in the Kurdish language. A more striking example, and one that caused me to understand the crucial role of photojournalism, was the Halabja chemical attack. Halabja is a Kurdish city in the Kurdish region of Iraq. On 16 March 1988, it was bombed by the Ba'athist regime under Saddam Hussein, killing 5,000 innocent people and injuring nearly 10,000 more. The chemical bombing is officially recognized as genocide by the Iraqi government and designated as a war crime by the international community. The photos of this massacre were taken by Iranian photographers and then later by international media outlets. Without these photos, this tragic event might have been trivialized or undermined since the neighbouring countries, as well as the Ba'athist regime, did not want the news to be covered.

Apart from capturing tragedy, these photos serve as raw materials for research on Kurdish life. For instance, whenever I want to see the historical dress or jewelry of a particular part of Kurdistan, I look for the work of photographers and travellers, and through them I find answers. Of course, these answers are inflected by the visitors' subjectivities, political views, and motivations. This is a paradox for me because, while I feel the importance of the scenes captured (and need them since they are the only photographic source of information we have), I know there is so much that was omitted from the photographic record, and that what does exist has been mediated and shaped in particular ways by the priorities and perspectives of foreign researchers. This paradox continues to this day, with an important and growing change. A young

generation of Kurdish photographers and photojournalists feel the
urge to create their own archive of images and documents. These
local photographers now take photos that act as a counterpart to
the work of international and foreign photographers, providing
more perspective and depth to a conversation that has mostly been
one-sided and one-dimensional.

Although some local Kurdish photographers did what we might
now consider photojournalism work in the twentieth century,
Kurdistan did not have local photojournalists whose full-time job
was searching for stories and taking photos until the late 2000s.
Their emergence was catalyzed by the formation of the Kurdistan
autonomous region in 1991 and the fall of Saddam's regime in 2003.
Some of these photojournalists were funded by the government and
presented an entirely pro-government image to the outside world.
However, a developing group of photojournalists challenged such
presentations and aimed for a more realistic image. This generation's narration challenges the accounts of both pro-government
locals and the foreigners that came before them. They are changing
the perspectives of Kurdish and Western communities by portraying
Kurdistan and the life of the Kurds in new ways. These local photojournalists have become representative sources for broadcasting the
news and stories of their own country and people, shaping how we
understand the region today and creating sources for future generations to look back upon. Despite their relatively recent rise, Kurdish
photojournalists now play an active role in creating a more accurate,
fleshed-out, and heartfelt portrait of Kurdish society that resonates
better with the people represented. With these portraits, they are
contributing in a crucial way to the process of forming Kurdish
memory and identity for generations to come.

This essay explores Kurdish photojournalists' contributions to
memory formation in the past two decades. The first section intro-
duces the photojournalists I interviewed for this oral history project.
In the second section, I write about the establishment of photojournalism in Kurdistan and the creation of the first photo agency in
the region, which helped support new Kurdish photojournalists.
Section three is about how these Kurdish photojournalists learned
their trade and how they are now involved in teaching the next generation. The fourth section deals with the present work of Kurdish
photojournalists, their aims, and the significance of their work. My
fifth section is about the history and identity formation of Kurds and

Figure 6.1 | A horse, used by Kurdish Iranian smugglers to transport alcohol from the Kurdistan region of Iraq to Iran, leaps after packages are placed on his back.

the photojournalists' role in this process. I conclude by exploring what the emergence of local photojournalism will mean for future generations of Kurds in Kurdistan and beyond.

INTRODUCING THE PHOTOJOURNALISTS

I have always been interested in the processes of documenting and archiving. When I was in college, I found photojournalism to be an effective tool. I was passionate to know more about it, but because we have few resources about photojournalism in Kurdistan, I was not able to understand the whole process. Now, through my research, I have gotten the chance to hear directly from photojournalists about how they use photography and narrative to document life in Kurdistan. Through interviews with five Iraqi Kurdish photojournalists, I explore both the history of photojournalism in Kurdistan and its present and future significance for Kurdish identity and memory. To begin, I introduce the five individuals interviewed and some of their most well-known works.

Ali Arkady, born in 1982, is a photojournalist and filmmaker from Khanaqin, Iraq. He graduated from Khanaqin's Institute of Fine Arts. He started to work as a freelance photographer in 2006. Ali is now a member of VII Photo Agency and won the prestigious Bayeux Prize for War Correspondents. His work has appeared in CNN, *The Telegraph,* and *The Times.*[3]

Hawre Khalid, born in 1987, is a photojournalist from Kirkuk, Iraq. He has a degree in journalism. Hawre started to work as a freelancer in 2007. His works have appeared in *Time Magazine,* the *New York Times,* the *Washington Post,* and the *Sunday Times.*[4]

Sartep Othman, born in 1990, is a photojournalist from Sulaimani, Iraq. He has been working as a local photojournalist since 2009. Sartep won the Open Eye Award in 2011. He now works as a daily photographer for a local website in Sulaimani. His works have appeared in *Time Lightbox, Universal News,* and *Rudaw.*[5]

Younes Mohammad was born in 1968 in Dohuk, Iraq. He has worked as a freelance photojournalist since 2011. He received his MBA from the University of Tehran. He has received many awards, including the MIFA and DAYS JAPAN. Younes is significantly older than most of the other photojournalists interviewed as he came to the work later in life, but he is now a very well-established freelance photojournalist whose work has appeared in outlets around the world.[6]

Sangar Akrayi, born in 1988, is a photojournalist from Erbil, Iraq. He first worked as a journalist and street photographer and has now been working as a photojournalist for four years. Currently, Sangar works as a daily photojournalist for Middle East Images.[7]

THE ESTABLISHMENT OF PHOTOJOURNALISM IN KURDISTAN AND THE KURDISH PHOTOJOURNALISTS

In 1991, the Kurdish people rose up against Saddam Hussein's regime, leading to the establishment of an autonomous zone for the Kurds called Iraqi Kurdistan. This autonomy led to greater freedom within the Kurdish part of Iraq, opening the region to visitors from foreign countries, as well as construction, multi-sector development, and international trade. This was the first step toward building connections with the media outside of Kurdistan. Before the creation of the autonomous region, local photographers and journalists had only limited connections with international news and media outlets.

Rafiq Mahmood Afandi, a Kurdish photographer from Sulaimani who inherited his studio (one of the first studios in Sulaimani, established in 1946) from his father, expressed this lack of connection beautifully. "Each one of us [photographers] worked alone and kept our secrets to ourselves. Nobody was allowed to contact people here," said Rafiq, who has since passed away, when he was interviewed by Susan Meiselas. "I didn't meet any journalists or photographers. Maybe they came and were with the leaders but nobody came to me to exchange ideas about photography."[8]

The role these new foreign media outlets played was mixed. On the one hand, they were a positive influence that opened doors for local media outlets that had been very restricted until then. They provided technical skills and taught new methods to local photojournalists that were emerging around the world. Furthermore, they helped showcase the Kurdish struggle at a time when the nation-states that had Kurdish populations were actively opposing representations of Kurds in the media. This was the case in the Halabja chemical attacks, where foreign media outlets helped draw international attention to the genocide.

On the other hand, these foreign outlets had a negative influence as well. Many times, they covered Kurdistan for foreign audiences and focused only on the bright side, depicting a Kurdistan that was reviving and flourishing. That is how the image was reported to them because Kurdish authorities wanted to showcase their land to the outside world. This also occurred in local media outlets, which received government support and in turn only presented Kurdistan in a positive light. Younes explained the phenomenon: "Their aim is to portray a fake personality [of Kurdish society] ... They help the foreigners because this might make the [foreigners] to discuss Kurdistan in a pleasant way."[9] These types of local media outlets wanted to present Kurdistan as a safe haven and to make the ruling powers of Kurdistan look good; photojournalism was one way to do so.

In contrast to government-funded photojournalism, Kurdistan's freedom led to more authentic and critical forms of photojournalism. This included the establishment of the first photo agency in Kurdistan, Metrography, which was founded in 2010 by Iraqi photographer Kamaran Najm and American photojournalist Sebastian Meyer. Metrography provided institutional support that helped shift the narratives told about Kurdistan by Western journalists to

Figure 6.2 | A peshmerga tank starts moving toward the villages around Mosul from the Khazir frontline, 17 October 2016, Mosul, Iraq.

those created by local photographers and journalists. Prior to this, as Meyer recalls, "Iraq's nuanced visual record wasn't being made by Iraqis."[10] This conjuncture of political and institutional changes created a space for Kurdish photojournalism to take root. Metrography soon gained worldwide recognition. Work from its photographers has been exhibited internationally and published in some of the most renowned media outlets around the world, such as the *New York Times, National Geographic, Time Magazine,* and the *Washington Post.* They promote themselves by saying that they "specialize in in-depth photo storytelling from the best regional photographers,"[11] and "represent local photographers who give us unrivaled knowledge and access to every corner of the region."[12]

Before Metrography, Kurds only had a few photographers and not a single photojournalist. Several of the photojournalists I interviewed shared how the agency affected them and their conception of their work. "What has been done in the past was not thought of as photojournalism, it was recording and archiving an event by a random choice," said Sartep. "We did not have the concept of photojournalism until the establishment of Metrography."[13] Ali thinks that "Metrography was the revolution" in photojournalism in Iraq back in the time when it was first established. However, things have changed somewhat since then. Tragically, co-founder Kamaran went missing in June 2014 while covering an encounter between the Peshmerga forces and ISIS fighters in an area around Kirkuk. His whereabouts are still unknown. His brother, Ahmad Najm, became the director of Metrography. Now, the agency focuses on setting up workshops and opening exhibitions in Iraq. In 2019, they brought the World Press Photo Special Exhibition "Best of Three Years" to three Iraqi cities. "Metrography's vision is not the same as before," said Ali.[14] Hawre shared this view, saying, "When Kamaran was still in Metrography, he was trying [to build photojournalism] in Kurdistan, but with Kamaran disappearing, it disappeared too."[15]

Despite the loss caused by Kamaran's disappearance, these younger Kurdish photojournalists had the opportunity to learn from the more experienced and educated generation of skilled foreign photographers and photojournalists that came before them. In 2011, Metrography offered a ten-day photography workshop by four renowned foreign photographers for twenty-three local, emerging photographers from cities across Iraq. Ali and Sartep participated in that workshop and said that this experience changed their lives entirely. "From that day my eyes opened, and not just that, my mind and everything changed. That master class imprinted courage in me to work, this was the point that took me to photojournalism," said Ali, who was a painter at that point and taught art classes in schools.[16] Ali recalled that after finishing the workshop, he went to his home, emptied his room, gave all his paintings to a friend of his, and "had the faith that this theme is more important than [the] art [of painting]," placing in his room only a single table with a camera on top of it. He started to take photos continuously, read exclusively about photography, and worked at his photography daily. Ali was amazed by the work of the foreign photojournalists he saw in Iraq and felt a great responsibility for taking this task on his shoulders. "Those foreigners came to work in Iraq, the place I was living, and their works were so professional," said Ali. Soon, he realized he would bring a different and more intimate perspective to the work than foreign photojournalists did. Ali added: "The stories were all around me. I even had more time and greater chances to work on stories from my home." Lecturers offered by the Metrography workshop helped Ali

Figure 6.3 | Raad Hindia, who is married with two children, worked in the mosque as a cleaner. He was arrested by an intelligence department and his mother cried for them not to take him in 2016.

develop his work. Without these lecturers, it would not have been possible for him to learn those skills. He recalls, "I learned and used all my experiences in art through journalism to produce my photos in the story that I made in these ten days with the help of my teachers." They showed the students photos produced in Iraq by foreign photographers and taught them how locals can work on those types of stories. Sartep, who also participated in this workshop, said that it built his understanding of photojournalism and how to make stories and that it was his first time being taught by professional photo editors and photojournalists.

LEARNING AND TEACHING THE TRADE: BECOMING PHOTOJOURNALISTS

Without formal training programs at universities or other institutions, most of the photojournalists I interviewed came from different academic backgrounds. This early generation of Kurdish photojournalists is now teaching new cohorts of photographers and photojournalists. For example, Hawre Khalid is teaching the basics of photography and photojournalism to students in Sulaimani. Through VII Photo Agency, Ali offers a twelve-week program in which he mentors the students and helps them publish their works at the end of the project. Sangar and Younes are some of Ali's students in this program. Younes also has one-on-one workshops for those who want to learn about photography.

Formal workshops and training are only part of the story. Kurdish photojournalists have also learned how to work in this field by teaching themselves and learning on the job. They read and learn about photography, as well as learn from the guidance of foreign photojournalists who come to work on assignment in Kurdistan. Often this contact occurs by working closely with foreign photojournalists as guides and fixers to show them around and bring them to their subjects. Younes, who now works as an international freelance photojournalist, said that, at first, he was working for free as a fixer just to be close to the photojournalists who come to Kurdistan on assignments. From them, he learned about photography techniques and how to build the relationships and connections with other photographers that helped build his career.

Indeed, some photojournalists I interviewed prefer informal training and learning on the job to formal classes and workshops. Ali thinks that it is not necessary to study photojournalism, as "they will give you a bunch of rules and instructions that you cannot go beyond." He emphasizes that "it is better to create your own experiences and your own works before that, you should have your own freedom of work and exploration." For these reasons, Ali thinks that master classes are the best approach to photojournalism education because they are independent and have fewer restrictions. According to Ali, "it depends on the capacity of the one who chooses photojournalism and their willingness to do the work. It requires someone to be patient and try to remain wise in the difficulties."[17]

Whether the journalists pursue formal or informal education and training, they all need to stay up to date with current events and photographic practices, often by following the work of other photojournalists. On this point, Sangar says that "seeing other photographers work" is a way to train one's eyes to look at photos, as "that is what every photographer has advised me to do as a good way to learn." With limited institutional infrastructure for learning

Figure 6.4 | Two Kurdish women make local Kurdish bread at the corner of their home in a village behind Erbil. Both are sisters and collaborate to make local bread at home. The bread, known in Kurdistan as "Nany Teeree," has a pleasant taste and has become part of Kurdish culture and culture in the four parts of Kurdistan.

their trade, Kurdish photojournalists must be committed to improving their craft when they can – taking advantage of the opportunities that present themselves and making use of available resources. They have decided to travel this often-difficult road to get into the field of journalism to tell the stories of their nation from their perspectives. "I feel responsible towards history, towards my people and those who are waiting for my works," said Younes.[18] Several of the journalists I interviewed shared how they gave up other careers to pursue photojournalism full time. Before becoming a photojournalist, Younes had two jobs in Hawler as a business administrator. He eventually quit both, saying: "I was not enjoying anything in my life anymore." He was searching for a career that could keep him excited about life and help him to learn every day. As for Ali, he was an art teacher in a small town near Darbandixan: "Every day after teaching I was going from school to Baghdad, Basra, Sulaimani or Hawler, staying for one day, working and then coming back because

I had to teach the next morning."[19] He then quit teaching and chose to be a full-time photographer. Sangar's career shift was less dramatic, as he had been working as a journalist before switching to photojournalism full time.

THE DISTINCTIVENESS OF LOCAL PHOTOJOURNALISM

Most of these Kurdish photojournalists believe that their proximity to their subjects, both geographically and culturally, helps them shed light on events and people in ways that are difficult or impossible for foreign journalists. However, they also acknowledge that there are unique challenges for local photojournalists that foreigners may not face. Some local photojournalists think that they are connected more to the stories of their country than foreign photojournalists who come frequently to produce a story and leave. "I am convinced that the way I know the society and the work that I can do, cannot be done by [foreign photojournalists] ... I can cover these images more effectively because I know my own people, I know their culture," Younes explained.[20] Since they are closer to the people and events of their country, they can build a better connection with the topic they are working on. In contrast to this view, Ali thinks that Iraqi photojournalists occasionally run into problems because of their local ties. They need to learn to accept the diverse community that inhabits their land to be able to do good journalistic work. If not, he says that sometimes foreign photojournalists work better in Iraq "because as a person they have less customs, traditions, [and other] related restrictions in this region, along with issues of religious acceptance or political issues."[21] He further explained how the foreign photojournalists can generally deliver their message in an unbiased way. Ali's perspective highlights how working as a local photojournalist in Kurdistan is by no means without its challenges and demands a great deal from those who take it on as a part- or full-time profession. Being enmeshed in the local context provides the possibility for rich and nuanced stories based on strong connections to and understanding of communities and histories but comes with its own set of difficulties.

If Kurdish photojournalists can bear their positionalities in mind, their knowledge of language, culture, and tradition is an enormous benefit to their work. Ali taught a master class to a group of Yazidi girls who survived the war against ISIS. He went to train them in the camp where they lived. "Their photos were deeper and stronger than mine in the camps, because it was their place," said Ali.[22] In Ali's opinion, photojournalists should gain experience both within and beyond their own communities. They may start out working locally, but as they develop as photojournalists, gain success in their region, and build confidence in their approaches, they will eventually gain the capacity to apply those skills and tell stories anywhere in the world. Ali thinks that by doing the work as a photojournalist, the stress and late-night work, they will receive the respect they deserve somewhere in the world: "They will see what you have done to be in your position." He can sense this now while he lives and works abroad.

Hawre Khalid, a Kurdish freelance photojournalist who left his life in Europe twice to cover the ISIS war within Kurdish borders, thinks that he can tell the stories of his people better than others because he shares their problems and concerns. This helps to produce a more heartfelt portrait of Kurdish society.[23] Younes also touched on this topic, saying: "I want to talk about the problems I see that are important around me [to the degree] that they have become an internal struggle for me and I feel responsible toward them, by making those stories I can solve this problem."[24] Younes wants to be the voice of his community and dig into the core of the problems that exist in his society: "I want to showcase the different reasons that made this situation for the Kurds other than politics and wars, then try to find a long-term solution for them." Younes thinks that although local photojournalists are not as well-respected as the foreign photojournalists, they have a heavier burden on their shoulders since they are closely related to the current and future situation of their land. The inequality in respect afforded to locals versus foreigners impacts the kinds of stories they are assigned. As Younes notes, "if an equal chance to work is given to both local and international photojournalists, the outcome would be different." This idea also surfaces in the writing of Metrography co-founder Sebastian Meyer: "While Kamaran and his colleagues were only asked to shoot instances of extreme violence, foreign photographers – like myself – were being assigned more subtle, in-depth stories."[25] Local photojournalists were not only implicitly considered less capable of producing subtle and complex stories, but also asked to put themselves at greater risk in their work. In return, Hawre said, "the

Figure 6.5 | A worker sitting in the middle of the Bazaar of Sulaimani, during the coronavirus pandemic in Iraq, 2020.

foreigner photojournalists and photographers are treated well and respected more than us even when they are not experienced enough in the field as much as we are."[26]

Hawre stated that Western photojournalists come to Kurdistan and tend to focus on one aspect of our lives. As he said, "it is important to me to see how a photographer from another country sees my homeland, but most of the time they cannot depict the complete picture, rather they deliver what they want or see to be important."[27] Kurdish photojournalists have more fleshed-out narratives that consider the roots of their people and country. "I care more about the stories of my country, which is why I can put more feeling into my work," said Hawre.[28] These local photojournalists are more detail-oriented, and their work has more dimension and depth. Sangar also thinks that he understands the details, rules, and restrictions of his country better than someone from outside.[29]

HISTORY AND IDENTITY FORMATION:
THE ROLE OF KURDISH PHOTOJOURNALISTS

Local photojournalists feel responsible for crafting an accurate image that could help in the future by shedding light on a lifestyle, event, or cultural dimension of Kurdish life that might disappear or only be remembered by a few. In this way, their work is as much about the future as it is documenting the present or recent past. Sartep Othman hopes that his works can have an impact on the way the history of the Kurds will be presented. "If the photos I have taken in the past few years could have a small contribution in writing a short history of Kurdistan or a city, I will be thrilled," he said.[30] Kurdish history was denied under Saddam's rule, and it is still denied in Iran, Turkey, and Syria. Because of that, there is always a fear in the heart of the Kurdish population that there might be another war, invasion, or attempted annihilation of Kurdish identity. That is why when Kurdish photojournalists talk about their mission, they always mention forming Kurdish memory and identity.

The constant conflict experienced by Kurds, as well as the fact that their traditional homeland is split between four nation-states, means that Kurds do not have a reliable recorded memory of the past. Some archives were destroyed by bombs or had to be abandoned in forced flight. Other archives have been destroyed by Kurds ourselves to prevent documents and information from falling to enemy hands.[31] Many Kurds have even burned their personal photo albums, leaving us with very few physical reminders of the past. The need to secure basic safety and survival meant that archiving and preserving historical documents and photographs could never be a priority. Younes suggests that the value of this kind of memory work was not yet widely understood.[32] Into this breach have stepped the new generation of photojournalists.

For Kurds, photojournalism is very closely connected with identity formation and memory preservation. Photojournalism is a way to actively participate in the shaping of Kurdish visual memory, providing future generations with an important legacy that past generations have not had. By having this reservoir of photos, which capture events, personalities, places, and practices that travellers, foreign journalists, historians, and government officials may not think – or want – to preserve, Kurdish photojournalists are using their present artistic and journalistic interventions with an eye to the future. This marks an important change in how Kurdish history has been created. Written history is new to the Kurds. In the past, Kurdish history, culture, and rituals were passed from one generation to the next through Kurdish songs called "Heyran'" and "Dengbêjî," as well as poems left by classical poets, letters between intellectuals, and official government documents. Apart from a few relatively elite Kurdish voices, Kurds had little opportunity to shape the documentary record that would go on to inform future generations' identities and histories. Photojournalism has changed this, allowing photojournalists to bring their understanding of Kurdish history to bear on their work, which will, in turn, shape future histories of the Kurdish people. As Ali said: "The things that I have seen in my childhood, my memories are gone undocumented, and Iraq was still going in the same direction, everything is diminished in a pit without being recorded. But no, now I am here and I should document them."[33] In this way the Kurdish photojournalists engage in the writing of modern Kurdish history through their lenses, merging their own experiences with their ideas of the forgotten Kurdish past. "I started to document everything so I can compensate for the things that I have seen in my childhood," said Ali about his attempts to recall his childhood. "I feel like I am filling the missing spaces of the things that I have seen before, by documenting them now."

Neil Shea, an American writer for National Geographic who has visited the region many times, shares Ali's view. He hopes that younger generations of Kurds see what their people have lived through and will be able to decide "how will we choose what to remember" through the work of their photojournalists. Indeed, he felt this process had already begun to occur. In commenting on Hawre Khalid's work, Shea observed that the impact of Kurdish photojournalists would not only be inward-facing, oriented toward community identity formation, but also that these photojournalists would have an impact on how the international community understands Kurdistan and its people. He stated that Hawre's work, and by extension that of other Kurdish photojournalists, can transcend geographical boundaries to join the wider community of photojournalists and image-makers around the world.[34]

By having their voices heard, these photojournalists can participate in writing the history of their people. They can leave their marks and craft their identity with their own hands. They are adding to the history of the world with their own history, through their own narration. Younes explained that this new photojournalism is different from what came before: "[what had been done before] was not done for the creation of a culture within our own society, or to solve a problem, rather it was only for displaying a side to the outside word that is in a way like an embellished face, an embellished nation to show [other] people."[35]

CONCLUSION

Although some local Kurdish photographers did work that we can define as photojournalism in the past, Kurdistan did not have local photojournalists whose sole job was searching for stories and taking photos until late the 2000s. This only occurred after the fall of Saddam's regime by US intervention in 2003 and the establishment of the first Kurdish photo agency in Iraq. All of this changed after the war against ISIS. The economy collapsed, Kurdistan was again on the frontline of a new war, and there were no longer any master classes or workshops for journalists. But there was a significant difference from the past, as now a handful of local Kurdish photojournalists that were internationally recognized. Emerging photojournalists can learn from this first generation of full-time photojournalists in Kurdistan. This will hopefully help the creation of a visual history for us Kurds, allowing us to take part in the process of forming Kurdish memory and identity for generations to come.

NOTES

1   Edward R. Kantowicz, *Coming Apart, Coming Together: The World in the Twentieth Century*, vol. 2 (Wm. B. Eerdman's Publishing Company, 1999), 160.

2   Susan Meiselas, *Kurdistan: In the Shadow of History* (Chicago: University of Chicago Press, 2008), xvi.

3   Ali Arkady, "Biography," https://www.aliarkady.co.

4   Hawre Khalid, Portfolio, DARS, http://darstprojects.com/hawre-khalid-portfolio.

5   Sartep Othman, interview by author, 26 July 2020, Sulaimani.

6   International Photography Grant, https://internationalphotogrant.com/winners-gallery/photogrvphy-grant-2017/photojournalism/hm/597.

7   Sangar Akrayi, interview by author, 29 July 2020, Sulaimani.

8   Meiselas, *Kurdistan*, 206.

9 Younes Mohammad, interview by author, 5 August 2020, Sulaimani.
10 Sebastian Meyer, *Under Every Yard of Sky* (New York: Red Hook Editions, 2019), 89.
11 Metrography, "Metrography is the First Photo Agency in Iraq" (Facebook), https://www.facebook.com/pg/metrographyagency/about/?ref=page_internal.
12 Metrography, https://metrography.photoshelter.com.
13 Sartep Othman, interview by author.
14 Ali Arkady, interview by author, 7 September 2020, Sulaimani.
15 Hawre Khalid, interview by author, 2020, Sulaimani.
16 All quotes in this paragraph from Ali Arkady, interview by author.
17 Ali Arkady, interview by author.
18 Younes Mohammad, interview by author.
19 Ali Arkady, interview by author.
20 Ibid.
21 Ali Arkady, interview by author.
22 Ibid.
23 Hawre Khalid, interview by author.
24 Younes Mohammad, interview by author.
25 Meyer, *Under Every Yard of Sky*, 89.
26 Hawre Khalid, interview by author, 12 August 2021, Sulaimani.
27 Ibid.
28 Ibid.
29 Sangar Akrayi, interview by author.
30 Sartep Othman, interview by author.
31 Meiselas, *Kurdistan*, xvi.
32 Younes Mohammad, interview by author.
33 Ali Arkady, interview by author.
34 Neil Shea, *Through the Smoke, Behind the Curtain* (Kurdistan: Karo Press, 2019), 10.
35 Younes Mohammad, interview by author.

PART THREE

Identity and (Un)Belonging: Constructing and Deconstructing Social Identities

Our final section grapples with identity, focusing on occupation and gender identities and their intersections. One of the threads that ties these essays together is a concern for what is often framed as a binary between tradition and modernity, and how evidence from the experiences of people posited to occupy one side or the other of this dichotomy complicates its rigidity. Time and temporalities, then, are particularly important for these essays, which address moments when traditions, and the identities imbricated in them, changed suddenly.

Phocas Maniraguha examines traditional healing practices in Rwanda, arguing that there is no sharp distinction between "traditional" and "modern" medicine – people choose methods based on access, financial burden, and efficacy, and often move back and forth between hospitals and traditional healers to find relief for their injuries and illnesses. However, recent attempts by the Rwandan government to impose standards on traditional healing have excluded many former practitioners and subjected those who are able to continue their work to new burdens of training and regulation. Following in detail the experience of one woman healer, Maniraguha sheds light on the tensions and contradictions inherent in this project of state-led modernization.

Ismail Alkhateeb's research on the experiences of Syrian women draws on his work as an activist and advocate. Addressing a myriad of factors, from education to gender-based violence to urban versus rural communities, he creates a complex panorama that is both attentive to the many challenges and inequalities that women in Syria confront and adamant about the possibility for change.

Finally, Sandrine Cyuzuzo Iribagiza considers the Intore traditional dancers in Rwanda who have become a symbol of national pride. As Iribagiza shows, however, the story of traditional dance is not one of stasis and continuity but rather of vibrant change. Looking back to the tenth century, she highlights how movements of people, ideas, and goods in the intervening centuries have shaped dance practices over time. She does this through careful attention to the costumes, instruments, and movements involved in different traditional dances, connecting them to the cultural and social contexts in which they originated.

These three essays have in common an attention to the social practices and material cultures that structure identity, as well as a sensitivity to the impact of forced displacement on identity and social belonging. They invite reflection on what tradition means and what it means to practice tradition in changing circumstances. They work to destabilize what we might think about received categories of thought and analysis, opening new ways to understand processes of change and continuity.

7

"Traditional Healers Save Lives": The Changing Relationship between Traditional Healing and Modern Medicine in Rwanda

Phocas Maniraguha

Dear Reader,

Conducting this research wasn't easy for several reasons, including the topic I chose and the timeline of this research's production. My topic – traditional medicine – is one many people in my community do not like to discuss. This made it more difficult to find interviewees, and the ones that I was able to speak with were often hesitant to share their perspectives and knowledge. The complications with the timeline are easily explained: while working on this project, I was also employed as a teaching assistant with other responsibilities and had to travel from Kigali to northern Rwanda for work. Limited access to research resources was another challenge.

However, I do consider this project a success. The research process helped me dig deeper into my community's history and see the impacts of traditional medicine in Rwanda. Looking at my research and my colleagues' projects, I found that we had similar experiences during the research process. For instance, one of my colleagues was researching the evolution of music in Rwanda. We were both studying and writing about Rwandan history and the ways traditional practices interact with new ideas. We were both thinking about how practices change over time, the influence of new forms of technology, and the conflicts and tensions that arise in these processes of change.

One important takeaway from my research is an understanding of the relationship between traditional healing and modern medicine in Rwanda. Even though many people do not want to discuss traditional healing, this essay shows that traditional healers are an important part of healthcare in Rwanda and people turn to them when modern medicine does not help their pain and suffering. Another takeaway that I learned through the research process was that there is a lack of research on this topic and on many other aspects of Rwandan history, particularly by members of communities affected by these changes. I hope many others will take up some of the questions I have considered here as we develop new narratives in Rwandan history.

Sincerely,
Phocas Maniraguha

INTRODUCTION

I grew up in the Muhoza sector of the Musanze district, known as Ruhengeri, in the northern part of Rwanda. Where I lived, traditional medicine was considered by many to be a sin, especially by those who believe in Christianity. Some believed that traditional medicine was performed by people working with the devil. One day, when I was fifteen years old, I asked my parents why traditional medicine was thought to be a sin in our community. My father told me that the reason is that people sometimes confuse traditional healers and witchcraft. He helped me to differentiate both practices. He told me that traditional healers are the ones who can cure you by using herbs and that they usually cure the poison and other diseases that a person can see such as asthma, pancreatic diseases, and others. Witchcraft, on the other hand, is the practice of people who still believe in traditional ways. They use magic or their ancestors to help solve problems. So, while both practices may go by the name traditional medicine, in this paper I will distinguish between traditional healing, which uses herbs but does not seek magical or ancestral intervention, and witchcraft.

This childhood experience inspired me to learn more about traditional medicine and its relationship to modern medicine and witchcraft. I distinguish between three types of healing practice: traditional medicine, modern or Western medicine, and witchcraft.[1] The

Figure 7.1 | An example of the herbs used by traditional healers.

second section of the paper explains these terms in detail. From the beginning, I knew that religion played a big role in shaping people's perceptions and willingness to use traditional medicine. Christians of different denominations are taught that traditional medicine is sinful and that they need to avoid it. However, there are some Christians

who use traditional medicine despite their religion. The first part of
my research question unfolds from here: What is the relationship
between traditional medicine and modern/Western medicine, and
what shapes people's decisions about the medical interventions they
seek out? Secondly, what is the role of religious and state institutions
in shaping this relationship and people's medical choices? Based on
oral history interviews with traditional healers and modern medical
staff, as well as participant observation, I argue that in Rwanda,
modern and traditional medicine are not always opposed but rather
often exist on a continuum. The government of Rwanda has made a
pragmatic decision to support this relationship between modern and
traditional medicine, while also seeking to mold traditional medicine
more in the shape of modern practices.

METHODOLOGY

This research draws on different methods, including participant
observation and oral history interviews. I was able to interview
traditional healers and modern practitioners. I also interviewed
patients who experienced both traditional healing and modern
medicine at least once in their life. I conducted semi-structured
interviews with traditional healers, using questions such as, "Are
there any childhood experiences that made you particularly interested in becoming a traditional healer? What is the difference
between witchcraft and traditional healing methods? What are the
impacts on the health system, people's opinions, and politics of the
practice that you do in your community? How is the government
supportive of your services?"

   For theoretical insight, I draw on the work of Rebecca Marshland.
From Marshland's research on Tanzania, I note the similar perceptions that people have of traditional medicine in Tanzania and
Rwanda (namely, the idea that all Indigenous medicine is "traditional" and all biomedicine is "modern," and that these exist in
tension).[2] The language that is used in both countries is also similar.
For instance, miti shamba (which Marshland translates as "trees/
bush from the field") is used by traditional healers in both Tanzania
and Rwanda.[3] I also used information from different organizations
including the Abavuzi Gakondo (AGA) Rwanda Network, which is
a semi-independent organization that brings together all Rwandan
traditional healers.

Figure 7.2 | Miti shamba, used by traditional healers in Rwanda. Traditional healers like Innocent wish to preserve knowledge of these herbs for future generations.

My chapter has a particular focus on Immaculate, a traditional healer with more than sixty years of experience. Through interviews and participant observation, I followed Immaculate's work and learned from her about the many changes she has experienced over her six decades working as a traditional healer. Learning from Immaculate was an interactive, iterative process in which her insights shaped the direction my research took, and I tried not only to focus on her ideas but also to use them to explore questions that had not occurred to me.

WHAT ARE THE DIFFERENCES BETWEEN TRADITIONAL MEDICINE, MODERN OR WESTERN MEDICINE, AND WITCHCRAFT?

The Rwandan Ministry of Health, drawing on the definition of the World Health Organization (WHO), explains that traditional medicine refers to "the sum of the total of the knowledge, skills, and practices based on the theories, beliefs, and experiences indigenous to different cultures, whether explicable or not, used in the maintenance of health as well as in the prevention, diagnosis, improvement or treatment of physical and mental illness."[4] The ministry uses the terms *alternative medicine* and *complementary medicine* more or less interchangeably with *traditional medicine*. These are defined as opposed to *conventional medicine*, which is itself not defined in the guidelines. The absence of a definition of conventional medicine is striking but not surprising; conventional medicine is, through its omission, framed as "normal" – a "baseline" against which "alternative" or "other" healing practices and conceptions of health are positioned. This juxtaposition contributes to the sense that traditional and conventional medicine are somehow opposite or incompatible. Also absent from the official guidelines is the difference between traditional medicine and witchcraft, and though it is difficult to draw a hard line between these, the Ministry of Health works with traditional healers who only use plants as their source of medicine, rather than those who invoke ancestors or other spirits. This is the distinction I work with in this essay.

Rwanda's traditional healers are currently represented by the AGA Rwanda Network, which brings all the traditional healers together. Of course, this means determining what is traditional healing and what is witchcraft, and deciding which practices qualify as traditional healing and which are unacceptable under this rubric. According to Immaculate, who is a practitioner of traditional medicine, "the witchcraft sometimes they do things which are dangerous and against the community belief which goes against the works of the good traditional healers."[5] So, according to her, "good" traditional healers and the practitioners of witchcraft differ in their methods of curing. As a traditional healer, she only uses herbs as medicine, while witchcraft sometimes involves calling on ancestors and other spiritual practices. Some of the dangers of using witchcraft include, but are not limited to, death, especially when they request you to provide the ritual price of a person. Immaculate also noted that traditional healers, especially in Rwanda, are not hidden. They practice publicly, while practitioners of witchcraft, whose practices are often frowned upon by Christian members of the community, tend to be more secretive and difficult to find.

The creation of the AGA Rwanda Network in 2011 helped formalize this distinction. Only traditional healers, not practitioners of witchcraft, could be members. To be a member of the AGA Rwanda Network, a healer needed to be able to cure at least three diseases and pay the registration fee, which is equal to 50,000 RWF (this is a significant amount of money; roughly a month's rent for a three-bedroom house). Joining the AGA network also meant agreeing to forms of government oversight, in contrast to those practicing witchcraft, who are not formally surveilled in this way. AGA members are involved in government agencies that test medicines by assessing their chemical properties to check that they can't harm people. Through all those processes, AGA members are licensed to perform traditional healing in their communities.

However, despite the certification and testing processes that have developed since 2011, traditional healers are not universally accepted. Many Christians continue to believe that traditional medicine is sinful and should not be practiced, often conflating it with what Immaculate describes as witchcraft. According to one interviewee, practitioners of witchcraft use black magic to tell people that they can cure them of different diseases and rely on ancestors such as Gihanga, Nyabingi, and others. Others believe that traditional healers are tricksters who only practice medicine to get money. According to Immaculate, some of these perceptions are accurate. She said that some called themselves traditional healers as a way of making money by saying they cure different diseases to gain money from patients.

Others suggested that because traditional medicine is not scientifically tested in the same way as modern medicine, it should not be held up alongside modern medicine as a healing practice. This is the view of Habiyaremye Martin, one of my interviewees. He works in laboratory science and told me, "It is difficult to believe traditional medicine because there are no specific measures or tests that were done for them."[6] He believes that there should not be any continuum with modern medicine. Immaculate, however, argued that there are controls in place to distinguish between those just trying to make money and qualified healers, and to ensure the safety of traditional medicines. She said that the government gathered all the traditional healers and took samples of their medicines and measured them. They checked the quality of the medicine and provided certificates to healers with effective remedies.[7] This certification system was not especially transparent, and the government's credibility was deeply undermined by the Rwandan genocide. Nonetheless, most traditional healers accepted government regulation because it helped them establish trust with the communities they served.

Martin's view reflects a common perception of a conflicting relationship between modern and traditional medicine. However, despite religious and scientific objections to traditional medicine, close to 80 per cent of Rwanda's population has used traditional medicine at some point in their lives.[8] The next section explores the various factors that lead people to choose traditional medicine.

WHY DO PATIENTS CHOOSE TO USE TRADITIONAL MEDICINE?

The Rwanda National Policy of Traditional, Complementary, and Alternative Medicine mentions that some of the reasons people choose traditional medicine include cultural and historical influences, inaccessibility of conventional medicine-based health services, failure of treatment, and the long history of traditional methods in Rwanda.[9] My interviews with patients corroborate the Rwandan government's summary while also showing that people are flexible, moving back and forth between different practices to meet their particular needs. Leonille Nyirabazihana, one of my interviewees, explained that she tried to use modern medicine for her sickness. She had a problem with her legs, and she went to various hospitals for treatment but could not find a treatment that helped. The doctors at the hospitals she visited could not tell her what disease she had – they didn't diagnose her. They provided her with pills but these did not work. The problem continued to grow. The pain in her legs got so bad that it was impossible for her to work at times. Still, the hospitals could not provide a cure for her pain. This led her to shift to traditional medicine, which was ultimately able to cure her sickness. As she said, "I tried modern medicine and I lost a lot of money traveling to the different hospitals, such as when I went to Kigali, but I didn't receive any cure to my sickness. But I was able to get the medicine from the traditional healer who used the plant with low money [i.e., that was cheaper]."[10]

Leonille's words show that she used traditional medicine for two main reasons: conventional medicine had failed to diagnose her pain or provide a cure, and it was becoming too expensive to continue pursuing hospital-based medicine. In 2005, she got support from the traditional healer and felt well with the cure. I asked her about the medicines used to cure her, and she told me that they used the plants as the base medicine. There were some medicines that the patient should drink, and others to put on the body. Also, she told me that they used another method called "Guca Indasango," where a laser is used to cut open the body to help the medicine enter better and more quickly.[11] Leonille is an example of one of the many people who use traditional medicine because modern medicine did not work or proved too expensive. Her account also shows that people move between the different healing modalities according to their needs and what seems to be working for their bodies and financial circumstances. Leonille used traditional and conventional medicine in complementary ways, turning first to modern medicine in hospitals and then seeking out a traditional healer when her pain was not resolved. The next section develops the idea that these ostensibly discrete forms of medicine exist, in practice, on a continuum, with people moving between different forms of medical intervention to get the relief they need in a way that they can afford and access.

HOW ARE THE PRACTICES OF TRADITIONAL AND MODERN MEDICINE RELATED? A TRADITIONAL HEALER'S VIEW

We have seen how some people moved back and forth between the traditional and modern medical systems to find cures for their ailments, whether because of price, accessibility, or efficacy. One question that remained was how similar and different traditional and modern practices were. To answer this question, I turned to Immaculate.

Immaculate told me that she receives different patients. Sometimes she receives patients from the local hospitals that are hoping to be cured with traditional medicine after hospital-based treatment proves ineffective. She said that most of them come after they have tried modern medicine and found that it did not work for them. She shared an experience where she visited one of the patients in the modern hospital located in the Burera district. At the same time, there was an old woman whose daughter was in labour. However, her daughter was not able to give birth but the doctors couldn't find any reason for this trouble and refused to operate. While they were thinking about what to do, the old woman saw Immaculate passing and recognized her as a traditional healer. The woman asked the doctors if they would allow Immaculate to help them. The doctors asked Immaculate if she thought she could help with that case. She accepted but she had to go to find medicine in a different forest. She went *guhamura* (in Kinyarwanda, "to go in search of plants in the forest") for medicine. Before she left, the doctors asked her if she used plants to cure people. I asked, "Why did they ask you that question?" She told me that they feared that she may be using other methods that might seem like witchcraft. Also, she asked them to take the patient to her home because the medicine was at her home, but the doctors refused. This caused her to work more than four hours searching for medicines. After she got them, she came back and provided the medicine, which helped the patient to give birth.

This interaction shows the complex relationship between traditional and modern medicine. On the one hand, modern doctors accepted the help of a traditional healer, and Immaculate was able to help the woman give birth when the modern doctors were unable to do so. However, it also shows the power imbalance between the two practices. Even though invited by the woman's mother to assist, Immaculate was met with suspicion and compelled to search for hours for the plants she needed because the doctors would not allow her to treat the patient in her home.

The relationship is further complicated because sometimes Immaculate will send her own patients to receive modern medicine. I asked if referring patients to modern medicine was a typical practice for her. She told me that it is. When she finds that a patient can be treated by modern medicine, she sends them to the hospital with an explanation of what they are suffering from so that they can get medicine quickly. I witnessed this firsthand. The first time that I visited her, there were three people also walking towards her home, which is about an hour's walk from the main road. I reached Immaculate's home first because some of the others were sick and moving slowly. When they reached her house, she went to see them. After not more than twenty minutes, she came back, and I saw them leaving. I asked her why they were going back and she told me, "One man who is sick has a problem with blood pressure. So, I sent them back to go to see the doctors." She said that there was a time that the hospital sent patients to her from the hospital to cure them.[12] She gave me an example where the hospital sent her a patient who was suffering from *Ubushwima* disease. This is a kind of disease where the belly gets big, like a woman about to give birth. So Immaculate received the patients and treated them.

Immaculate's account left me wondering whether there were similarities in the way traditional and modern practitioners work. That is, we have seen that people turn to both forms of medicine as complements. But are there ways in which the practices overlap? The first practice I considered was the consultation performed in both traditional and modern medicine. For traditional medicine, I interviewed Immaculate and John, another traditional healer. They told me that the consultancy is done using the hands and eyes. Immaculate told me that she asks the patients what problems they have. After that, she can touch the blood vessels of the hand and feel how the blood is flowing in the patient's body. She only uses her hands to examine during the consultation. This may seem very different from the practices used in a hospital setting but I found many similarities. Martin, a laboratory specialist, told me that consultations are done by asking questions and making an examination if necessary – much like Immaculate and John's practice. Unlike in traditional medicine, technology (such as blood pressure monitors) is used to help in an examination. While the questions are similar, the methods used to answer them are different.

Likewise, I observed many similarities in diagnosing and treating illness. Modern medicine has general measures, signs, and symptoms of disease that help practitioners know the medicine that they need to provide to their patients. For traditional medicine, it is very much the same. John told me that he evaluated a patient's illness and then began the process of selecting a treatment. Immaculate told me that in her practice, the choice of medicine is also careful. However, unlike in modern medicine, there is not a general or standardized measurement of medicine for a certain disease. For modern medicine, the research has already been done, which makes it easy for the doctors to know the medicine and the dose that the patient can take. Immaculate, instead, determines the amount patient by patient, rather than using a standardized prescription or course of treatment.

Practitioners of modern medicine and those involved in teaching new generations of doctors often see great value in traditional medicine, offering further evidence of the complementarity of the two approaches. Dr Raymond Muganga, a pharmacy lecturer at the University of Rwanda's Department of Medicine and Pharmacy and a representative of the National Pharmacy Council, thinks that traditional medicine should be taught to the young generation. His grandfather was a traditional healer, and he expresses feeling a sense of loss at not having his grandfather's skills.[13] In a similar vein, the chemist and herbalist Jeremy Nkusi said that traditional herbs are powerful, and he gave examples of some diseases that can be cured by traditional herbal medicines more easily than by modern medicine. He said that asthma, amoeba, hepatitis, and obesity can be easily treated by traditional medicine compared to modern medicine because traditional medicine doesn't produce the cumulative repercussions or side effects.[14]

The follow-up process with the patient is also quite similar. Immaculate told me that her patients make sure that they go back home when they have finished all the medication. If the medications are not working, she requests them to come back. This is similar to modern medicine because if the medicine doesn't work, the doctor makes sure that you come back to get new medicine or an examination.[15]

OFFICIAL PERSPECTIVES ON TRADITIONAL MEDICINE

As the Ministry of Health's report on traditional medicine shows, the Rwandan government is increasingly involved in defining, regulating, and setting the parameters of traditional medicine.[16] One method of state intervention has been to attempt to regulate traditional healers' activities by forming them into cooperatives. This would allow all people to have access to both practices and would make traditional medicine operate more like modern medicine in some ways. However, it is important to understand why people continue to choose traditional medicine over modern medicine. Many people make this choice because modern medicine is much more expensive. There are also important cultural reasons why people prefer traditional to modern medicine, but for now, I will focus on the issue of accessibility and affordability.

According to the Ministry of Health of Rwanda, inaccessibility of conventional medicine-based health services is one of the reasons that people opt for traditional medicine.[17] In Africa, there is one traditional healer per 500 people, while the ratio of physicians to population is one per 40,000.[18] The greater number of traditional healers makes traditional medicine more accessible. Because many people look to traditional medicine for primary care, the government is keen to establish greater control over traditional healers. According to Dr Theophille Dushime, who oversaw the General Clinical Services in the Ministry of Health of Rwanda, the government, through the Ministry of Health, recognizes traditional medicine so that it can establish greater control over primary healthcare.[19] There is an ambivalence in the government's posture toward traditional medicine: the state recognizes, on the one hand, that it is how the majority of the population accesses healthcare, and that modern medicine is not affordable or accessible to most people. On the other hand, it attempts to mold traditional medicine in the image of modern medicine through various forms of regulation.

Traditional medicine is such an integral part of how people access healthcare in Rwanda that the government felt a need to incorporate it into its healthcare planning. However, we have not yet examined how this incorporation occurred in detail or the relationship between traditional and modern medicine from the perspective of the state. While we have seen that for patients, moving back and forth between traditional and modern medicine is a way to access better care at a lower cost, we have not yet considered the government's perspective on different medical practices or the ways that people use them. One of the government's goals is to increase the efficiency and professionalism of traditional medical practitioners.

Immaculate told me that the government provided traditional healers with training in professionalism, while also examining their healing practices.[20] They gathered all the traditional healers and they asked them for some samples for their examination. This was in 2003–04; even before the 2011 report, the government recognized the importance of traditional healing and tried to find ways to regulate it. After the examination of all the medicine, they chose the best medicines. Immaculate's medicine was among the few that passed the exam. However, Immaculate told me that examination system was not transparent, and the traditional healers didn't know the criteria that were used to determine which medicines passed the exam. One reason for this is that all the exams were done in Kigali, while she lived in the Nyabihu district in the northern part of Rwanda. Nonetheless, she passed the exam and received permission to continue her practice, while those who did not pass were prohibited from practicing traditional medicine any longer. Those who passed were asked to fulfill additional requirements before starting to practice medicine, including having a specific place to practice and belonging to an association of traditional healers. Those who didn't meet the requirements were asked to stop practicing. There were different punishments imposed on those who didn't follow the rules, such as losing their licences to work as traditional healers and being fined.

The government also intervened to organize traditional healers by helping to create and recognize the AGA Rwanda Network, the purpose of which is to "sustain and improve Rwandan Traditional medicine in line with modern development therefore fully exploit the related wisdom in Rwandan culture."[21] Among the supports provided by the government to the network was the protection of forests where traditional healers find their medicinal plants and herbs. The formation of the network has given traditional healers a platform to advocate for the needs and interests of the profession. These include preventing the felling of some tree species that are used as medicine. So, the AGA Rwanda Network, which works as an independent organization, is an example of the way that the government is willing to work with traditional healers to create a cooperative relationship between traditional and modern medicine, rather than an antagonistic one.

HOW ARE TRADITIONAL HEALERS TRAINED?

In 1980, the government of Rwanda established the Traditional Medicine Service in the healthcare division of the Ministry of Health. They also started the University Centre for Research in

Pharmacopoeia and Traditional Medicine. This centre was in charge of drafting a national policy on traditional medicine and coordinating, implementing, and establishing Rwandan traditional pharmacopoeia. The centre prepared basic documents to make sure that traditional medicine and health practitioners were integrated within the framework of primary healthcare.[22] Immaculate, who was one of the traditional healers at that time, mentioned that there was also a priest called Telesphone Kayinamura[23] who was appointed by the government to follow up with traditional healers. He visited all the traditional healers and invited some of those he considered the best to train at the centre. In addition to providing training in professionalism and patient interaction, the centre functioned to assemble all the traditional healers so that they could learn from each other. Each traditional healer had their specialty, so the school was a way for them to come together and teach and learn from each other. Immaculate was one of those who were supposed to attend that school. However, she couldn't attend as her husband refused to let her go because the school was located in the Huye district, far from their home.

Immaculate's experience illustrates how well-intentioned attempts to help healers learn from each other could actually exclude women and others unable to leave their families and lives and travel to the centre for further training. Indeed, many of the steps the government has taken to regulate and improve the provision of traditional medicine have also made the practice more exclusive. The goal has been to improve the quality of medical care; however, as Immaculate's long experience shows, one could offer exceptional medical services and still find oneself excluded by the government's programs. Despite her own exclusion, however, Immaculate is an advocate for greater training of traditional healers. She wanted to recommend the government and other people put more effort into improving the research on traditional medicine. She sees forms of modern scientific research as a way to improve traditional medicine. She also wants to write the book as a way of keeping her knowledge in a safe place that can be useful to other people in the future. There is a sense that despite the increased oversight of traditional medicine and its closer formal integration with modern medicine, the knowledge and skills of the current generation of healers will not be passed on. For this reason, Immaculate also thinks it would be better if traditional healers were allowed to have schools to teach people about their practices.

CONCLUSION

Far from being opposed practices, traditional healing and modern medicine in Rwanda exist on a continuum. People move between different medical practices in response to their perception of how well the practice is treating their ailments, their ability to afford different treatments, and the availability and accessibility of practitioners. For most Rwandese, the lower cost and greater number of traditional healers make them a significantly more accessible option than modern medicine, even as modern medicine is given a privileged place by the Rwandan government. At the same time, Immaculate's experience shows a symbiotic, if unequal, relationship between traditional healing and modern medicine.

There are many questions that remain for future researchers to consider. For instance, what are the networks of medical knowledge and practice that currently exist in Rwanda, and Eastern Africa more broadly? To what extent is local knowledge of plants, people, and medicines paramount, and to what extent does traditional healing knowledge work across the boundaries and contexts by understanding the transnational linkages between traditional healers in Africa? What is the impact of closer government regulation on traditional medicine, both in terms of the kinds of practices employed and who can practice?

Indeed, one of the key insights of this essay is that while many Rwandans rely on both traditional and modern medicine to meet their healthcare needs, and while the government has taken some steps to facilitate the provision of traditional medicine, traditional and modern medicine are not on equal footing in the eyes of the state. Modern medicine retains pride of place and ultimate authority in arbitrating what forms of medical practice are and are not legitimate, even though it remains expensive and inaccessible to many Rwandans.

NOTES

1   Rwandan Ministry of Health, *National Policy of Traditional, Complementary, and Alternative Medicine* (2019), 4. For the purposes of this chapter, modern, Western, and conventional medicine are used interchangeably. Traditional healing and traditional medicine are also used interchangeably.

2 Rebecca Marshland, "The Modern Traditional Healer: Locating 'Hybridity' in Modern Traditional Medicine, Southern Tanzania," *Journal of Southern African Studies* 33, no. 4 (2007): 751–65.

3 Ibid., 754.

4 Ministry of Health, *National Policy of Traditional, Complementary, and Alternative Medicine*, 4.

5 Immaculate, traditional healer, interview by author, 2019, Nyabihu district.

6 Martin Habiyaremye, laboratory worker, interview by author, 2019, Kigali.

7 Immaculate, interview by author.

8 Ministry of Health, *National Policy of Traditional, Complementary, and Alternative Medicine*, 5.

9 Ibid., 8.

10 Leonille Nyirabazihana, interview by author, 2019.

11 Lasers are used today for creating an open space on the body of the patient. However, in the past, they used other traditional materials such as bamboo parts and others.

12 Immaculate, interview by author.

13 Francis Byaruhanga, "Why Traditional Medicine Needs Support and Preservation," (2017), https://www.newtimes.co.rw/section/read/220939.

14 Ibid.

15 Immaculate, interview by author.

16 Ministry of Health, *National Policy of Traditional, Complementary, and Alternative Medicine*, 8.

17 Ibid.

18 Ibid.

19 Byaruhanga, "Why Traditional Medicine Needs Support and Preservation."

20 Immaculate, interview by author.

21 Jean Ntampaka, AGA *Rwanda Network Census*, (2012) retrieved from https://www.slideshare.net/jeanntampaka/aga-rwanda-network-census-14170967. This is a SlideShare that shows the census that was done by AGA Rwanda Network.

22 Ibid., 40. After the genocide, the Centre was changed into the Centre for Research in Phytomedicines and Life Sciences.

23 Msgr. Telesphone Kayinamura was a Monsignor and he created a village called Village of Mutendeli, which is known as Mutendeli at Kayinamura. This village is a center of traditional medicine, which is still there even after his death. Information related to Monsignor Kayinamura, Catholic Diocese of Kibungo, retrieved from http://www.diocesekibungo.com/fr/paroisses/bare/.

8

Until New Dawn ... New Day:
The Development of Gender Awareness
across Generations in Syria

Ismail Alkhateeb

Dear Reader,
I grew up in an Ismaili community in the middle of Syria. I have
a bachelor's degree in English literature and a master's degree in
translation. Between 2007 and 2014, I participated in multiple
programs with the Aga Khan Development Network in my hometown. This has granted me the opportunity to help engage the local
community in sustainable development. After the war that stormed
Syria in 2011, I participated in establishing a women's network
for peace building. This was an eye-opening experience in terms of
understanding how Syrian women challenged stereotypical gender roles during the war years. Thankfully, I worked closely with
inspiring women who found a way to lead the change despite the
hardships caused by the Syrian conflict.

I moved to France in 2018 and am currently in my second year
at Sciences Po Paris studying social sciences. I am particularly interested in community engagement in governance, as well as gender
studies and minority studies. As a women's rights activist and
Syrian citizen, I bring a unique perspective to understanding the
different contexts in which gender awareness changed, especially
regarding equality in access to education, financial resources, and
the labour market. Therefore, I was interested in learning about
those aspects and how they changed in the past decades. To do so,

I interviewed women who lived through the 1980s and 1990s to create a narrative of their realities, concerns, and priorities.

My passion to explore the unwritten history of women's struggle for equality started during my three-year journey with groups of Syrian women who lived through the hardships of the civil war while attempting to create peace in a war-torn country. I realized that those incredible women have not only changed their communities but also resisted the authoritarian narrative that always excluded them from the headlines. However, this struggle started many decades before the war, even though it has not been well documented. Therefore, I wanted to shed light on individual stories of Syrian women who resisted the oppressive patriarchal system and tried to change its narratives within their families and communities. I wanted to offer a perspective that is more detailed and personal than that provided by government surveys. For instance, one of my interviewees said that women's margin of liberty varies within different religious and cultural groups, but the same systems of oppression are imposed on women regardless. I believe this reflects the complexity of traditions and systems that need to be considered when studying changes in women's roles and challenges in the past three decades.

Oral history enables individuals to express their experiences in and on their own terms. Particularly because I am interested in the experiences of women from different generations, oral history has provided me with a valuable tool for understanding and weaving together these stories. It is also a way to include the nuance and complexity that I think are so important to understanding women's lived experiences of change and continuity in their lives, their communities, and wider society.

Sincerely,
Ismail Alkhateeb

INTRODUCTION

This research presents a narration of certain aspects of Syrian women's lives to offer a qualitative understanding of women's experiences, concerns, and priorities, as well as how those have changed (or remained the same) during the past three decades. During this period, the development of gender awareness went through radical changes and shaped women's status in Syrian society. However, there was also a great deal of continuity, particularly with respect to women's economic status. Drawing on both oral history interviews and survey data compiled by different NGOs and grassroots networks, this chapter offers a panorama of women's experiences in the past thirty years.

In March 2011, peaceful pro-democracy demonstrations broke out in Damascus and other cities and inspired thousands of people to participate in demands for their political liberties. However, the Syrian government responded to those demonstrations with deadly violence. Violence provoked violence and caused the country to slip into one of the worst civil wars in recent years, leaving hundreds of thousands dead or injured and millions of refugees. Women have been especially affected by the Syrian conflict as violence against women increased dramatically. In particular, sexual violence against women was used as a weapon of war. In addition, women had to endure the burden of displacement and the absence of male breadwinners. In the light of the war's consequences, gender roles in Syria started to shift, and many Syrian women's associations, groups, and organizations took the initiative to mobilize support to ensure the empowerment of Syrian women and to shield their rights and dignity.

Syrian women have long encountered political and economic exclusion as well as social suppression, which has limited their participation in decision-making and minimized the opportunities and possibilities available to them in comparison with men. In theory, Syrian women should have had equality with men since the Syrian civil and commercial codes granted women the right to control assets and access to education and labour market. Nevertheless, social norms continued to restrict women's participation in political, social, economic, and cultural life. Therefore, it is essential to look beyond governmental surveys to understand the challenges women continue to face and how to overcome them.

The research was undertaken in the form of semi-structured interviews and short life stories with two women from different minority groups in Syria. Heyam Almouli is a fifty-seven-year-old retired teacher, born and raised in Salamieh, Syria. She studied at the Teacher Preparation Institute and started her career as a teacher at the age of twenty. Coming from an Ismaili family, she was brought up in a progressive community that promoted women's rights and gender equality. She taught for more than thirty years in remote villages in Hama Governorate.

Figure 8.1 | Heyam Almouli, a retired teacher from Salamieh. Heyam taught for more than thirty years in remote regions of Syria.

Rola Ibrahim is a forty-six-year-old sociologist born and raised in Homs, Syria. She studied sociology at Damascus University and graduated in 1999. She was brought up in a traditional family that belongs to the Murshidis minority. She has worked as a gender-based violence (GBV) coordinator and psychological counselor with multiple organizations. She writes articles on gender issues and provides psychological support for GBV survivors. Together, through personal and professional experience, these women offer in-depth perspectives on the struggle for gender equality in Syria and how it has developed over the past three decades.

Working with only two interviewees means my chapter is not representative of all women in Syria; however, I draw on larger surveys and other data sources to provide a more well-rounded picture. The advantage of working with two women in such detail is that their stories and perspectives can be treated holistically, as narratives valuable in and of themselves, rather than as discrete data points only

Figure 8.2 | Rola Ibrahim, a researcher and counselor. Rola is a sociologist who works on issues of gender-based violence in Syria.

treated in aggregate terms. I have also chosen to include excerpts of our conversations in which I participate as an interlocutor to reflect the ways our interviews were co-created with both narrator and interviewer playing important parts in shaping the direction, flow, and subject of conversation.

Because of the wide array of contexts in which women have struggled for greater equality and rights, this paper is divided into a series of sections that address some of the most important areas for gender equality. In particular, it examines the following issues, each of which is taken up in turn over the course of the essay: first, I address discrimination in education. Women's access to education correlates with the development of their status and indicates the improvement of gender awareness. Second, I consider economic empowerment: investing in increasing women's economic independence paves the way for more equality in decision-making in all aspects of life. Third, I turn to gender awareness, by which I mean the process of changing attitudes, behaviours, and beliefs that reinforce gender inequality and are crucial to countering gender injustice. Fourth, I examine domestic violence, as there is a significant correlation between a society's level of gender inequality and rates of domestic violence. Relatedly, I look at child marriage because a root cause of child marriage is gender inequality, and the practice is sustained by social norms and religious beliefs that reinforce injustice toward women and girls. Finally, I take up reproductive health. Many of women's reproductive health problems are consequences of discrimination and lack of power to decide whether and when to bear children. It is an indicator of whether women have authority over their bodies or not. When observing the development of women's rights in Syria from the point of view of individuals who represent certain cultural groups from specific backgrounds, one can appreciate the diversity of women's experiences as individuals rather than thinking of women as a homogeneous social group.

DISCRIMINATION IN EDUCATION

The Syrian government approved the Convention on the Elimination of All Forms of Discrimination Against Women (CEDAW) in 2002. This convention, first adopted by the United Nations (UN) in 1979, strongly recommends that girls' and women's right to education is a central obligation of state parties. If parents refuse to educate their daughters, the government can take legal action against them. Nevertheless, the barriers to girls' education in Syria have proven resistant even in the face of the government's recent commitment to their schooling. To understand the roots of educational discrimination against women, we need to look back to the decades before the government approved CEDAW.

In the 1980s and 1990s, some women took the lead in breaking the societal barriers that excluded them from education. Those women paved the way for generations of Syrian girls to demand their educational rights. Heyam shared her experience in the 1980s when she pursued higher (postsecondary) education. In the first half of the 1980s, the vast majority of girls in Salamieh chose to become teachers by attending the Teacher Preparation Institute in Hama. Such a decision was shaped by societal factors – teaching was stereotypically the best career for women as they did not have to work with men and earned a good salary with limited working hours. This institute was also located in a nearby city so girls from Salamieh did not have to move away from their families. Nevertheless, a few girls from this city had taken the initiative to challenge the traditions by moving to more distant and larger cities such as Damascus or Aleppo to pursue their studies in fields other than teaching. Because those girls were few back then, their stories went viral as pioneers and have influenced many other girls.

In 1994, Rola challenged her family and society by moving from Homs to Damascus to pursue a degree in sociology. In her case, it was unusual for an eighteen-year-old girl to leave her city to seek education on her own. In the following excerpt from our interview, Rola shared the challenges and opportunities that came with her decision:

> ROLA: There were some things that I refused. I could get married in the tenth grade, but I refused and this has caused me problems. I also had to pursue my studies in Homs, but I refused and moved to Damascus and this has caused me problems.
> ISMAIL: So, what you did was unusual at that time even in your community.
> ROLA: Exactly, and this was a revolution that turned my life upside down, but this also has opened the door for other women after that.[1]

Rola's words reflect a sense of connection between her generation and the younger generations – the notion that the challenges she faced in defying convention and moving to Damascus were worth it, not only (or even mainly) for her own life but also, and more importantly, for the women who came after her. Rola mentioned that she observed notable changes during the first half of the 1990s as girls from more traditional communities started seeking further education: "The proportion of girls in universities has risen relatively. I used to see girls from Dara'a and other provinces coming to the university. Thus, this was a reasonable proportion in comparison with the past."[2] However, even as young women began pursuing education away from their hometowns and families, they remained bound by restrictive practices. Rola remembered a young girl who went away to college to study medicine, only to be called back by her family to be married. She noted, "The gender awareness among the girls was low. Girls used to go to university for some reasons like free higher education and dormitories. Regarding gender awareness, it was low."[3] In other words, Rola perceived that while young women may have gone to university in prior decades, they did not necessarily see higher education as having a political or social valence with respect to gender-based inequality.

Importantly, even though girls from all classes and communities in Syria faced similar kinds of oppression when seeking higher education, this oppression was not equally distributed, especially among cultural groups. For example, in Salamieh in the 1980s, Heyam believes that women's education was more appreciated and accepted within the Ismaili community than in other cultural communities. As she said:

> I noticed that the Ismaili community is aware of the importance of women's education and work more than others. Other groups favored girls to get married at a young age rather than pursuing their education. Such was the case where we used to live. For example, in my family, all of us were girls who pursued their education and graduated. Whereas in our neighbourhood, the majority of girls got married at a young age. Those belong to a different cultural group (other than Ismailis). We, as Ismailis, never thought of getting married before graduating and completing our studies. It is because of what we have learned through observation; that women who are not productive and [who are] economically unstable, their life quality is poor. This is where I personally stand on that.[4]

The situation in Homs in the 1990s was not very different. Rola noted that religion played an important role in determining group attitudes toward women's education and women's freedoms, more generally. She mentioned that girls from groups other than Sunni Muslims were more aware of their right to access education.

ISMAIL: In Homs city, where there is a cultural diversity, was there a common oppression in all cultural communities?

ROLA: Yes, but in an uneven way. We, who belong to non-Sunni Islam, are more liberated. And the most liberated are the Christian people (as girls). This was the general atmosphere back then.[5]

Rola also mentioned that even high-profile decision-makers have not taken women's right to access higher education seriously: "I remember that one day a girl went to meet the rector of Damascus University in 2002 to ask him for a dormitory as she was pursuing a master's degree. The rector answered her sarcastically: 'Go home and get married, that is much better for you!'"[6]

Resistance to women's education finds fertile soil not only within religious communities where women's freedoms are broadly restricted but also in the very institutions of higher education that are meant to serve all Syrians. When women do access higher education, often over the objections of their families and communities, and even the institutions where they enroll, their participation in tertiary education is heavily restricted to certain fields. Nevertheless, more and more women are finding their way to pursue higher education degrees in the past decade. By 2010, for example, women PhDs outnumbered men in fields like medicine, agriculture, math, and information technology (IT).

This would not have been possible without women fighting against the norms, societal oppression, and stereotypes that restricted their access to and participation in higher education. Unfortunately, the outbreak of war in 2011 has had negative consequences for women's education, despite the incredible achievements made by women students and scholars. The war, which caused both a crisis of displacement and the destruction of many educational facilities, has affected Syrian girls the most.

The Syrian civil war has been distinguished by a brutal targeting of women. The United Nations has gathered evidence of systematic sexual assault of women and girls by combatants in Syria and described rape as "a weapon of war." For instance, radical terrorist groups such as the Islamic State (ISIL) have increased the brutal treatment and sexual enslavement of women and girls in the areas under their control.[7] This violence against women affects their opportunities for education. Parents, fearing for their daughters' safety and "honour," are more reluctant to allow their daughters to travel long distances to attend school. The net enrollment rate for primary education dropped from 92 per cent in 2004 to 61 per cent by 2013 (61.1 per cent for girls and 62.4 per cent for boys) and for secondary education, from around 72 per cent in 2009 to 44 per cent in 2013 (43.8 per cent for girls and 44.3 per cent for boys).[8]

ECONOMIC EMPOWERMENT

Syrian law ensures women's equal rights to own property, run businesses on their own, and initiate legal processes. According to the Syrian legal system, Syrian women have full and independent control over their income and assets and are free to enter into business. Nevertheless, the reality does not match women's formal legal rights. Women who own property via inheritance or their own financial means may face social restrictions when attempting to make use of that property. Also, women are not expected to save their income and use it for their own purposes. Therefore, many Syrian women don't have authority over their major life decisions, including education, career, marriage, divorce, and so on. Heyam mentioned that in her community, women started to realize the significance of women's work and the importance of controlling their income as a way to gain rights, reject men's domination over their lives, and improve their quality of life. In her view, economic independence before marriage is one of the most important factors in shaping women's lives:

> Out of what we have observed, women who are not productive and not economically independent have miserable lives. This is my personal point of view. Those women are devoted to their children, households, and spouses. In addition, they suffer from oppression, persecution, and deprivation of their right to be free. They are not free to move, they can't speak their minds. In contrast, women who were raised to prioritize education and career, they postponed marriage till they were able to be economically independent.[9]

This changed during the 1990s when women were freer to move to other cities and choose the careers they preferred. As Heyam noted, "People became more aware of the significance of women's economic independence. This was derived from the fact that women contribute more when they are economically independent, and also because it is human right to decide what they want to do with their lives." She twined together two important ideas: that it is better for Syrian society (from an economic point of view) when women can lead independent lives, participate in higher education and the work-force, and not be financially dependent on male relatives or spouses; and that such freedoms are a basic human right for women.

When looking at women's status in rural areas, the situation has always been difficult. Women contribute to their household incomes by spending most of their time working in agriculture. Still, they rarely own any shares in the property they manage, such as the land, animals, or real estate. In cases of divorce, women are often left without any type of financial guarantee or other sources of income. Heyam talked about women in rural areas, specifically in the villages of Hama Governorate. There, women are given some freedom to go out on their own, but apart from that, men dominate all aspects of life. In addition, women work on the farms, feed animals, and do heavy agricultural labour. Rola also mentioned the findings of a sur-vey she conducted in the countryside of Damascus while completing her sociology degree. Women spent their time working on the farm and taking care of animals. Still, in comparison to what they contrib-uted to their households' economy, they owned nothing to support themselves if their spouses abandoned them. In short, during the 1980s and 1990s, women in rural areas were not treated as partners, but as labourers. In cases of separation, women were often unable to take care of their children as they lost their livelihoods. Therefore, they were often compelled to leave their kids. As an example of this, Heyam talked about the story of a woman in a village who left her four-year-old daughter to her former husband as she did not have any way to support herself in raising a child. She also mentioned the story of another woman who had to abandon her three children after she got divorced. Neither she nor her family could afford to raise three children, despite her supporting her household when she was married.[10]

In the 1980s, efforts were made to empower women to take con-trol over their life decisions and become economically independent and self-sufficient. Many women sought training and education to improve their careers – with many becoming successful business-women, influential managers, and even ministers. Rola talked about the changes that occurred during the 1990s and the 2000s when Syrian women became more independent in comparison to the 1990s. She said, "I remember many women in that period were successful:

such as TV journalists with remarkable charisma. Also, many women proved to be high-profile leaders of institutions and organizations. One of the factors that contributed to such developments is simply having childcare centres in their workplaces."[11] However, according to the Central Bureau of Statistics in Syria, women's participation in the labour market barely changed between 2001 and 2010. There was a dramatic shift away from agricultural occupation to work in the service sector, with the percentage of women in agricultural jobs falling by more than half. This suggests that while women remained employed at overall the same rates over this decade, there was a remarkable shift in the kinds of work women did.

Of course, these figures do not reflect all the domestic labour performed by women, which remains unevenly distributed between men and women even when women are employed outside the home. And, as Rola noted, what income women do earn by participating in the waged economy is typically handed over to their husbands, meaning they do not control this money. Thus, women's labour is under-recognized, and the income they do receive rarely offers them financial autonomy.

GENDER AWARENESS

So far, this narrative has documented important instances of gender-based inequality in Syria. However, many social factors normalize these inequalities, making them seem easy to take for granted. One of these factors is a system of social values that considers women as inferior to men and in need of male guidance and discipline. It is important to understand how people come to recognize these inequalities as such – how inequalities have been denaturalized and transformed into parts of society that can be changed. Families play an important role in entrenching or challenging these norms within the domestic space, as Heyam and Rola's experiences illustrate.

According to Heyam, she was raised in a family that tried to break the pattern of normalizing discrimination against women. When I asked her how she started developing her awareness toward the cycle of gender injustice, she answered:

This is thanks to my family and the way I was brought up. We observed in our neighbourhood how girls were oppressed and had no rights or freedom at all. They were not even allowed to express themselves. Those families, like mine, realized that girls should be given the opportunity to be empowered before thinking of getting married. Unfortunately, this was not the case for all families.[12]

Rola had a very different experience in which her gender was used to limit her autonomy within her family. The following exchange illustrates some of the ways gender operated in the context of her family:

ISMAIL: When did you feel the difference in the gender roles in the family?
ROLA: I felt like I was segregated. Plus, the phrase "because you are a girl (female)" was repeated over and over again. Because you are a girl you have to do this, you can't stay late outside. Because you are a girl you can't study outside Homs (in a different city). There was a long list of forbidden things.
ISMAIL: And was this during your middle school?
ROLA: Yes. It was always repeated that "because you are a girl" you have to do housework. No going out and no staying out late.[13]

Nevertheless, she came to realize that such discrimination is not normal. This was thanks to a book she read during middle school:

ROLA: I read a book that has lit a lantern in my head and changed my mind. It is what drove me to gender awareness prior to all girls in my surrounding. It is *An Introduction to the Psychology of the Oppressed Man* by Mustapha Hejazi.[14] When I read it, I was in the tenth grade and it changed many things that used to be facts to me in terms of gender and women status. The book has a whole chapter about women. This is what granted me awareness before going to college.
ISMAIL: So, you felt that you could see the gender differences?
ROLA: Exactly.
ISMAIL: After you read this book and you gained awareness, how did you transfer this awareness to your personal and social life?
ROLA: It has changed a lot. Also, there was another book, *An Introduction to Studying the Arab Society* by Hesham Sharabi.[15] I mean, there are social aspects, customs, and social traditions that are needed in our lives and we need to live with them as

they are. But after reading these two books, I gained a critical perspective at the women's reality, and I felt that the women's status isn't right. And this was reflected on me as I wasn't a typical woman anymore.

For both Heyam and Rola, different experiences denaturalized gender inequality and helped them form opinions and beliefs that challenged the status quo. From relatively young ages, they started to distinguish among the various forms of injustice being inflicted on women in their community as well as in other communities. In her testimony, Heyam mentioned that she observed in the 1980s even worse social injustice towards women when she left to teach in the rural area of Hama Governorate.

> I observed many social norms that led to the girls lacking self-confidence. The parental approach for bringing up girls made them think that whatever they do they are wrong. Even to express their opinions or to laugh was considered socially unacceptable. In the villages, where I used to live to teach in the 1980s, the social norms were very different from my own community. Women there have some type of freedom to go out and have fun, but they were not given any essential freedom or value. Men were dominant and in possession of everything.[16]

Change has been slow to come to these rural areas, as Rola observed during a study she conducted in 2000 as part of her undergraduate studies. This study surveyed women in the rural area of Damascus Governorate. She came to similar conclusions as did Heyam.

> ROLA: I have conducted research with a professor in Damascus City and the countryside of Damascus. The topic of the study was about the role of women and their social status. The study was based on a very well-designed questionnaire. We had samples from Damascus and the countryside of Damascus. This was in the year 2000 and the sample was pretty wide, with a very strict validation methodology. The results showed that women's role is significant, and it doesn't fit with their social status at that time.
> ISMAIL: Could you clarify what do you mean by "role?"
> ROLA: What she is doing. Simply, how she spends her time. She spends her day in housework, childcare, and agricultural work,

as we studied agricultural societies too. Also, some women do household repairs (like gas bottle installation), while these tasks are usually connected to men. And this, in comparison with what she owns (like land) and she doesn't own the delegated divorce right, means she owns nothing.[17]

ISMAIL: So, this research is extremely important as it showed that her productivity is much higher than her social status. And my question here is: Is this situation justified in traditions and in law as well?

ROLA: Not in the law generally. But in family law status laws and in women-related laws: yes. But in fact, traditions are stronger than the laws.

Once more, Rola's research showed a significant gap between the formal laws governing women's rights and the social and family practices that constrained those rights in daily life. Even the Syrian Commission for Family Affairs' 2014 report stated that women in rural areas experience gender-based violence more frequently than do women in urban areas.[18]

As a sociologist, Rola believed that gender awareness in Syrian society has not developed significantly and meaningfully in the past three decades. She came to this conclusion based on the fact that there is no plan on raising awareness of gender-based inequality and violence on the national level. Such a plan, she expressed, would help decrease inequalities between men and women. It may also help develop methods for understanding how gender roles and norms are changing, something that, according to Rola, does not yet exist.[19] While people may reference superficial aspects of women's liberation, such as modern clothes, smoking in public, and engagement in the workplace, these do not capture all the forms of inequality and oppression that affect Syrian women.

DOMESTIC VIOLENCE

As with other forms of gender-based inequality, gender-based and domestic violence are normalized in Syria to the extent that it is difficult to understand the scope of the problem. Women often hesitate to speak up against their abusers who are, most of the time, their brothers, husbands, boyfriends, or fathers. For instance, Heyam mentioned that during the 1990s, very few women could dare to speak up about being abused at home by their male family members or husbands.[20]

> Not many women have spoken in public about domestic violence. Only those women who could not carry on their marital lives with their spouses due to excessive violence. The majority of women kept silent and swallowed their families' abuse and spouses' violence just to maintain their marriage and household. Only when things get to the point of separation, those women would speak up. That was very common during the 1990s. Even in the 2000s, I could not notice any remarkable progress. Violence against women was not being spoken about in public. Nevertheless, divorce is becoming more common nowadays due to domestic violence. I am not sure what the reason is. It could be women's awareness about the right to stop violence in their households, that is in particular after 2011. Such violence was considered a personal issue that should not be revealed. It was not considered normal, but she would compromise to save her marriage.[21]

The normalization of domestic violence has led many women to suffer in silence. Heyam shared a story about one of her best friends who endured a long abusive marriage, even though she had serious heart failure. This story left me speechless, so I had to stop recording for five minutes before I could resume the interview.

> I knew one of the victims who died after a long, abusive, and miserable marriage, who died in the end. She endured her husband's cruelty and violence so much. She was seriously ill; her heart was failing. She never spoke up about it, she kept silent for the sake of her children. She was not working as well. Her heart's condition in addition to the abusive relationship led to her death young. She knew that it was not normal to be physically abused this way, but she never thought of seeking separation. Even her family let her down. This also has affected her children dramatically, even when they became grown-ups.[22]

She also added that in the 1970s, divorce bore a social stigma. Therefore, women who were being abused at home often remained silent about their experiences to avoid divorce. Those women who did not have alternative sources of income or any properties tolerated much violence rather than seeking separation.

In 2014, the Syrian Commission for Family Affairs surveyed 5,000 women over eighteen years of age. The study's report concluded that women are subjected to different types of physical violence ranging from threatening, punching, slapping, and kicking to the use of knives, belts, sticks, and even rifles. For instance, over 45 per cent of surveyed women said that they were being punched, slapped, or kicked. Also, 16.3 per cent of them mentioned that they were hit with objects that caused severe pain or led to a serious injury. When asked about the identity of their abusers, 68 per cent answered that it was their spouse.[23]

Rola mentioned that between 2000 and 2010, gender-based violence was referred to as violence against women. Back then, speaking up about violence against women was unacceptable. It was particularly difficult to discuss this issue in the public media. She added that even now there are many women who consider domestic violence normal.

Heyam agreed with this description and added that domestic violence against women increased in the years after the war. She told me about an incident she witnessed in Salamieh's courthouse:

> I have met a young woman with her two daughters when she was in the process of delivering the children to her former husband to finalize a custody case. Although they were divorced, her former husband insulted and verbally abused her in front of the courthouse staff. Even though he is [now] alien to her, he dared to abuse her.[24]

Incidents such as this show that women's status has not improved very much as men still abuse women without any form of social or legal restrictions or consequences.

Murder is the most extreme form of domestic violence. One form of murder occurs when the man claims to be defending a woman's "honour." Honour crimes are rarely discussed in public and honour crimes are not considered first-degree murder. The Syrian penal code still tolerates lenient sentences for murders committed in the name of "honour" despite a recent reform that brought increased penalties and abolished the possibility of complete vindication for certain "honour crimes."[25] In the 1980s, Heyam thinks that honour crimes were more common. Now, this kind of murder seems to be less prevalent, perhaps because more of the population rejects it. However, in prior decades, many men killed their wives, daughters, or sisters. Their sentences did not exceed ten or twelve years, whereas the Syrian penal code imposes a sentence that ranges between twenty years and capital punishment for the crime of murder.[26]

In part, the reduction in honour crimes can be connected to activism surrounding the issue. Civil society and feminist activists struggled, campaigned, and advocated for reforming the Syrian penal code to remove honour crimes as a mitigating factor in the early 2000s. Rola talked about one of the many attempts to stiffen the penalty for such crimes and consider them as first-degree murders.

> In 2009, I was a member of the national team to protect children from violence. There wasn't a significant amendment [to the penal code] regarding the so-called "honour crimes." And what is strange is that some influential figures like judges and clerics stood against changing it. And plenty of intense debates led to a secret vote. I think the ultimate decision was political. I don't think that secularists are the ones who won. And there were rumors about fraud. The amendment was, instead of putting the convict in jail, the punishment became between a sentence of one year and a half to three years. There was also an amendment in the family law but it was cancelled (out of nowhere) despite the great efforts made to achieve it. There were laws correlated to protect children from violence and family protection and women protection. And all of them failed. The only achievement was the one related to honour crimes.[27]

She also mentioned that even high-profile figures such as judges and academics opposed the project of amending the laws surrounding "honour crimes." They argued that such an amendment would lead to women breaking social norms. They did not consider this unfair law a problem but rather saw it as a "social guardian" that would keep women in their designated subordinate places.

Despite some legal and societal advances in combatting gender-based violence, after the outbreak of war in 2011, domestic violence has reportedly been on the rise. For instance, field research conducted by the I Am She Network in 2018 showed that the majority of women in Idlib Governorate are subjected to physical violence, with a slight variation between the city and the rural areas.[28]

CHILD MARRIAGE

Child marriage is not a new phenomenon in Syria. Before the Syrian civil war, 13 per cent of Syrian women aged twenty to twenty-five were married before the age of eighteen. Conflict and disasters compound the pre-existing poverty, gender inequality, and lack of education that cause child marriage to happen in the first place. However, there is significant regional and cultural variation in the prevalence of child marriage. For example, Rola could have been forced to get married at the age of fifteen if she had submitted to the social norms in her community in the 1980s.[29] On the other hand, Heyam mentioned that in her surrounding, very few incidents of child marriages of thirteen- or fourteen-year-old girls occurred during the eighties and nineties. Even in rural areas, where she used to teach, child marriage was rare. Girls were not allowed to get married before the age of fourteen.[30]

After the outbreak of war in 2011, child marriage increased dramatically. Important aspects of child marriage also changed in the context of mass displacement. I saw some of this firsthand. While I was working as senior program coordinator for Women for the Future of Syria, I contributed to a qualitative study on child marriage in internally displaced person (IDP) camps in the north of Syria. The study came to several conclusions. First, most girls married willingly and were not forced by decision-makers at home. Nevertheless, most of them were not aware of the dangerous health, psychological, and social consequences of getting married at this young age. Second, most of them stated that they did not receive any type of support from their families or their spouses after marriage. In addition to asking how the decision to marry was made, we asked young married women about how marriage had impacted their well-being. The majority of women experienced feelings of isolation and permanent restlessness; loss of ability to enjoy activities; decreased ability to achieve; lack of independence; and lack of feeling safe.[31] Heyam also mentioned that after the war, she heard about cases of girls who got married at the age of thirteen and fourteen. She considered this as a major backslide of women's status even in comparison to the 1980s and 1990s.

In 2019, the Syrian Parliament approved amendments to the Status Law, whereby the legal marriage age is set at eighteen, and marrying below this age is criminalized. However, given that a high percentage of marriage contracts that are not registered in the courts are performed on underage girls, the problem remains more social than purely legal.

REPRODUCTIVE HEALTHCARE

Reproductive healthcare is closely related to gender-based violence. For many women, inadequate access to reproductive healthcare is an indicator that women do not have authority over their bodies. In fact, violence against women, or even the threat of violence, is manifested in the fact that many women do not have the ability to control their own reproductive health and to plan their own families. Likewise, women who experience emotional or physical violence or other forms of abuse within their relationships may also have less ability to negotiate the use of condoms or other contraceptives with their partners to protect themselves from unwanted pregnancies and related negative health outcomes. The stigma related to abortion remains one of the most dangerous forms of gender-based violence as it leads to many women losing their lives during pregnancy.

Heyam talked about the 1970s when birth control was unheard of in the environment in which she grew up. Women's role was to bear children as long as they could, regardless of whether they wanted to or not.

> During the 1970s, birth control was not heard of at all in the community I grew up in. As long as they are fertile and can bear children, they keep on doing so. There were no ways to control this or even awareness regarding this matter. Sometimes, they gave birth to up to ten or twelve children. They were not aware of the health risk on the mother's body or the child's. Women had no right to say whether they are willing to get pregnant or not.[32]

Also, she mentioned that abortion was taboo except when the pregnancy threatened the mother's life. Apart from that, abortion was generally rejected and considered as socially prohibited.

Lack of access to birth control was a problem experienced among all social classes and cultural groups, according to Heyam. During the 1980s, however, there was a change, as health centres started raising awareness about family planning, and birth control methods such as pills and helix contraception became available. Heyam noted, "In the beginning of the 1980s, things started to change as contraceptives became available. Also, because women started to participate in the labour market, they needed to plan their families and economize on having children."[33] Once again, we see the links between economic arguments about women's productive potential and women's bodily autonomy. In this way, reproductive choice was instrumentalized as part of a larger argument that to be as productive workers as possible, women needed to control their fertility.

During the second half of the 1980s and throughout the 1990s, the Syrian government, in cooperation with the UN Population Fund, launched a project for reproductive health. This led to positive changes in family planning and women's reproductive health. Heyam summarized the results of this program:

> Family size decreased due to the fact that women became aware of the risky consequences of repetitive pregnancies. Also, women needed to control birth as they started focusing more on their careers. Well, health comes first. So, they became aware that they need to maintain their well-being. Contraceptives became available along with raising awareness campaigns on family planning.[34]

Before those changes occurred, women did not have a sense of ownership over their bodies. They were "indoctrinated" by the social norms that their duty after marriage was bearing children for as long as they were capable. However, the 1980s brought significant changes as women prioritized their well-being and decided when to get pregnant. The changes of the 1980s have had positive effects on other health indicators in the decades since. Statistics show that maternal morbidity decreased between 2001 and 2004, as there were fifty-eight cases out of every 100,000 live births in 2004 in comparison with 2001, when the rate was almost 65.4 out of every 100,000 live births. Also, in 2004, newborn morbidity was 3.1 per cent.[35]

However, these opportunities for family planning did not come without activism on the part of women. Rola talked about the role that the General Union of Syrian Women (GUSW) played during the 1990s in campaigning for family planning. The GUSW aimed to mobilize Syrian women while developing their education, political activism, and other skills to help women become more effective members in socioeconomic settings. They attempted to raise awareness of the significance of birth control to practice effective family planning. Nevertheless, they encountered opposition in some areas. She mentioned that a centre in Dara'a was vandalised as people considered family planning and birth control to be religious taboos.[36]

Heyam noted that women have historically been blamed for the composition of their families and the sex of their children:

> During the 1970s, there was a widespread misconception that women were responsible for determining the child's gender. Therefore, women were being blamed for bearing female children, as the society favors male children over females. So, women felt frustrated and guilty. In this case, women kept getting pregnant until they gave birth to a male child. Even during the 1980s, this issue remained despite the development of awareness. This also has continued throughout the 1980s up to the beginning of the 1990s. Many families had more than five female children until they could have a male, but when it did not happen, they stopped trying when the women could not bear children anymore. Some of these women were highly educated, and they know that the man is biologically responsible for determining the child's gender, still they submitted to social pressure.[37]

As with many other aspects of women's rights, after the war that started in Syria in 2011, there were dramatic setbacks in women's access to reproductive healthcare and family planning options. For instance, several studies have shown that since the start of the war, the use of contraceptives has declined while menstrual irregularity, unplanned pregnancies, preterm birth, and infant morbidity have increased.[38]

Rola talked about her observations in IDP camps and shelters when she was providing psychological support to displaced women. When she interviewed women who recently gave birth, they said that they bear children so their spouses don't abandon them. Others said that they have many children in the hopes that they may help improve the household's financial security in the future.[39]

Heyam mentioned that in some communities, using contraceptives is religiously prohibited. For some women, there is a lack of knowledge and access to contraceptives due to the war; for other women, this was a more long-standing problem that predated the conflict. Heyam said:

> In some remote villages, families don't practice any type of family planning, so the family size is still big. Mostly, the reason for not using contraceptives is religious. In other cases, it is the lack of awareness or the inaccessibility to healthcare that prevents women from practicing birth control. In addition, due to repetitive pregnancies, there are many [cases of] infant morbidity and abortions due to health complications.[40]

She added that women in remote villages may undergo abortions by themselves or by unspecialized midwives, regardless of the risks of not having antibiotics or sterilizers. Syrian law restricts the granting of abortion in the Practice of Medical Professions Law, which stipulates that a doctor or a midwife shall be prohibited from performing an abortion, by any means, unless the continuation of pregnancy is a threat to the life of the woman.[41] Also, it does not permit abortion in cases where girls have been raped, according to articles 525–532 of the penal code. The consequences of this for women are severe, as Heyam observed:

> Health centres and practitioners refuse to provide abortion without any medical causes, because it is considered as a crime. Nevertheless, women still seek abortion illegally and secretly without specialized supervision. In fact, abortion is legally rejected, but it is not socially denied. Therefore, many abortions happen behind closed doors.[42]

She added that there are no rehabilitation programs for women who have received abortions in health centres. Even when women are able to access abortions through the medical system, they do not receive follow-up medical, psychological, or social support for what they have experienced.

Rola believed that women's ownership over their bodies is essential and they should be the only ones who can decide whether to get pregnant, give birth, or have an abortion. Complicating this, as Rola added, is the fact that women who have abortions bear a sense of shame, even if they are married.[43] So, while there were some important advances for women's reproductive healthcare motivated by activism and organizing around these issues, long-standing religious and cultural norms, coupled with the displacement of the war, have frustrated efforts to increase access to safe reproductive healthcare in the twenty-first century.

CONCLUSION

The past four decades have witnessed both changes and continuities in Syrian women's rights. Girls and women participate in education and higher education at rates similar to those of boys and men, rates of child marriage have declined, and some laws barring women from full economic participation have been changed. However, particularly following the outbreak of the Syrian conflict in 2011, many women continue to struggle to access reproductive healthcare, experience high rates of gender-based violence, and remain economically dependent on their male relatives. Nevertheless, some women have become more aware of the gender inequality they are subjected to in different forms and have used this awareness to advocate for change in their communities and at the national level. These women have paved the way for future generations to continue their struggle for women's equality in Syria.

NOTES

1 Rola Ibrahim, interview by author, 5 July 2020, online.
2 Ibid.
3 Ibid.
4 Heyam Almouli, interview by author, 11 August 2020, online.
5 Rola Ibrahim, interview by author.
6 Ibid.
7 Olivia Caeymaex, "How to Stop Sexual Slavery in Conflict Zones," United Nations University, 12 November 2014, https://unu.edu/publications/articles/how-to-stop-sexual-slavery-in-conflict-zones.html.
8 Marta Guasp Teschendorff, "Loss of Access to Education Puts Well-being of Syrian Girls at Risk," United Nations University, 17 September 2015, https://ourworld.unu.edu/en/loss-of-access-to-education-puts-well-being-of-syrian-girls-at-risk.
9 Heyam Almouli, interview by author.
10 Ibid.

11 Rola Ibrahim, interview by author.
12 Heyam Almouli, interview by author.
13 Rola Ibrahim, interview by author.
14 Mustapha Hejazi, *Social Backwardness: An Introduction to the Psychology of the Oppressed Man* (Arab Cultural Center, 2015).
15 Hisham Sharabi, *Neopatriarchy: A Theory of Distorted Change in Arab Society* (Oxford: Oxford University Press, 1992).
16 Heyam Almouli, interview by author.
17 In Islam, a man can delegate the right to divorce to his wife or another third party.
18 Syrian Commission for Family Affairs, *Report on Domestic Violence* (2014), http://musawasyr.org/?p=1134.
19 Rola Ibrahim, interview by author.
20 Heyam Almouli, interview by author.
21 Ibid.
22 Ibid.
23 Syrian Commission for Family Affairs, *Report on Domestic Violence*.
24 Heyam Almouli, interview by author.
25 UNICEF, "Syria: MENA Gender Equality Profile" (2011), https://www.unicef.org/gender/files/Syria-Gender-Eqaulity-Profile-2011.pdf.
26 Heyam Almouli, interview by author.
27 Rola Ibrahim, interview by author.
28 I Am She Network, "The Impact of War on Syrian Women" (2018).
29 Rola Ibrahim, interview by author.
30 Heyam Almouli, interview by author.
31 Centre for Civil Society and Democracy, *Lost Childhood…Child, Early and Forced Marriage in Syrian IDP Camps: Causes and Effects* (February 2016).
32 Heyam Almouli, interview by author.
33 Ibid.
34 Ibid.
35 Rim Duhman, "Reproductive Health in Syria: Increase in Birth and Decrease in Morbidity," http://musawasyr.org/?p=2418.
36 Rola Ibrahim, interview by author.
37 Heyam Almouli, interview by author.
38 Syrian American Medical Society, "Women's Health Services Lacking for Syrian Refugees," 14 February 2019, https://www.sams-usa.net/2019/02/14/womens-health-services-lacking-for-syrian-refugees/.

39 Rola Ibrahim, interview by author; Rola Ibrahim, "The Other Dimension of Motherhood in Camps," 6 February 2020, https://swnsyria.org/?p=12155.

40 Heyam Almouli, interview by author.

41 Practice of Medical Professions Law, Legislative Decree No. 12 of 1970, Art. 47(B).

42 Heyam Almouli, interview by author.

43 Rola Ibrahim, interview by author.

9

The Impact of Migration on Intore Traditional Dance

Sandrine Cyuzuzo Iribagiza

Dear Reader,

My name is Sandrine Cyuzuzo Iribagiza. I graduated from Southern New Hampshire University through the Kepler program and hold a Bachelor of Arts in healthcare management with a concentration in global perspectives. I live in Rwanda, where I took my BA classes through the College for America platform. I have been an academic intern at the Rwanda Biomedical Center in the HIV prevention unit. My responsibilities included assisting in preparing and training people on HIV testing services and the prevention of mother-to-child transmission of HIV. In addition, I conducted training on the use of HIV nutrition tools in the Karongi district and participated in structuring the National Strategic Plan on HIV/AIDS for 2020–22. I am currently working for World Vision Rwanda for my professional internship in the design monitoring and evaluation department. Outside of my work, I am interested in reading (fiction and non-fiction books, magazines, news, etc.), being involved with charities, playing team sports (football, cricket, basketball, tennis, etc.), learning new skills, and being a member of social, environmental, and animal rights groups.

Learning in a classroom with a global mix of students was a great experience because of the differences and creative ideas we all brought to our projects. In particular, working together with refugees and host-community students as my colleagues, rather than focusing on our different legal status, was important to me.

The differences in our backgrounds make our collective experience better whether we are refugee students or host-country students. In fact, it was in class that the idea for this project came to me as someone mentioned a story about a famous African president criticizing Intore dancers. This started me on a path of asking questions about the history of Intore dance and its relationship to Rwandese culture and migration.

My research was carried out during six weeks of interviewing and field research. I also used videos and images of Intore dancers to understand the different movements and practices. Furthermore, I attended two traditional dancing events to see how they matched with data collected from interviews and other research. While my research involved some sensitive questions, I felt supported and welcomed by the people I interviewed and am grateful for their contributions to this paper. Doing research was a challenge as it was the first time I had done a project like this, and for a long time I could not settle on a research question. However, through talking to people and starting interviews, I came to sharpen my focus on the impacts of migration and displacement on Intore traditional dance. However, another important challenge was language. While I conducted interviews in Kinyarwanda, I needed to translate them and write this essay in English. Translations can change the sense or the meaning of the question and answer, so determining how to express ideas communicated in Kinyarwanda to English was its own challenge. One of my interviewees even taught me to perform some steps of Intore dance before we sat down for an interview.

For me, part of the "right to research" is also sharing the work I have produced, and so it is with great pride that I share this chapter, "The Impact of Migration on Intore Traditional Dance." I am very proud of this story and feel that readers will learn a great deal about the impact of migration on Intore dance.

Sincerely,
Sandrine Cyuzuzo Iribagiza

INTRODUCTION

On 16 May 1985, Libyan leader Colonel Muammar Gaddafi visited Rwanda. Intore traditional dancers welcomed him with a performance of their traditional dance. However, he made fun of them and mentioned that he would donate handcuffs to arrest all the Intore dancers. He thought they were mad based on their dance moves and styles. I don't know if this happened – whether it's a true story or apocryphal. Whether it happened or not, it inspired me to learn more about the history of Intore dance and how this tradition has changed over time, as well as how dancers have been received by the audiences and what those performances are meant to communicate. In particular, I will show how it has changed because of the cross-border mobility of people, both to and from Rwanda, since the late 1950s.

I begin by describing the long history of Intore traditional dance, which has its roots very early in the Rwandan kingdom. Understanding the social and political context in which Intore dance began is important for contextualizing how dance practices, and their symbolic resonances, have changed since the founding of the Rwandan kingdom. Then, I describe the different tools, outfits, and practices used in Intore dance, as well as their symbolism. This brings me to a discussion of the different kinds of Intore dance and how they have been affected by voluntary and forced migration over time. Throughout the chapter, my focus is on both the material culture of Intore dance, and the embodied movements that dancers use in their performances.

BACKGROUND

Rwanda's kingdom was founded in the late tenth century by a king named Gihanga Ngoma Ijana, which in English means "the creator or founder of one hundred kingdoms." The kingdom of Rwanda had three main leadership categories including the monarchy, which was headed by the king and other nobles. The second category was called abiru, which can be translated to "advisors" in English. Abiru were ritual loyalists who lived in the palace of the king. They had to advise the king and forecast the future. Because they were old people, it was thought they could use their experience to know what might happen in the future. Lastly, there were the chiefs, who helped the kingdom in social, political, and economic actions. Within this group, there were three types of chiefs: the cattle chiefs, the military chiefs, and the land chiefs. Social actions were controlled by the land chiefs, political actions were controlled by military chiefs, and economic actions were controlled by the cattle chiefs because cows or cattle were the standard measure of the wealth of a person.

Intore traditional dance was used in all three of these sectors of the kingdom. Intore dancers were young men selected after receiving a privileged education and choreographic training to entertain the masters in the kingdom during certain occasions, like winning a war or at a ceremonial event like Umuganuro, a celebratory harvest feast (discussed in more detail in Aime Parfait's chapter on Burundian drumming). In political actions, Intore dancers danced as a sign of victory after expanding the country by conquering the other kingdoms or winning a battle against their enemies. Intore dancers also danced as a way of expressing joy or happiness. For instance, if people gave each other land or cows, the Intore danced to show joy and appreciation. In addition, when a person gave birth, the Intore danced to thank God and the family for a newborn in the community. In economic actions, whenever a person gained cattle since the person's wealth was increasing, the Intore would dance as a sign of showing happiness for the improvement. To sum up, Intore was danced primarily for happy reasons like achievements and improvements on the societal or personal level. The word *Intore* itself means "the selected one" or "the chosen one," reflecting the fact that the dance is practiced only by selected men with certain achievements. Lastly, the tools and clothes worn by Intore dancers had special meanings in accordance with Rwandan values, beliefs, and traditions.[1] The vibrant costume of the Intore dancers consisted of long or short skirts, ankle bands, headbands made of various beads, headdresses with grass wigs, and small hand-painted shields and sticks.

Though the specific social and political contexts in which Intore dance first developed have changed dramatically, the dance is still practiced in Rwanda today. I wanted to understand how the dance has changed over the centuries since its creation. Drawing on oral history interviews with Intore dancers, cultural experts, and museum professionals, as well as participant observation and careful study of recorded dance performances, I show that migration has been one of the most important influences on Intore dance. To protect interviewees' identities, I refer to them only by their first names.

Before delving into the specific migration patterns that have shaped
the dance, I describe the tools and costumes that are worn by the
dancers – the focus of the next section.

TOOLS USED IN INTORE TRADITIONAL DANCE

Intore traditional dance has tools that help dancers to perform their
dances and imbue them with meaning. While there are different
kinds of Intore dances, the tools used by the dancers are typically
the same across these different styles. For instance, the drums used
in making the beat and imirishyo (the sticks drummers use to beat
the drums) are common across the types of Intore dance. However,
some tools are specific to particular kinds of dance. Here, we begin
to see the impact of migration on Intore dance as the histories that
have shaped the tools dancers use are also histories of migration
and displacement.

The first important tool in Intore dance is the Ingoma, or "drum"
in English. In Rwandan culture, Ingoma or drums stood for the
reign, royalty, and the kingdom. Ingoma is covered with a membrane
of animal skin. The top of the drum is larger than the bottom. The
Ingoma is usually cylindrical in form, tapered only in the lower part
of the instrument. There are four main types of Ingoma: Ishakwe,
Inyahura, Inumvu, and Ibihumurizo. Each produces a slightly different sound, and together these varied sounds are used to create
the rhythm of the dance. Inyahura is the base rhythm to which
Ishakwe responds. Then comes the Inumyu drum together with the
Ibihumurizo. Another way to think of them is like a chorus, with
Inumyu being the bass, Ibihumurizo the tenor, Ishakwe the soprano,
and Inyahura the alto.[2]

To play the drums, drummers use Imirishyo, or wooden sticks.
There are approximately twenty-two types of Imirishyo. Here,
I will discuss five. As will become clear, different types of Imirishyo
could have rhythmic or symbolic functions or both. The first type,
Umugendo, follows the rhythm of the dancers. The second, Ibihubi,
is used when the king's advisors gathered to advise him or make
other decisions about the kingdom. The third type, Imirindi, symbolizes that soldiers are going off to war or to rescue people or goods
stolen from the kingdom. On the other hand, the fourth type, Inege,
is used when the soldiers are on parade before the people or king.
And finally, Umuterero, the fifth type, is used to end the dance.

Drums are not the only sonic element of Intore dance. Dancers may also wear Amayugi, a series of small bells tied together and worn around the ankle. One bell is called iyugi and is about three or four centimeters in size. In Rwandan culture, Amayugi are used to protect against spirits, herd livestock together, and keep robbers at bay. When the dancers move in unison, the Amayugi all produce a rhythm together that accompanies the beating of the drums.

Also worn on the dancers' bodies are Umugara, or headgear. During the Rwandan monarchy, headgear was worn by the king as a symbol of royalty. That is why the Intore traditional dancers put on headgear: they were the chosen ones, too. Umugara is closely related to understandings of the natural world, as it is meant to resemble a lion's mane, and the lion was considered the king of the jungle or forest, above all of the other animals. In this way, Intore dancers use Umugara to show their power. They even mimic the behaviour of the lion, shaking their heads in imitation of its gestures. A further demonstration of their power comes from the shields and spears the dancers carry. Ingabo and Icumu (shield and spear, respectively) are held by dancers in their hands. These were used in ancient Rwanda by the soldiers in battle; Intore dancers were also responsible for being prepared for battle, so using shields and spears had both practical and symbolic functions. Now, the use of these implements is mostly symbolic.

For fancier performances, dancers may wear Ibitako, or jewels. These consist of long necklaces made from sparkling blue and brown jewels combined with thread, as well as bracelets. Lastly, Ibitako includes two crossed small cloths that dancers wear before putting on their necklaces. Intore wear this piece of cloth from the neck to the low belly. Other optional elements used for some dances include Agasuka (a small hoe) and Ifirimbi (a whistle). Depending on the type of dance, Agasuka is used to show how agriculture was the lifestyle of some Rwandans, and whistles were used to produce or augment the song's rhythm. Other tools were connected to Rwandans' livelihoods, too. Inkuyo is a tool that is used by Intore traditional dancers in a type of dance called Igishakamba. Normally, Inkuyo is a collection of dry grasses that can fit in the hand and is used by shepherds to help cows sleep and feel well. In Kinyarwanda this is called *kwagaza*. Therefore, Intore traditional dancers use these grasses when dancing Igishakamba to show that Intore helps people to feel well, just as Inkuyo does for the cows, as well as to symbolize the importance of cattle-raising for Rwandan society.

The final component of Intore traditional dancers' outfits is their dress. Around the waist and upper thighs, they wear a covering made from animal skins. According to Rwasamirera, the Rwandan cultural expert I interviewed, the animals selected to make these outfits are revered for their power.[3] They include lions, cats, cheetahs, tigers, and leopards. These are, among others, the most preferred costumes for Intore.

This overview of the outfits and tools used in Intore traditional dance highlights the symbolic importance of dancers' dress and accoutrements, as well as the ways the dance reflects Rwandan livelihoods. They also show the intimate relationship between components of Intore dance and the local environment, with animals, both wild and domestic, and local flora physically incorporated into, and symbolically represented by, different Intore dances. In the next section, I show in greater detail how the dances, as reflections of social, cultural, and economic practices in wider Rwandan society, have been shaped by different migrations, both voluntary and forced, over time.

THE RELATIONSHIP BETWEEN MIGRATION AND INTORE TRADITIONAL DANCE

Now that we have considered the different tools and outfits used by Intore dancers, we can consider how the dances they perform have changed over time as the result of many factors, among these geography and migration. In the following section, I describe different types of Intore dance and how migration has affected each.

Nkombo dance is from the western part of Rwanda, on an island called Nkombo, which neighbours the Democratic Republic of the Congo (DRC). The movements of the dance mimic people boating on the water. This reflects the geography of the region – as the island is covered in bodies of water and people rely on boats for transport – and the livelihoods of most people on the island, which depend on fishing. Nkombo developed as a way for people to dance and entertain themselves while boating. People on Nkombo would sell their fish to people in the DRC, and migration between the island and the DRC is common. These movements of people have affected the dances they practice, with Congolese dances shaping Nkombo dance and vice versa. Peter, one of my interviewees, observed that there are significant similarities between Ndombolo Ya Solo, a Congolese dance, and Nkombo dance, especially in terms of the movement of the hips.[4] These similarities suggest the mutual influences of the different dance practices on each other and the place of migration in shaping both.

A second example is offered by Ikinyemera traditional dance, which originated in Gisenyi in the northwestern part of Rwanda. This area borders Uganda and is the area where a clan known as Abagogwe resides. In Ikinyemera, dancers lift their hands and arms above their heads to symbolize the horns of a cow, as cattle-raising is the main occupation in Gisenyi. The wealth of a person is determined by the number of cows they own. The music used in Ikinyemera is also shaped by the geography of the region, which is very mountainous. You find that one person might live on a mountain and their neighbours might live in a valley or on another hill. This is symbolically represented in the high tones used in the songs accompanying the dancers.

The Abagogwe, the clan in which the Ikinyemera dance originated, has its origins in Rwanda, particularly in the Tutsi ethnic group of ancient Rwanda. In 1959, when the Hutu came to rule the first republic, they tortured the Abagogwe, as they did other clans of Tutsi. As a result, Abagogwe, who mostly lived in Gisenyi, near Goma in Congo, migrated to Masisi and Rutshuru in the DRC. Today, there are some Abagogwe who are still refugees in the DRC, while others already came back to Rwanda after the 1994 genocide. Therefore, this migration of Abagogwe from Rwanda to the DRC brought Ikinyemera to the DRC in those places where the Abagogwe were living.[5]

A dance with a more recent history shaped entirely by the consequences of migration is the Igishakamba traditional dance. Igishakamba originated in Umutara, located in the eastern province of Rwanda. This type of dance was introduced between 1960 and 1970 after the merging of the Ekitagururo dance from the Bahima clan in Uganda and the Umuhamirizo dance from Rwanda. It was created after the migration of Tutsi Rwandans who were forced into exile after various violent incidents done by Hutus taking over the power from Rwandan monarchy, which was led by Tutsi kings. As a result, many Tutsi went to Uganda in exile and started making life there. Entertainment was an important part of this, which is where dancing comes in. Therefore, the Ugandan dance of Ekitagururo was merged with Umuhamirizo of Rwanda, which produced the Igishakamba of today. After mixing life in exile, dances were merged, too. The tools or instruments that are used when dancing this type of dance show the occupation of the people. Normally, the general way of life was semi-pastoralism because of the scenery of flat areas and dry seasons that revolve around animal husbandry, and cows were the most valuable form of property. Therefore, the male dancers use sticks and whistles, while the female dancers use whistles only. In animal husbandry, the cowherd uses sticks for guiding cows, and when dancing, sticks are used for directing the performance. In addition, all parts of a cow's body are used, including as parts of the dance. The skin of the cow is used to make the covering for the drums that are played during the dance.

Igishakamba has another connection to migration. Once it developed as a mix of Rwandan and Ugandan dances in the 1960s, it was introduced in Burundi due to the migration of Rwandans there. While there are variations between the different types of Igishakamba, the similarity that all of these dances share is the movement of hips, according to Rwasamirera.[6]

A final example is Ikinimba, a traditional dance style that originated among members of the Abacyiga clan in the northern part (Ruhengeri) of Rwanda, in what is today the Musanze district. This is a part of Rwanda that borders Uganda. Movement through Ruhengeri is still the most common way to travel between the two countries, even though there are now other ways available. This frequent movement from one country to the other shaped the culture on both sides of the border. Ikinimba is performed in both countries in the same way, completely because of the migration of people. As with other kinds of dances, the geography and scenery of the region have shaped the dance. This part of Rwanda is known to have volcano stones (Amakoro) everywhere – one reason for the dance's origins. This dance is done by jumping, as if there is something that the dancers are hitting on the ground; it requires a lot of energy. Both women and men participate in this dance. Drums are used to produce the melody or rhythm of the songs, and other additional instruments like whistles are optional, according to Peter.[7]

CREATING A NATIONAL DANCE TRADITION

Beginning in the 1940s and 1950s, Intore dancers began to perform the dances of different cultures, combining dances from the west, east, north, south, and central parts of the country. They performed to celebrate the return of the army. To this day, the dancers are invited to almost every special celebration and ceremony, including weddings and public events. Their significance is deeply emotional for many Rwandese: according to Munyampundu Charles, a Rwandese who spent time in exile, missing ceremonies with Intore performances was one of the saddest things in exile.[8]

The blending of different regional dance practices to create a national dance culture meant that the dances developed in border regions have been transformed into a distinctively "Rwandan" tradition. This process inevitably implies tensions, particularly in the post-genocide context. The push for a unified national identity in the aftermath of the genocide has helped elevate Intore dance as a symbol of cultural unity; the inclusion of regionally specific dances in troupes' repertoires is meant to highlight the universality of Intore dance as a part of *all* Rwandans' culture. However, as this chapter has shown, different dances are intimately linked to the geographic, social, economic, and cultural contexts of the regions and clans where they originated, as well as to specific patterns of cross-border movement. Some – particularly the older generation of Intore dancers, many of whom trained before the genocide – feel that the subsumption of these different practices into a homogenizing "national" culture represents a loss, as new dancers may not be from, or even know about, the regional traditions whose dances they now perform.[9]

The possibilities for Intore dance to fulfill a unifying national function are further limited by the continued exclusion of women from many aspects of the dance. According to Gahamanyi, a traditional artist who was one of my interviewees, in Rwandan culture, only men performed Intore traditional dance due to the difference in the work done by different genders.[10] Women were expected to take care of the home and children while men were in charge of hunting, fighting in wars, and doing other physical works. Political change to ensure gender equality has also allowed women to participate in Intore dance in some ways – mainly as drummers. However, they still do not perform as dancers in traditional troupes, though they do perform as dancers in other (non-Intore) dances.

CONCLUSION

The continued exclusion of women from full participation in the tradition in some ways reflects the limitations of Intore dance as an instrument of homogenizing national unification. As this essay suggests, attention to the historical development of Intore dance and to the heterogeneous, diverse influences that have shaped its different regional incarnations perhaps offers an alternative perspective on the possible role of Intore dance in national life. Rather than viewing it as a distinct national tradition with an instrumental political function, it can be seen as a kaleidoscope of historically and socially contingent practices that capture in embodied form some of the changes and continuities experienced not only by the Rwandese but also by the various national and ethnic communities who have shaped Intore dances. Intore traditional dance is not the product of one culture but rather different cultures combined in unique regionally and socially specific ways. Moreover, as this essay shows, it has been – and still is – deeply impacted by the forced and voluntary movement of people across national borders.

NOTES

1 Philip Briggs and Janice Booth, *Rwanda: The Bradt Travel Guide* (Bradt Travel Guides, 2006), 29.
2 Nsanzabera Jean de Dieu, "Inkomoko…"
3 Rwasamirera, interview by author, 2 July 2019, Kigali, Rwanda.
4 Peter, interview by author, 23 July 2019, Kigali, Rwanda.
5 Veritas, "Inkomoko Y'igihugu Cy'u Rwanda N'abanyarwanda (igice Cya Kane)," *Veritas Info News*, 17 January 2015.
6 Rwasamirera, interview by author.
7 Peter, interview by author.
8 Charles, interview by author, 2019, Kigali, Rwanda.
9 Carine Plancke, "Contemporary Dynamics in Rwandan Dances: Identity, Changing Creativity and the Globalisation of Affect," *Dance Research* 34, no. 2 (2016): 150–69.
10 Gahamanyi, interview by author, 2019, Kigali, Rwanda.

Conclusion

Ismail Alkhateeb, Sandrine Cyzuzo Iribagiza, Aime Parfait Emerusenge, Alain Jules Hirwa, Phocas Maniraguha, Richesse Ndiritiro, Muna Omar, Marcia C. Schenck, Kate Reed, Lazha Taha, and Gerawork Teferra

To craft this conclusion, we all responded to a set of questions: What is research? What does it mean to be a researcher? What does dialogue mean, and what is its role in research and writing? What are the strengths and limitations of narrative and storytelling, both in the abstract and in the particulars of your work? Our answers are brought together here, not to reflect consensus or finality but to highlight points of confluence and divergence, lingering questions and tensions, and ongoing conversations. (Though, in reviewing our reflections, it became clear that there were many more moments of convergence than the opposite.) To that end, we have adopted grammatical conventions that allow us to write together while preserving our individual perspectives: the collective first person is used only for statements with which we all concur. Personal reflections are placed in quotes with first names provided. This reflects, partially, the fact that attempting to write together surfaces in microcosm many of the larger issues at stake in this project: whose voices speak from these pages? What does it mean to write as a collective when we come to this volume from such different places and perspectives? What does it mean to "include" eleven voices in one text, particularly when those voices often disagree? Of course, we do not have answers to these questions, which serve rather as a word of caution to the reader, but also as an invitation to think through these issues with us, not in pursuit of a single answer, but to acknowledge the difficulties and imperfections inherent in a project whose fundamental orientation is one of hope.

BECOMING RESEARCHERS

"As a refugee from the camp pursuing higher education, I have been a target of many [research projects]," Richesse says. "I have never seen any conclusion or presentation of the research I participated in." His experience is familiar to many contributors to this volume. Research, as a consequence, might seem distant, impossible, other: "I could not picture myself as a researcher before this," Lazha writes. Others, like Ismail, had conducted research projects before; for him, this prior experience informed ways of "turning [stories] into a tool for advocacy." And Phocas came to identify research as a way to "understand ... and learn more about [the] community" to "support [the researcher's] community." Richesse, Lazha, Phocas, and Ismail's reflections speak to the importance of research not only for its own sake but also for the possibility of using knowledge creation to effect meaningful change. They speak to an awareness of the stakes of historical research and representation – and of how high those stakes are.[1]

To conclude this volume, we wish to turn our developing orientations as researchers back onto ourselves and this project to offer some reflections about the volume's creation and publication and how participation in this project has affected all of us.[2] A commitment to transparency about "the process and life behind what is finalized as the scholarly text" is integral to our work, which questions and unsettles often-tacit assumptions about history as both process and product.[3] This includes aspects of the research process from our positionalities as researchers and writers, to the obstacles that shaped our work, to the ways that this work has shaped us. In short, our presence in the contributions to this book – made explicit in the prefatory and concluding notes accompanying each essay – is something we wish to highlight rather than efface. Following Adom Getachew, who posits that universalism begins in specificity and that the practices of those who are marginalized inaugurate new ideals and ways of being, rather than simply realizing those ideals conceived at the "centre," we seek to draw attention to the situatedness of the knowledge shared in this volume and the historians who created it.[4] In so doing, we reinforce the claim staked at the outset: that a right to research ought to be, and can be, universal, but its "realization" (perhaps, transformation?) will require rethinking what we mean by historical research, as we attend more fully to the necessary particularities of doing research from positions outside the traditional bounds of university, archive, and nation-state.

We focus our final reflections around four themes: first, rethinking what it means to do research and be a researcher. Second, the challenges and setbacks contributors faced, both particular to their projects and embedded in structural inequalities. Third, the ways that working on these projects has shaped each of us personally in the ways we think about the role of research in our lives and those of our communities. We end the volume by articulating some of the ways we hope our work contributes to the ongoing project of transforming historical scholarship, which entails, we argue, a concurrent transformation of the conditions in which that scholarship is produced – that is, a transformation of the world.

RETHINKING RESEARCH

One set of questions we addressed for this conclusion revolved around the meaning of research and whether our understanding of this question changed over the course of the project. Many of us felt that the project helped us build more expansive notions of research. Research became at once more quotidian, more democratic, and more complex. For instance, Marcia observes that she has debunked her professionally imbued and restrictive notions of research as a purely scholarly exercise and now views research as a more egalitarian process, a set of steps that encompasses "being able to formulate a question, know where to look for answers, analyze the information you come across, evaluate it, and frame your results in a narrative." That question can range from "a complex [one] about which you write an article" to "a more practical question like, how do I get a passport?" Gera, similarly, notes that the recipe he uses to make dinner, "that only demands one plate, one spoon, one cooking pot, one cap, [and that] has helped me conserve water, labour, and fuel came as a result of several days experiments, and I call it research." Sandrine puts it succinctly: "a researcher is someone who asks, investigates, interprets, and collect[s] all the possible information for the purpose of finding something out."

At the same time, many of us have emerged from this research and writing process with more complex ideas about what research can be. Much of this is bound up in ideas of narrative and intersubjective experience – the notion that research requires us to step outside the bounds of personal experience and preconception to more fully understand others' narratives about their lives and the world. As Gera notes, "When I started [my] research project, I didn't recognize [the preservation] of stories as an important [or] meaningful goal of research." His previous research experiences were more concerned with "reducing complexities or simplify[ing] complex reality" by controlling the environment and removing outliers, while (oral) historical research instead emphasized the very complexity and contingency that more experimental settings sought to minimize. Ultimately, he identified the complexity of his research, and its multifaceted representation of life in Kakuma refugee camp, as its principal strength. Alain, likewise, now thinks of a researcher as "someone who sets [out] to find out and document the story of something that would otherwise go undocumented" by "interacting with people and materials to find out what gap[s] might exist in how the histories ... of those people or their culture ... are told." In no small part, this is attributable to the ways conducting oral history interviews required contributors to "jump the empathy wall," as Gera says, paraphrasing Arlie Russell Hochschild. For Aime Parfait, the concept of sharing between researcher and community became central, with research offering an "opportunity ... through dialogue, [for] knowledge sharing."

Even as we shared a newfound appreciation for the power of dialogue, we did not always agree about the conversations in which we wanted to take part. With limited time and resources, was it important to focus on academic publications? Or was it more important to think about ways for the research conducted under the auspices of Global History Dialogues to enter into community conversations?[5] To be sure, there are ways to bridge both imperatives, facilitated by the opportunity to publish these essays on an open-access basis. But in devoting substantial time and energy to navigating the academic publishing process, we have foreclosed, at a minimum, more immediate opportunities to exchange and debate the ideas raised by these essays in the contexts in which they were researched and written. We have also had to work around severe obstacles, including a lack of internet access, during important steps of the review process. Many contributors continue life on the move and often on the margins of their respective host societies and in host societies that restrict internet use.

CHALLENGES AND SETBACKS

If a more democratic vision of research, one that honours the complexity of everyday life, was a significant result of this project, it did not come about without a more acute awareness of the unevenly distributed obstacles that make such research more difficult. Another common thread that wove through our reflections about the research process was a newfound appreciation for the difficulties of conducting rigorous research, particularly in conditions that we might generously describe as less than ideal. Even as the possibilities of oral history illustrated a more democratic form of historical research, the lack of access to libraries, databases, archives, internet, travel grants (in many cases, even the possibility of legal travel), and more, was a frustrating impediment. Muna, for instance, "would stay up after midnight until mornings, as it is the time people sleep so the network might not be pressured and use VPNs to unblock sites" as she conducted most of her research from Yemen. For Richesse, travelling from Kigali to Mahama refugee camp – a distance of over 156 kilometers – posed a different kind of challenge. And as Gera writes, when he found, after months of research, a book chapter that laid out an argument very similar to his own, it felt as if someone "pour[ed] cold water on my paper ... [and] made me think that I spent time and energy to answer a known thing." It is perhaps facile but still worth saying, that a right to research is inseparable from other basic rights that continue to go unfulfilled: rights to mobility, security, education, and healthcare. The list goes on.

Gera's experience led him to raise the question: "How [can we] liberate those answers to our problems (knowledge) from such institutions that protect them from [the] public with password[s]? ... Is knowledge a private or public good?" He goes on to note that he would not be comfortable with any restrictions on access to his chapter "because of the fact that I played a role in assembling information from my twenty interviewees and twenty-seven written articles." The realities of academic publishing mean that open-access publication remains prohibitively expensive, particularly for scholars without generous institutional support. It is our immense fortune to work with a press that shares our commitment to making this volume freely accessible in digital form. Of course, this does not remedy the underlying problem also alluded to in Richesse's reflection at the start of this chapter: too often, the subjects of historical or social scientific research are not the direct beneficiaries of it (let alone the creators of it), especially when access remains limited to those with sufficient institutional affiliations or resources. This is another way in which material inequality is bound up with the production of knowledge, as those without access to scholarly conversations are implicitly denied the opportunity to participate in them on anything resembling an equal footing.

In addition to the difficulties that confronted different contributors, there were more common obstacles. Building trust with interlocutors so that they would feel comfortable speaking about sensitive topics, and then doing justice to their stories in the writing phase, were frequently mentioned as difficult but ultimately fulfilling aspects of the research process. For instance, Phocas notes that his research topic (traditional healing and witchcraft in Rwanda) was controversial enough that few people were willing to speak with him at first, and it took time to develop trust and learn how to broach the subject with different narrators. The possibility to learn from and share with members of the community resulted in richer research as well as personal growth as we rethought what research meant and how it could fit into our lives and those of our communities. As we are clear about the structural inequalities that have shaped this volume, and that make it – unfortunately – such a unique one, we also want to celebrate how this project has affected us, allowed us to see things differently, and inspired us with hope about the possibilities for continued and deepened dialogue.[6]

PERSONAL CHANGE

Global History Dialogues is global in scope and encourages student-researchers to see global connections between their projects and those of distant peers. But the project operates at many scales, from the global down to the personal. All of us, in addressing the questions that shape this conclusion, wrote something about how we personally were affected by the process of creating the essays that appear in this volume. Many expressed feelings similar to those shared by Lazha, who writes, "I am one of those [people] who is shy to share their thoughts and speak their ideas in a crowd … but this [project] helped me to value my understanding of the things I know and find a way to share them." A sense of confidence in one's skills and ability to create and share knowledge was a through line in our reflections; some of us, like Richesse, have gone on to research intern-ships because of our work in Global History Dialogues. Others, like Kate, have used the methods taught in Global History Dialogues to carry out research projects of personal or family significance.

In addition to instilling a sense of confidence in our capacity to conduct rigorous historical research, the conversations that formed the bulk of the primary materials in this volume often worked to shift contributors' thinking. "Refining preconceived ideas, biases, and prejudices about refugees, humanitarian organization, bureau-cracy, etc., has been critical," Gera writes. Through this process, this notion of research as an "orientation to the world," as Kate writes, we were compelled to confront and take seriously perspectives that differed markedly from our own, both while interviewing narrators and in thinking about in what form(s) to share the pieces gathered here with a wider audience. Ismail identified the "dynami[sm]" of the research process – its inclusion of many voices and perspectives and the importance of interaction and exchange – as central to thinking about the tensions that inevitably emerge in projects of this scope.

A final impact of the research process on many of us was the ways it shaped our approach to our everyday experiences and interactions. As research came to seem more accessible and more useful for parsing everyday life, the methods of historical analysis and interpretation – as Muna describes them, "having the spirit of, 'maybe this is not right,' delving in more deeply, being open to new ways of looking at the research problems, and always asking the question 'why'" – became easier to deploy in daily life. In this vein, Lazha notes that for her, research has become a way to seek clarity for herself and others about questions connected to their lives. Going through the experience of planning, carrying out, and sharing an extensive research project provides a set of approaches and tools of enormous applicability, whether those tools are applied to the creation of a personal archive to commemorate a deceased family member, the devising of the most economical supper recipe possible, or the continued exploration of topics of personal or community importance.

CONCLUDING THOUGHTS

Our hope is that this volume serves as a doorway to ongoing con-versations about the epistemological and material changes needed to alter the way historical research and analysis are produced. The nine essays gathered here might do so in several ways. First, as Ismail observes, the somewhat disparate nature of the volume might leave readers wondering about the relevance of the pieces to each other. But, he continues, they are all connected in their implicit affirmation of the historical importance of the perspectives they draw upon, as well as the authority of the contributors themselves. It is thus the polyphonicity of these texts, both as entities unto themselves and in their juxtaposition, that provides one catalyst for further discussion and action.

Second, the attention paid throughout the volume to the conditions of production of these histories, as well as the content of many of the essays themselves, underscores the material inequalities that structure the creation of historical knowledge. Attending to the embodied and situated creation of historical knowledge is a political act that reinforces the inseparability of economic, political, and legal inequality from epistemological inequality. Both scholars and scholarship from the so-called margins face the entwined difficulties of lower funding, less access, and so on, and a greater justificatory burden. Scholars are confronted with demands to justify why they are present, why their work is relevant, and how their scholarship converses with the work that has come before them – work that has long excluded them.[7] Making these inequalities more visible does not remedy them; that will require sustained and systemic action.

Third, we hope the shortcomings and lacunae of this volume instigate further work and reflection. Its Anglocentrism, the gender imbalance among contributors, the power imbalances between editors and contributors – these, and many others, are weaknesses of this volume and the project from which it grows. We have worked to be open about the ways we have experienced these shortcomings and their impacts on our work and do not position this project as a model for others to follow. Indeed, we continue to disagree among ourselves about what collaborative forms of history teaching, research, writing, and publication can and should be, and we invite readers to participate in those disagreements with us. Marcia describes how our ability to work through these differences is founded on trust: "A lot can go amiss when the message travels from sender to receiver in any everyday conversation. Imagine meeting this challenge, not only across age differences, genders, classes, cultures, languages, time zones, and physical distances of thousands of kilometers, but never having met in person, purely online … It works through trust."

Fourth, we continue to harbor the hope that sharing narratives about displacement, refugeehood, human rights violations, and other forms of marginalization, from the perspectives highlighted in this volume, leads to action. As Muna writes, "We need to tell multifaceted and complex stories about refugees and immigrants ... By combining different voices [to] cover all angles of the topic, [we can] help raise awareness ... and generate social change." The nuanced and critical studies in this volume, which underscore the limitations of humanitarian paradigms, encourage us to think more systemically about (im)mobility and its causes and consequences. At the same time, these essays only scratch the surface of critical questions: the place and provision of education in "crisis" settings; the intersections of gender, (forced) migration, and labor; the processes we use to document the present; and many others.

Finally, we are leery of the language of experimentation, cognizant that the exigencies of humanitarian emergencies and the unequal distribution of power between refugee and migrant people and humanitarian intervenors make possible the justification and implementation of experimental logics that would be considered unacceptable in many other contexts.[8] At the same time, the injustices that characterize the status quo – even if we constrain our lens to focus on access to education – require something other than, well, the status quo. Thus, while we do understand this project as experimental, it is so in a collaborative, dialogical way, one in which the position of "expert" shifts from the original teaching staff to the student-researchers as they develop and embark upon their own research projects and share their findings and analysis with their colleagues. This malleability is part of a broader unboundedness of the Global History Dialogues project. As Kate writes, "framing the space as experimental implies a certain willingness to adapt, to change, to transform – grounded in a process of constant and searching reflection." It is in this sense of experimentation that we hope readers consider this work, our ultimate hope being that this volume eventually becomes less unique, less exceptional – that there emerges a myriad of spaces and ways for community historians who are also refugees, displaced, or otherwise marginalized, to speak, be heard, and taken seriously.

NOTES

1. See also Eunsong Kim, "Petty Materialism: On Metaphor & Violence," *Michigan Quarterly Review* (23 December 2020).

2. For another example of "bringing academic knowledge 'back home,'" see Sara Ahmed, *On Being Included: Racism and Diversity in Institutional Life* (Durham: Duke University Press, 2012), 11.

3. Kim, "Petty Materialism."

4. Adom Getachew, "Universalism after the Post-Colonial Turn: Interpreting the Haitian Revolution," *Political Theory* 44, no. 6 (1 December 2016): 821–45.

5. For further reflection on these questions from a group of Global History Dialogues students, see Mohamed Zakaria Abdalla et al., "Opportunities and Challenges of Oral History Research through Refugee Voices, Narratives, and Memories: History Dialogues," in *Global South Scholars in the Western Academy: Harnessing Unique Experiences, Knowledges, and Positionality in the Third Space*, ed. Staci Martin and Deepra Dandekar (New York: Routledge, 2021).

6. Recently, more work has emerged in which refugee voices are included – albeit often in a pretty heavily edited form, and mostly as authorities on their own lives, rather than as a researchers. *Voices from the Jungle* sets out to reveal the personal stories of a few inhabitants of the Calais camp to a broader public, while *Making Mirrors* is a collection of poetry by and for refugees working with professional poets. In the same vein, *The Displaced* assembles work of successful refugee authors. The latter two projects differ in terms of who is speaking from both the Calais Project and this book. See Jehan Bseiso and Becky Thompson, eds, *Making Mirrors: Writing /Righting by and for Refugees* (Northhampton, MA: Olive Branch Press, 2019); Marie Godin, Katrine Moller Hansen, Aura Lounasmaa, Corinne Squire, Tahir Zaman, ed., *Voices from the 'Jungle' Stories from the Calais Refugee Camp* (London: Pluto Press, 2017); Viet Thanh Nguyen, ed., *The Displaced: Refugee Writers on Refugee Lives* (New York: Abrams Press, 2018).

7. On justification, see Kristie Dotson, "How Is This Paper Philosophy?," *Comparative Philosophy* 3, no. 1 (30 December 2012): 3–29.

8. See, for instance, chapter 35 in Benjamin Rawlence, *City of Thorns: Nine Lives in the World's Largest Refugee Camp* (New York: Picador, 2016). Rawlence describes a dubiously ethical experimental program that trained women refugees to install solar lights, but that primarily took advantage of their vulnerability and desperation.

Contributors

ISMAIL ALKHATEEB is a Syrian translator and women's rights activist. He helped coordinate the I Am She network, a network of community-based women's groups or "peace circles" led by Syrian women working to reinforce effective political, economic, social, and cultural participation of women to realize peace, freedom, justice, representation, and transparency for all Syrians.

SANDRINE CYUZUZO IRIBAGIZA graduated from Southern New Hampshire University with a degree in healthcare management and a concentration in Global Perspectives, studying through the College for America platform from her home in Kigali, Rwanda. She has interned with the HIV Prevention Unit of the Rwanda Biomedical Centre and contributed to the National Strategic Plan on HIV/AIDS for 2020–22. Beyond her academic and research work, Sandrine enjoys reading and playing team sports, like cricket and football.

AIME PARFAIT EMERUSENGE is a Burundian refugee living in Rwanda. He graduated from Southern New Hampshire University with a degree in management and a concentration in logistics and operations. Now, he works with a British organization called Jigsaw Consult as a youth researcher, assisting with their research about post-primary education for refugees in Rwanda and Pakistan. He is interested in education, history, business, and technology, and enjoys reading about all those topics in his free time.

ALAIN JULES HIRWA is a poet and writer studying for an MFA. His creative works have appeared in a variety of publications. He is also a graduate of Southern New Hampshire University, where he completed a bachelor's degree in communications. From 2018 to 2020, he served as a teaching assistant in communications at Kepler Kigali University Program. His hobbies include writing, photography, and fashion design.

PHOCAS MANIRAGUHA is a graduate of Southern New Hampshire University through the Kepler program in Rwanda. He majored in healthcare management with a concentration in global perspectives. He has skills in social enterprise creation from Acts of Gratitude and holds a certificate from the Global Health eLearning Center in logistics for health commodities. He has worked as a teaching assistant and senior learning assistant at Kepler, where he supported students with their academic work. Currently, he serves as a public health intern at Agahozo Shalom Youth Village where he provides different forms of support to young people. His hobbies include listening to music, dancing – especially Rwandan traditional dances – and supporting other people and community works. He is passionate about transforming healthcare and education systems.

RICHESSE NDIRITIRO is a Burundian refugee living in Rwanda. He holds a degree in healthcare management with a concentration in global perspectives from Southern New Hampshire University. As a Kepler scholar, he has been a Refugee Student Ambassador and a Student Refugee Representative in the Connected Learning in Crisis Consortium (CLCC).

MUNA OMAR is Ethiopian but was born and raised in Riyadh, Saudi Arabia, where her parents met after fleeing violence in Oromia after crossing the sea from the Horn of Africa to the Arabian Peninsula. After her father was deported, her mother struggled to raise her in Saudi Arabia and the two eventually moved to Yemen. Recently, after living for seven years in Yemen, Muna was able to move to Addis Ababa. She has studied business management and obtained certificates and badges in public health and humanitarian leadership programs from John Hopkins and UNICEF, as well as other humanitarian agencies. In addition, she has worked for various NGOs and educational organizations in different capacities.

KATE REED is from the United States, and she now travels between her US hometown and the United Kingdom as a graduate student in economic and social history. She researches labour, land, and migration in Latin America, and worked as a teaching assistant for the Global History Dialogues project during its first two years. In addition to her research and teaching in history, Kate has served as an interpreter and English teacher with several immigrant and refugee rights groups in the United States and Mexico.

MARCIA C. SCHENCK is professor of global history at the University of Potsdam. She holds a PhD in history from Princeton University, where she first became involved with the project that developed into this anthology. She created the Global History Dialogues course as part of the Global History Lab run by Jeremy Adelman at Princeton. Her research is about labour migration and refuge-seeking in Africa, and she works with global history, oral history, and microhistory approaches. She has published widely, also in academic journals such as *Africa, African Economic History,* and *Labor History,* and her latest book is the co-edited open-access volume *Navigating Socialist Encounters: Moorings and (Dis)Entanglements between Africa and East Germany during the Cold War*, edited with Eric Burton, Anne Dietrich, and Immanuel R. Harisch (De Gruyter Oldenbourg, 2021).

LAZHA TAHA is from Iraqi Kurdistan. She holds a degree in media studies from the University of Sulaimani, where she has lived her whole life. She currently works as a researcher and translator of Kurdish literature at Kashkul, the Center of Art and Culture at the American University of Iraq, Sulaimani. She is part of a team that is working on translating a selection of articles written by the early twentieth century Kurdish journalist, writer, and poet, Piramerd. Her hobbies are reading, watching movies, designing jewelry, going on long walks, and taking photographs.

GERAWORK TEFERRA successfully completed Princeton University's Global History Lab and History Dialogue Project, learning to use historical research methods, oral history, and storytelling. He coauthored "Hope Disrupted: Refugees in Limbo" together with Dr Staci Martin, based on the Psychosocial Peace Building training she conducted in the camp. Currently, he is working as an academic advisor under a Jesuit Worldwide Learning (JWL) tertiary-level education program that offers associate and bachelor's degree programs in collaboration with South New Hampshire University. Above all, he has lived in Kakuma refugee camp for ten years teaching at secondary and postsecondary level and interacting with a diverse community, which has made him wonder about human nature, hope, and different forms of establishments. Consequently, wondering, contemplating, reading, and nowadays listening to YouTube talks have become his hobbies.

Index

1917 Protocol Relating to the
Status of Refugees, 8, 84. *See
also* Geneva Convention
1951 Convention. *See* Geneva
Convention

abafaransa. *See* Twa
Abagogwe, 233
abaterambere. *See* Twa
Abavuzi Gakondo (AGA) Rwanda
Network, 186, 188–9, 196
abortion, 219–22
Afandi, Rafiq Mahmood, 167
agency, 16–17, 20, 26, 39
Ahmed, Sara, 12
Akrayi, Sangar, 166, 171–5
Anglo-Boer War, 6
Appadurai, Arjun, 12–13, 33n6
archives: access to, 4, 77, 241;
creation of, x, 11, 129;
destruction of, 162–3, 176
Arendt, Hannah, 16, 26
Arkady, Ali, 166, 169–74, 177
Assab. *See* Eritrea
asylum: asylum story, 18–20; in
Kakuma refugee camp, 65

Bahutu. *See* Hutus
Balai Citoyen, 155
Batutsi. *See* Tutsis
Batwa. *See* Twa
Bellino, Michelle J., 55, 57, 67
Bideri, Clemence, 137
birth control, 219–22
Black Americans, 148–52
Bombaataa, Afrika, 150
borders, 14, 28, 45–6, 140,
148, 236
Burundi: 2015 political crisis in,
120; colonization of, 118–22,
135–8, 144; independence of,
111, 119, 138; monarchy of, 29,
111–16, 119, 124, 133–5
Burundian drumming: commodification of, 121–5; and masculin-
ity, 116–18, 121; symbolism of,
114, 122
Burundian refugee drummers,
109–10, 120–4

Central America, 8
Charry, Eric, 151

citizenship, ix–xi, 8, 9, 11–13, 33n6
Cold War, 6
colonization: as brainwashing, 119;
    of Burundi (*see* Burundi: coloni-
    zation of); of knowledge, 1, 24
Compaoré, Blaise, 155
conditions of production, 10,
    26, 244
Convention on the Elimination of
    All Forms of Discrimination
    Against Women (CEDAW), 205
co-researching, 22. *See also*
    research
corruption, 94–8
Crane, Susan, 5
criminal gangs in Yemen, 81, 87,
    93, 96
Cuba: connection to hip-hop, 151;
    refugees from, 17; soldiers in
    Ethiopia, 91

decolonization: in Africa, 8; of
    knowledge, 21, 41
Democratic Republic of the Congo
    (DRC), 232–3
Derg, 79, 90
D'Halluin, Estelle, 19, 38n58
dialogue, x, 5, 21, 31, 32n2,
    237, 240
diaspora, 28, 152
disobedience, 21–2
displacement, 4–14, 23, 26–8; and
    Burundian drumming (*see*
    Burundian refugee drummers);
    durable solution to, 53, 65, 71;
    external, 138, 142; forced, 133,
    144; internal, 85, 134–6, 218;
    and Intore dance (*see* Intore tra-
    ditional dance); in Sub-Saharan
    Africa, 78; in Syria, 202, 218

Djibouti, 82, 86, 89–91, 93
DJ Kool Herc, 149
domestic labour, 85, 101–2,
    106, 211
domestic violence. *See* gender-based
    violence (GBV)
Dotson, Kristie, 16, 18
Dryden-Peterson, Sarah, 53–6

East Africa: East Africa Got Talent,
    122; historical connections with
    Yemen, 81; migration from,
    79–80, 85, 100
economic migrants, 20, 39, 86
education: camp schools, 47–8, 51,
    53–7, 59, 63; community-based
    training, 69; computer literacy,
    60, 61; discrimination in educa-
    tion, 205–9; in emergency
    settings, 51, 70; integration
    of refugee and host country
    systems, 55–7, 64, 71; over-
    crowding, 59, 67; post-school
    opportunities, 56–7, 67, 71;
    quality of, 58–9, 70, 85; refugee
    access to in Yemen, 85; refugee
    teachers, 56, 67; schools as social
    spaces, 52, 59, 62, 71; student
    performance in, 59–62; symbol-
    ism of, 57–64; tertiary level, 56,
    67, 68; two-shift system, 60, 66
Eritrea, 79, 84, 90
Ethiopia, 7, 72, 76, 82, 90;
    migration from, 76, 85–8, 93–4;
    Oromia region of, 76, 88, 93,
    104, 105
ethnic violence, 133, 138, 153
Everill, Bronwen, 7
experimentation, 4–5, 239, 240,
    245, 246n8

family planning, 219–22
Fassin, Didier, 19, 38n58
Feast of the First Fruits. *See*
    Umuganuro
feminism, 23, 103, 155, 217
forced marriage, 79
Freitag, Ulrike, 11

Gaddafi, Muammar, 228
Gatrell, Peter, 27
Gatsinda, Jean Paul (J.P.), 150
gender awareness, 211–14
gender-based violence (GBV), 87,
    91, 96, 104–5, 118, 203, 214–23;
    domestic violence, 205, 214–17;
    honour crimes, 216–17; rape, 79,
    87, 89, 91, 94, 208; sexual
    exploitation, 79, 98; stigma
    associated with, 215; as weapon
    of war, 202, 208
General Union of Syrian Women,
    220
Geneva Convention, 6, 8, 84–5
genocide, 6, 90; in Iraq, 163, 167;
    in Rwanda, 138, 156, 190, 235
Getachew, Adom, 238
Global Education Strategy (GES),
    55–67, 71
global history, 4, 6, 9, 42n83
Global North, 13–14, 49
Global South, 3, 13–15
Great Lakes Twa. *See* Twa
guhamura, 192

Halabja chemical attacks, 162–3,
    167
healing: traditional versus Western,
    30, 181, 189, 192
healthcare, 100; refugee access to,
    84, 93, 100

Hejazi, Mustapha, 212
Herero, 6
Hergum, Hans Petter, 137
Himbaza Club, 122–3
hip-hop, 147, 149–51; as foreign,
    152; Kenyan Hip-Hop
    Parliament, 153–4; as resistance,
    154–5; use of slang in, 156–7
honour crimes. *See* gender-based
    violence (GBV)
hope, 12, 45–8, 50, 59, 63, 100,
    106, 237
Horn of Africa, 79, 81–6, 105
host community, 28, 31, 56
Houthis, 85, 94
humanitarian intervention, 17, 80
humanitarianism, 6–7, 39
humanitarian law, 84, 97. *See also*
    international law
human rights, 23, 103–4; violations
    of, 28, 77, 79, 80–1, 96, 106,
    245
Hutus, 133, 134, 138, 233

I Am She Network, 217
Igishakamba dance, 231, 233–4.
    See also Intore traditional dance
Ikinimba dance, 234. *See also*
    Intore traditional dance
Ikinyemera dance, 233. *See also*
    Intore traditional dance
implementing partner organiza-
    tions, 55, 65–7; Lutheran World
    Federation, 55, 65–6, 69;
    Windle International Kenya, 56,
    65–6, 69
inclusion: in knowledge-
    production, 5, 20–6, 31; in
    refugee education policy, 50, 53,
    55–6, 60, 64, 71

inequality, 9, 156, 174, 205, 207, 211, 214, 242–4

Ingoma, 230

internally displaced people, 4, 78, 85, 218

international law, 6, 8, 11. *See also* humanitarian law

International Organization of Migration, 6, 7, 86, 98

Intore traditional dance, 30; attire in, 230–2; drumming in 230; exclusion of women from 235; relationship to migration, 232–4; as symbol of Rwandan nationalism, 235. *See also* Igishakamba dance; Ikinjmba dance; Ikinyemera dance; Nkombo dance

Iran, 162–5, 176

Iraq, 29, 129, 161–78

Islamic State (ISIL, ISIS), 178, 208

Ismaili community, 200, 202, 207

Italy, 15

Jackson, Michael, 16, 36n37

Jacobsen, Karen, 22

Jensen, Katherine, 19

Kakuma refugee camp, 47–72. *See also* education

Karyenda, 113–14, 118, 122

Kenya: educational system, 50, 55, 56, 59, 61; Hip-Hop Parliament, 153–4; Kenyan Secondary Certification Examinations, 84, 86

Keyes, Cheryl, 150

Khalid, Hawre, 166, 169, 171, 174, 175, 177

Kibona, Msia, 152

Kurdistan: archives of, 162; creation of Kurdistan autonomous region, 162; photojournalism in, 162–78

labour, 99–100, 210; in academia, 10, 22; domestic labour, 85, 101–2, 106, 211; in refugee camps, 6

Landau, Loren, 22

Latinos, 148–52

League of Nations, 7, 118

Mahama refugee camp, 29, 46; Burundian drumming in, 120, 123; Twa pottery in; 132–40

Malkki, Liisa, 11

Marsh, Charity, 153

Marshland, Rebecca, 186

material culture, 151, 182, 228

Mbembe, Achille, 21, 40n70

Meiselas, Susan, 162, 167

memory, 156–7, 161, 163–5, 176, 178

mental health, 93

mental migration, 130, 148–9

Metrography, 167–9, 174

Meyer, Sebastian, 167, 168, 174

migrants, 4, 7, 20, 39n63; challenges of researching migrant experiences, 78, 81, 87; discrimination against, 79; journeys of, 86–7; relationship with humanitarian agencies, 79 97–8; smuggling networks, 86–7, 96–7; voluntary repatriation of, 98; vulnerabilities of, 83, 87, 96, 106

migration, 22, 27–8, 79–82, 232–4. *See also* mental migration

Millennium Development Goals
(MDGs), 50, 54–5
miti shamba, 186, 187
mobility, 27, 110, 129, 133–6, 144–
6, 241, 245; education as a
means of, 52, 57, 63
Mohammad, Younes, 166–7, 171–8
Muwalladīn, 82, 93, 96

Najm, Ahmad, 169
Najm, Kamaran, 167
Namibia, 6
Nansen Passport, 7
narrative, 9–11, 15–20, 48, 80, 87,
129, 149, 151–8, 162, 165, 167,
203, 245
nation-state, 7, 23, 158, 162,
167, 176
Nayeri, Dina, 15–16, 19–20
New York Declaration for Refugees
and Migrants, 104
Nibbs, Faith, 17–18
Nkombo dance, 232–3. See also
Intore traditional dance
Nkurunziza, Pierre, 120
Ntafatiro, Patrice, 116
Nyanzi, Stella, 155

objectivity, 19–20, 22, 25
oral history, 9, 15, 27, 52, 77, 112,
132, 140, 161, 186, 201–2, 229,
240–1. See also research
oral tradition, 19, 134
organizational capacity, 66
Othman, Sartep, 166, 168–70, 176
outcome-based accountability, 64–6
Overby, Jonathan, 151

participant observation, 149, 186,
188, 229

pastoralism, 133, 137, 234
patriarchy, 201. See also gender
awareness; gender-based violence
(GBV)
Perez Sheldon, Myrna, 23
Petty, Sheila, 153
photojournalism, 129–30, 206–22;
and futurity, 176; and identity
formation, 176–8; introduction
to Kurdistan, 166–70; local
versus foreign, 173–5; training,
170–3
Polly, Jay, 152
positionality, 4, 9–10, 14, 21, 23,
28, 31, 173, 238
power, 10, 24–5, 49, 111, 112,
114–18, 125, 192, 231–3, 240–5

rape. See gender-based violence
(GBV)
refugee camps, 6, 139; and concentration camps, 6; and education
(see education); protracted
refugee situations, 11, 35, 51,
55–6, 70–1. See also Kakuma
refugee camp; Mahama
refugee camp
refugeeness, 4, 16–17, 26, 48, 64
refugees: Burundian refugee drummers (see Burundian refugee
drummers); decision to leave,
86–94; definition of, 4, 8, 11,
39n63, 45; discrimination
against, 70, 82, 85, 100, 101–2,
133–40, 143–4; effects of refugee
status, 12–13, 61, 64; healthcare,
84, 93, 100; as historians, 4,
23–6, 26–8; identity, 4, 16–17,
26, 48, 64; media coverage of,
17, 80; objectification of, 17–18;

relationship to history, 4, 26–8, 238; women (*see* women)

religion, 185–6, 207

repatriation, 7, 53, 65, 98

repertoires of contention, 29

reproductive health, 219–23

research: challenges of, 24–5, 48, 77, 78, 110, 239, 241–2; as conversation, 13–15, 22, 24–6, 30–1, 237, 240–4; co-researching, 22, 41n73; limitations of, 12; oral history experiences, 47–50, 77, 81, 110, 132, 186, 202–4, 227 (*see also* oral history); and relationship-building, 13, 242; right to, 12–16, 20, 21, 27, 31, 33n6, 227, 241; stakes of, 238; writing process, 5, 10, 13, 31, 239

researcher: identity as a, 12, 31, 238–9; insiders and outsiders, 12, 22, 48, 162–3

resettlement, 7, 17, 20, 61, 65, 94, 97–8

right to research, 12–16, 20, 21, 27, 31, 33n6, 227, 241

Russell Hochschild, Arlie, 240

Rwanda, 109, 120–4, 133–45, 156–7, 184–98, 228–36; genocide in, 138, 156, 190, 235; Ministry of Health, 194–6; National Policy of Traditional, Complementary, and Alternative Medicine, 190; refugees in (*see* Mahama refugee camp); Traditional Medicine Service, 196–7

Sall, Macky, 155

Santería, 151

Saudi Arabia, 76, 85, 93–6

Segato, Rita Laura, 21, 23

Selasie, Taiye, 152

self-censorship, 16, 49

Senegal, 149, 152, 154–5

Shadle, Brett, 7

Sheng, 154, 158

Shire, Warsan, 157

silencing, 10, 11, 16; practices of, 16, 20

slang, 156–7

Smith, Bonnie, 4, 23

Smith, P.G., 157

smugglers, 86–7, 96–7

Sobral, Anna, 155, 157

socioeconomic rights, 64, 84

Somalia, 79, 86, 93, 100

sovereignty, 7, 114, 119, 123

Soviet Union, 162

Spivak, Gayatri, 10

storytelling, 16, 48, 77, 168, 237

Sunni Muslims, 207–8

Sustainable Development Goals (SDGs), 55–6

Syria: civil war, 200, 202, 208, 218, 221; Commission for Family Affairs, 214, 216; Hama Governorate, 202, 210, 213; Homs City, 203, 206, 207, 212; Kurds in, 162, 176; refugees from, 80, 102; Teacher Preparation Institute, 202, 206; women in, 200–23 (*see also* General Union of Syrian Women)

Táíwò, Olúfẹmi O., 25

Tanzania, 120, 186

testimonial quieting, 16–17

testimonial smothering, 16, 18

traditional healing, 183–98; accessibility of, 181, 190–1, 195;

certification of practitioners,
189–90; consultancy, 193–4;
regulation of, 194–6, 197–8; ver-
sus witchcraft, 184
Traditional Medicine Service
(Rwanda), 196–7
translation, 24, 29, 227
translocal, 11, 29
Trouillot, Michel-Rolph, 10, 24
Tuff Gang, 156, 159n21
Turkey, 162, 176
Tutsis, 116, 133–8, 233
Twa, 116, 129, 132, 133–45

Ubushwima disease, 193
Uganda, 30, 62, 120, 132–4, 149,
155, 233–4
Umuganuro, 111, 113–16,
119, 229
unaccompanied minors, 71–2,
86
United Arab Emirates (UAE), 15
United Nations (UN), 50, 154, 157,
205, 208
United Nations High
Commissioner for Refugees
(UNHCR), 6–8, 51–6, 65–71, 80,
94, 138, 143–4
United Nations Office on Drugs
and Crime (UNODC), 86
United Nations Population Fund
(UNFPA), 80, 220
United States, 3, 7, 8, 9, 36, 148,
150–6

voluntary return. *See* repatriation
von Oppen, Achim, 11

Wade, Abdoulaye, 155
witchcraft, 184, 186, 188, 189, 192

women: and Burundian drumming
(*see* Burundian drumming);
discrimination against, 197;
economic independence of, 202,
205, 209–10, 220, 223; employment of, 85, 101, 197 (*see also*
domestic labour); and Intore
traditional dance (*see* Intore
traditional dance); migrants,
78–106; and property ownership, 209–10; violence against
(*see* gender-based violence
(GBV)); vulnerabilities of, 79, 81,
96, 102, 104, 106
Women's Refugee Commission
(WRC), 80
Woolley, Agnes, 8, 18
World Health Organization (WHO),
188
World University Service of Canada
(WUSC), 61
World War I, 6–7, 118
World War II, 6–7

Yemen: and 1951 Convention, 84;
civil war in, 96; criminal gangs
in, 81, 87, 93, 96; discrimination
in, 100–1, 104; migration to,
78–106

Zulu Nation, 150